CHINA UNDER DENG XIAOPING

China under Deng Xiaoping

Political and Economic Reform

David Wen-Wei Chang
University Rosebush Professor of Political Science
University of Wisconsin–Oshkosh

Foreword by Robert A. Scalapino
Institute of East Asian Studies
University of California, Berkeley

St. Martin's Press   New York

First published in the United States of America in 1988

Printed in Hong Kong

ISBN 0–312–01682–4

Library of Congress Cataloging-in-Publication Data
Chang, David W., 1929–
China under Deng Xiaoping: political and economic reform/by
David Wen-Wei Chang.
p.   cm.
Bibliography: p.
Includes index.
ISBN 0–312–01682–4: $40.00 (est.)
1. China—Economic policy—1976–   2. China—Politics and
government—1976–   3. Political planning—China. I. Title.
HC427.92.C333   1988
338.951—dc19   87–34906
                                                            CIP

To my wife Alice
and sons Christopher and Victor

Contents

Foreword

Professor David Chang spent the fall of 1985 with us at the Institute of East Asian Studies, University of California, Berkeley. In addition to his research and writing, he organised a seminar that brought together our visiting scholars, enabling an exchange of ideas among a variety of intellectuals from East Asia. It was an idea sufficiently valuable to be continued after Professor Chang's departure.

Now, he presents us with the broadly gauged study upon which he was working at Berkeley. It is a highly instructive work, covering the major facets of recent political, economic and social developments in China. Ample in data, provocative in its analysis of personalities and events, and carefully balanced, this work captures much that is China at a particular point in time. The author is the first to acknowledge that predictions regarding China's future are fraught with difficulty, with various scenarios possible. Even in recent months, unexpected developments have occurred, particularly in the political realm. However, he provides us with many of the facts pertaining to recent Chinese history that should make possible a deeper understanding of the challenges that lie ahead.

Upon reading this work, one has a stronger realisation of the advantages of being thoroughly at home with the culture and language of China, able to communicate with the diverse individuals who make up this highly complex society. It is with the aid of scholars like David Chang that all of us will be able to grasp new aspects of an old society at a transitional point in its difficult journey toward modernity.

Berkeley, California   ROBERT A. SCALAPINO

Preface and Acknowledgements

This book is the result of six summer trips to the People's Republic of China, two of which were university study tours. The others were either lecture tours when I was invited by the External Affairs Bureau of the Chinese Academy of Social Sciences, or private travel in which I visited relatives. I have been to several dozens of major cities and many parts of rural China. As a former native of the land, I was easily able to reach many people of different ranks and responsibilities. They allowed me interviews, formally and informally, with no restrictions to any kinds of questions so long as I would not identify them with specific answers. They were teachers, professors, factory managers, commune leaders, governors, party functionaries, personnel directors, students, workers, county government officials and special economic zone directors. As a result, I feel able to fully share their views of their own lives and their genuine expectations for their country. After thirty years under communist rule, many of them had much to tell or to reflect in order to impress me often deeply with a personal message of protest or new expectation. At the policy-making level, I am grateful to many party and government officials in Beijing and in the provinces.

I am grateful to the Institute of East Asian Studies and its center for Chinese Studies of the University of California, Berkeley for allowing me as their visiting scholar in 1985. The University of Wisconsin–Oshkosh, my home institution, granted me the sabbatical leave to make my stay at Berkeley possible. My research tours to Taiwan and Hong Kong were partially sponsored by the Pacific Cultural Foundation in 1984 and 1985. I am grateful to the foundation for its generosity.

This publication represents a personal summary of what I have learned about China after thirty years of communist rule, its people, culture, progress and problems. In the last one hundred years, the country has undergone several major reforms and revolutions. Yet it is still struggling in revolutionary transition to achieve, politically and economically, what Japan and other east Asian countries have long succeeded. The story of communist rule is much the story of Mao Zedong's failure in misleading his party and the masses toward excessive revolutionary radicalism. The success of Deng Xiaoping's reform so far has been pre-determined by Mao and his followers whose knowledge of the outside world was too limited for them to realise that they were wrong. Today, under Deng, much has to be changed. New economic standards and political reforms have to be adopted. Mao's ideological idealism has to be modified or abandoned. Practical solutions must be found to new problems in many fields. This book is a description of Deng's partial policy response to some of the problems. However, the emphasis is on the following: Deng's reform itself is a challenge for more basic innovations to come; factional conflict within the Communist Party makes reform difficult to achieve or implement; rural and urban economic reform is critical to the livelihood of the people and the modernisation of the country; and challenges from Hong Kong and Taiwan and a solution for their return to the motherland must be found. These problems are further compounded by new demands for more institutional and democratic reforms. It is my personal view that, at long last, China will have to find a new way to reconcile three fundamental traditions, namely, the Confucian historical tradition, the modern tradition introduced by the revolution of 1911, and the Marxist revolutionary experience itself. It may take many decades of chaotic struggle within the Communist Party and throughout the country before China is able to catch up with the rest of the world in economic standard and in genuine democracy. Hong Kong's continuing prosperity, Taiwan's political evolution, and the Japanese model of democracy through party politics and open election may, in the end, be strong influences on the Chinese people in pursuing their modernisation effort.

For their individual assistance, I wish to thank the following: Professor David M. Jones, Carol Klein, Linda Olsen, and Janet Bohn of the Political Science Department of the University of Wisconsin–Oshkosh; Professor Robert A. Scalapino, director of the Institute of East Asian Studies, and his staff, especially Elinor Levine, of the University of California, Berkeley; Professor Chao-Cheng Mai of the Institute of the Three Principles of the People, Academica Sinica of Taiwan, and the library staff of the Institute of International Relations, Mucha, Taipei, Taiwan; Professor Kwang-sheng Liao, Professor Byron Wendy and Dr Terry Lautz of the Chinese University of Hong Kong; and those in the People's Republic of China including Mr LuoYuanming, Senior Economist of the State Economic Commission; Mr Wang Yibing, Division Director and

Researcher of Policy Research Centre of the State Education
Commission; Mr Yang Shangkun, Vice-chairman of the Communist
Party Military Commission; Mr Hu Qili, member of the Politburo
and a member of the Party Central Secretariat; Mr Hu Qiaomu, a
leftist Marxist theoretician; Madame Deng Zingchao, a former
member of the party politburo and wife of late Premier Zhou Enlai,
and Mr Xi Zhongxun, a present member of the party Central
Secretariat. I am particularly grateful to Vice-chancellor Fang Sheng
of Shenzhen University for his stimulating views as a well-known
economist on economic reform in China today. To many others in
rural China and urban factories or elsewhere as teachers, officials and
housewives, etc., I am most grateful for allowing me to share their
views and feelings relevant to my study. None of them, however, is
responsible for what I have said in this book.

University of Wisconsin–Oshkosh   DAVID WEN-WEI CHANG

Prologue

This book concentrates on the broad outline of Deng Xiaoping's political-economic reform which began seriously after 1979. The reform on such a grand scale followed Deng's own political victory in factional struggle against former Premier Hua Guofeng. His return was made somewhat inevitable by the crude and cruel manner in which Mao had earlier dismissed him in January 1976, thus also destabilising the communist regime. Deng would have been happily endeared as the logical and pragmatic successor of Mao as the party leader had Mao died earlier than the late Premier Zhou Enlai, who had, since 1973, succeeded in convincing Chairman Mao to bring Deng back as his First Deputy Premier to undertake all of Zhou's own duties while the latter was ill and long hospitalised, The 'Gang of Four' would not have attempted to achieve power had Chairman Mao himself not been so cruelly selfish and politically self-misguided. This long history of leadership struggle was Mao's own making since the cruel period of the Cultural Revolution (1966–76). Readers may wish to consult my other book on the crisis of Communist leadership struggle (*Zhou Enlai and Deng Xiaoping in the Chinese Leadership Succession Crisis*, 1984).

By the end of 1987, one can safely comment that Deng's economic and political reform, at long last, has proved to be successful in itself and overwhelmingly desired by a huge majority of the population. The only critical opposition comes from the ideological left-wing faction from within the Communist Party itself. The leftists are fighting a losing battle, even though they put together temporary coalitions to block the progress of reform. Politically or personally it is understandable that they fight to retain their high positions of power and influence. The leftist opposition is in fact defensive ideologically, given the intellectual new atmosphere of the post-Mao anti-leftist movement. Factional conflicts will continue because Deng's 'grand reform' will require decades before its general goals are achieved or when the 'four modernisations' are considered accomplished. Until then, China will remain in a state of continuous transition and rapid peaceful change. Indeed, there is a long and zig-zag road ahead in transforming Mao's China to an industrialised socialist state, to practise 'socialist legality and socialist democracy'.

This publication concentrates on an outline of political-economic reform as introduced during the few years since 1978. It avoids making detailed evaluative analysis of the reform performance. To do so would require much more statistically reliable data from the Chinese government. Emphasis is on the gradual experiment and extension of the economic reform from the rural to the urban spheres. Until recently there was much less effort in political-structural reform. Political reform has lately been increasingly urgent and unavoidable. Serious political reform was promised in the 1984 reform declaration. Recent experience has demonstrated that it is far more difficult in political restructuring of the communist system than in the area of economic change. This has been so primarily because of Deng's refusal to employ the cruel Maoist method of political purge against opponents in the party. Demands for greater democracy, better bureaucratic performance and new measures against corruption are far more serious and obvious now than just a few years ago. It seems theoretically possible to assume that lesser economic reform success breeds the needs for more economic reform and that success in the economic sphere breeds popular demands for more fundamental democratic reform. The current reform has, indeed, been able to generate its own momentum. Many reform measures continue to be at the experimental stages.

The experimental nature of the Chinese reform may be divided into three periods: (1) the first stage was in rural management and production changes, and in transformation towards commodity privatisation between 1979 and 1982; (2) the experiment in urban factory management autonomy to improve production efficiency and profit-sharing between 1980 and 1984; and finally, (3) the adoption of the grand reform resolution of October 1984 in favour of an overall economic restructuring that has required more reform measures in almost every production and management sphere, including prices and wages, currency, trade, taxation, etc. In short, China has been committed to brave peaceful reform in order to achieve the 'four modernisations' before the end of the twentieth century. This commitment requires the opening up of the country to the outside world and the introduction of a degree of capitalism at home. To achieve both depends on the further opening up of the political process through decentralisation and liberalisation. Given the ideological inflexibility and the lack of a new reform theory, political conflicts and economic debates have multiplied problems for the Chinese leadership. However, the reform group under Deng's leadership has won the struggle. At the party's 13th Congress in

October in 1987 the reform leadership again appeared to be in full control. Deng's successors are now in charge to map out the long-term strategy for the coming decades, while Deng and his old colleagues have retreated from the political front stage. The following paragraphs summarise parts of Premier Zhao's speech relevant to reform as reported to the 13th Party Congress in October 1987.

In Premier Zhao Ziyang's report, a new blueprint for greater reform in political restructuring was unavoidably and seriously emphasised. The reform leadership seems more conscious now that, without political power, decentralisation, democratisation and institutionalised limitations against party dominance, economic, social and intellectual reform cannot succeed. Socialist legality and socialist democracy cannot long remain as empty promises without encountering intellectual and social (student) unrest. He declared that during the next sixty years China would still be at the 'primary stage' of socialist development. Zhao's report has also offered some theory to guide the ambitious blueprint. A political restructuring will soon take place throughout the country. Basic principles and content of the new reform have been mapped out in Zhao's reports. These include elimination of functional confusion between the Communist party and the government, dismantling of over-centralisation of power, administrative overstaffing, inefficient bureaucracy and the imperfect socialist democratic system. In separating the government from the party, the latter shall concentrate only on itself as 'the core of the leadership of China's socialist cause, without interfering in the day-to-day administrative affairs of the government'. The political leadership of the party will focus on 'setting political principles and political orientation' in policy decisions and personnel recommendations. The party shall work among the citizens to motivate them to follow 'party principles and policies'. Against overcentralisation, Zhao's report proposes to delegate power to 'the lower levels' to allow local affairs to be 'handled by the locality, and affairs of the people by the people themselves'. Unwieldy government organisation and bureaucracy, from top to bottom, will be 'amalgamated or simplified' to separate governmental administration from production enterprises. The State Council (cabinet) will proceed immediately to implement the proposed changes and report to the 7th National People's Congress in the spring of 1988. A civil service system will be established to increase administrative merit efficiency. A new system of 'public consultation and dialogue' will be established to promote

communications between levels of government and groups among the
people to overcome problems of corrupt bureaucracy.

The practice in the principles of democratic centralism will be
improved through the system of the People's Congresses, multi-party
cooperation and political consultation under the Communist
leadership. These are new systems considered appropriate for the
Chinese traditions. The National People's Congress will improve its
own performance, and strengthen its downward legal supervision.
The Chinese People's Political Consultative Conference (CPPCC), as
a patriotic united front, and other democratic political parties will
also regularly conduct 'political consultation and democratic supervision' over major issues of state policy. The election system has been
singled out for reform to institutionalise democratic life at the
grass-roots levels. The achievement of these reform goals will help
lay the ground for socialist democracy. In short, political reform has
become unavoidable to meet the needs for deepening economic
reform and the need for democratisation in socialist modernisation.
How all these will be implemented and received by the people in both
urban and rural China will be closely watched by all concerned
parties inside China and the outside world .

Premier Zhao declared that 'profound changes' have taken place in
the country in the past nine years: 'The national economy has
registered a sustained and stable growth to double the gross national
product, state revenue and average citizen's income. During the
nine-year period, 70 million urban residents have found new jobs,
while some 80 million rural citizens have now shifted partially or
wholly from farming to industry. Market supplies have greatly
increased to reduce the acute shortage of consumer demands.' The
imbalanced development in the major sectors of the economy has
improved. These successes, Zhao reported, prove that the policy line
of the party since 1978 has been correct. He praised Deng Xiaoping
for 'his courage in developing Marxist theory, his realistic approach,
his rich experience and his foresight and sagacity'. In advancing the
ideology of the 'peaceful revolution', Zhao pointedly declared that
China is now in the primary stage of socialism. It will be 'at least 100
years from 1950s to the time when socialist modernisation will have
been in the main accomplished'. Uniquely different from Marxist
application elswhere, this is 'the specific stage China must go through
while building socialism under conditions of backward productive
forces and an underdeveloped commodity economy'. Zhao went
further to assert theoretically that 'we must persevere in socialism

and never deviate from it' and, second, 'we must proceed from this reality and not jump over this stage'. He warned those who might disagree by saying: 'Under the specific historical conditions of contemporary China, to believe the Chinese people cannot take the socialist road without going through the stage of fully developed capitalism is a mechanistic view on the question of the development of revolution, which is the major cognitive root of right-deviationist mistakes. On the other hand, to believe that it is possible to jump over the primary stage of socialism in which the productive forces are to be highly developed is a utopian view on this question, which is the major cognitive root of leftist mistakes.' Thus the correct and basic theory at this 'primary stage' must be for the party to lead the nation in a united, self-reliant and pioneering struggle to convert China into a rich, strong, democratic and modern socialist state by concentrating on economic development as the central task without abandoning the four cardinal principles (democratic dictatorship, the Communist leadership, Marxism-Leninism and Mao Zedong Thought, and the socialist path). In policy practice, Zhao's report accentuated the need rapidly to advance educational, scientific-technological and economic development through rational reforms at home and widening the contacts with the outside world. The 13th Congress has adopted Zhao's theory of 'primary-stage socialism' unique to China alone. This itself is a major revision of Marxism to add 'Chinese Characteristics'.

On economic restructuring, Zhao emphasised socialist reforms to include different types of ownership, maintenance of predominant public ownership, and development of private sectors in the economy. The main focus is to change the 'managerial mechanism of enterprises' and to institute 'systems of planning' on investment, allocation of resources, finance, currency policy and international trade. Together these measures will enable China to establish a basic 'framework for a planned commodity economy' which should be able to integrate planning with the market. The Premier admitted the difference in ownership as the major variation between socialist and capitalist commodity economies. In short, he asserted in the report that 'the state regulates the market, and the market guides the enterprises'.

On party-building, Zhao reported that the existing policy is correct in making ranks of cadres 'more revolutionary, younger, better educated and more competent'. This reform effort should be implemented at the central level among leading bodies of the party.

The central committee must practise 'collective leadership and democratic centralism'. He advocated in the speech the following: (1) establishing a system of regular working reports to the Political Bureau by its Standing Committee and to the plenary sessions of the Central Committee by the Political Bureau; (2) increasing the meetings of the plenary sessions of the Central Committee each year to augment its collective decision-making opportunities; and finally (3) establishing work rules and a system for holding democratic meetings of the Political Bureau, its Standing Committee and the Secretariat of the Central Committee to assure an institutionalised collective leadership so as to 'put central party leaders under strict supervision and control'. Zhao insisted in the report that party effort against 'self corruption' must continue and 'corrupt members' must be expelled.

In conclusion, Zhao's long report was a blueprint of long-term reform and transformation to institutionalise a new system of leadership for efficiency and revitalization to lay a foundation for socialist democracy and socialist economic modernisation. (He made no serious proposal to institutionalize an election system to produce central level leaders accountable to the general public.)

Can the Party put into practice all these reform proposals? Can Zhao and his reform colleagues forge ahead in strong collective leadership acceptable to the military and to other factions? The four cardinal principles, especially the leadership of the party, convey a rigid sense of a single-party dominance in a progressively democratised industrialising society. Can the new forces resulting from economic progress be easily contained by the restructured political framework? Can intra-party conflicts be silenced or balanced peacefully after Deng's complete departure from the political scene? On the other hand, Zhao's report represents a complete victory of the reform leadership over the leftists in the party. In practice, this report suggests that Marxism-Leninism has been further put aside. China is on her way to blaze a new trail of theory in socialism that will inevitably bear 'Chinese characteristics'. In other words, the criteria of socialism, democracy and the rule of law of the West may, in the end, lose their original moral persuasion and institutional implication when they are variably understood and skilfully implemented by the Chinese communists. However, success in political and economic reform will inevitably continue to generate new conflicts. China is likely to remain in a state of peaceful transition until a popularly acceptable political harmony is achieved between the government on the one hand and the people on the other. Such a new state of affairs presume the existence and practice in fundamental constitutional rights by the population throughout the country.

Many China-watchers in Asia are doubtful of major successes in political-institutional reform in the immediate future. To maintain peaceful stability requires factional consultation inside the Communist Party. For example, it took a full summer for the factions to reconcile their differences in order to show a smooth unity at the 13th Party Congress. Experts do not believe that, in the short run, the proposed greater intra-party democracy and collective leadership are possible. Such frequency of meetings between members of the Political Bureau and the Central Committee will probably increase the 'unwanted influence' of the older and retreating generation. Many observers fear that the next Central Advisory Commission and the Commission for Discipline and Inspection may exercise a strong pressure on the new collective leadership under Zhao because these commissions have large numbers of old-guard conservatives. One bright prospect, however, is likely to be progressive development of a new socialist legal system by the next National People's Congress whose new head is known to be the present Deputy premier Wan Li. He is said to favour the need for legal and institutional reform. He may encourage that partial experiment in direct popular election at the provincial, and even national-level elections may be instituted to give the regime popular representation.

What concerns China-watchers most is the continuing need for Deng to remain as the arbiter to balance conflicts between the reformers and the conservatives in the party. Deng needs to move fast to build an institutional stability. Should Secretary-General Zhao Ziyang fail to assert and dominate the next Standing Committee and its Political Bureau (the standing Committee consists of Zhao himself, Hu Qili, Qiao Shi, Li Peng, and Yao Yilin) a continuing power struggle beyond Deng is unavoidable. Deng is aged 83. After him, there may be a short moment of leadership adjustment and instability. Certainly there will be some period of power struggle between the reformers and the leftists or the conservatives. Reform progress will no doubt continue beyond Deng's time. It may however suffer from a slower pace. There is no real likelihood of a military coup or a conservative takeover after Deng's departure. Popular demands for major political liberalisation and economic forces for greater economic reform are likely to remain of paramount importance for a long time to come.

D.W.-W.C.

1 Introduction

This book is an interpretation of events in China from which various conclusions can be drawn. What has happened in China since Deng Xiaoping's last return to power has occurred within a time span of only a few years. There is a continuing sense of revolutionary urgency for change, adjustments, reorganisation, decentralisation or broad reform. The process in Deng's words is 'an experiment'.[1] Indeed research into the last several years on public policy indicates that Deng and his administrators did not at first have a blueprint for policy changes on many fronts. They have carefully allowed minor and regional initiatives in economic development, for example, to experiment and to succeed before the adoption of a major policy by the central government. This process of peaceful reform is so great in its ultimate impact that Deng Xiaoping, the leader of the regime and the mastermind of all major changes, has called the process 'a second revolution'.[2] This book will pinpoint and interpret some of these changes in the current revolutionary process in China. The author fully recognises the risk and danger involved in making this 'simplified' description and 'preliminary' or tentative interpretation of some of the possible or likely consequences of Deng's experimental and revolutionary reforms in China today.

My interpretation will be influenced by my understanding of changes since the Hsinhai Revolution in 1911 under Sun Yat-sen's non-Marxian democratic leadership. I must admit also that my understanding of Imperial China's more than 2000 years of institutional and cultural heritage has strongly influenced my judgement. Some of the revolutionary leaders have, in fact, exercised their political leadership with only minor behavioural changes in themselves from that of past tyrannical emperors. Furthermore, the monumental ideological and economic differences between Sun's democratic revolution of 1911 and Mao Zedong's Marxist revolution of 1949 have turned out to be of no major significance to the broad masses of the nation, although such an 'ideological divide' caused many battles for decades among Chinese intellectuals, who themselves have gone through many uncomfortable times in twentieth-century China. They now find a new ideological climate in the nation.

My interpretation of current events will focus on the two major revolutions of 1911 and 1949 and several other major and bitter events. I shall not review the history of major events in detail. However, I trust that informed readers will easily see my views (and biases too) which can be taken as reflections of a former citizen of that nation who attempts to understand and interpret changes and events within the Chinese historical and modern revolutionary context. These views may seem somewhat out of line or strange to my Western colleagues, but I simply convey the views of many other Chinese in China. I am still affected by my past education in China some thirty years ago. In this book, more than anything else I am more concerned about trends of future change, ideology in politics, and the long-term consequences of current major policies which have been relentlessly implemented since Deng's return to power. China experts, especially policy makers of the West in the last seventy years or so, have also frequently changed their views about China. Often they were caught by unexpected surprises that suddenly occurred in China contrary to their expectations or earlier conclusions. The same is also typically true even for some Chinese intellectuals who for forty years argued about the corruption of the Nationalist government before 1949. They were themselves soon suppressed and humiliated by Mao Zedong during the cultural revolution. They have, today, awakened to a new reality that truth and ideology can only come from practice. In fact the whole Chinese population has come through a nightmare it experienced during Mao's last decade as an 'imperial ruler' in China. My position has been greatly influenced by research and interviews with many simple or educated Chinese who are factory workers, farmers, schoolteachers, party cadres, factory managers, university intellectuals, merchants, and students. I have also held discussions with a few of high-level party officials in China today. What I have seen and what they have told me during the last few years constitute the basis for my views in this volume of interpretation. I am grateful to those who spoke to me in plain Chinese language with such intimacy not usually extended to a Westerner. I am equally thankful to those cadres and officials who asked me not to quote their names and positions in the government.

Briefly, this book will concentrate on Chinese political leadership succession, ideological void, socialism with Chinese characteristics, rural economic change, urban economic restructuring, and the problems concerning Hong Kong and Taiwan. All of these issues have been central to Deng's careful examination of policy making. These issues are intimately related to the ideologically struggling factions now within the communist party, or to their emotional commitment to unify the country through a formula of 'one country, two systems'.

Thus, the following chapters cover Deng's leadership and the suspension of the ideological battle, the 'Socialist State with Chinese Characteristics', a new model of rural economic prosperity and industrialisation, urban economic restructuring, and 'One country, Two Systems'.

1.1 SOURCES OF RESEARCH MATERIALS

My researched materials have involved a variety of sources. First of all, over a period of six years, I have visited China five times in different capacities, as a private tourist, study tour director, and an invited lecturer at the Chinese Academy of Social Sciences in Beijing. These tours have secured me opportunities for visits to schools, universities, factories, communes, and hospitals. I attended many private meetings, speaking forums, seminars, and interviews as I travelled to the four corners of the huge country.[3] Altogether I have been to some fifteen cities and their rural suburbs, to my isolated village of birth in northwestern China, a special interview tour to Nanhai county in South China, and the Shenzhen Economic Special Zone. My interviews in Beijing included Hu Qiaomu, Ma Hong, Huan Xiang, Hu Qili and a few others. These visits and interviews provided me with certain original points of view and interpretations of the way my hosts see things. I shall not attempt to alter their views as I come to describe them. My second source of material comes from my trips to Hong Kong where interpretations of events in China are quite diverse and divided. Yet, Hong Kong provides one of the most valuable sources of interpretation for academic research on the People's Republic of China. In addition, the return of Hong Kong itself in 1997 calls for a common challenge to the people there in the interests of maintaining their autonomy as agreed upon during the Sino-British negotiation. Hong Kong itself is a challenge to the Beijing government's ability to keep it as a free port and self-governing during the next sixty years.[4] As a result, Hong Kong's free press is able and eager to cover all major events happening on the other side of the border. I have also collected extensive data in Taiwan on the issue of unification. The policy positions of Taipei and Beijing are presently far apart. Yet both continue to insist that unification is a common goal for the future. On the other hand, the majority of people in Taiwan maintain a unique third position in favour of rapid Taiwanisation in political and democratic development. One of the most difficult problems to anticipate is whether the two societies, one under the Communist and the other the Nationalist Party, will either move closer in internal development or still keep further apart. Much of the answer depends on the evolution of events surrounding the future of Taiwan and on liberalisation on mainland China.[5]

This study will not cover any discussion of aspects of China's foreign policy or such international issues as are relevant to China's internal development, or of Beijing's change of direction in response to external challenge. In respect of politics, discussion will be limited to ideological issues, leadership succession, party reform. local election, etc., to the exclusion of such other major issues as freedom of the press, development of independent political parties, human rights, judicial independence, and intellectual freedom. The discussion of rural and urban economic development will exclude many important aspects of transportation, energy supply, applied science and research, although these are closely related to rural and urban development. If these related issues are mentioned, they are mentioned only to highlight their general importance but not to discuss them in detail.

1.2 NEW DYNAMISM IN THE REFORM

In Mao Zedong's time, Chinese policy-making was preceded and followed by mass mobilisations which always produced high momentum for tension, stress and mobility. Today such mass involvement is no longer intensive nor visible in the street. However, the politics of mobilisation for economic development is still an important element in China. There seems, however, a strong popular acquiesence or genuine approval of the official campaign to succeed in birth control, economic progress, party reform and educational reorganisation. The masses fully enjoy the current politics in rural economic innovation, expansion in domestic commerce and free marketing, decentralisation toward enterprise decision-making autonomy, the campaign against the 'iron rice bowl' (job security), and the retirement of senior leaders in favour of the young leadership alignment. Current media campaigns seem both rational and necessary for the nation to maintain a long-term political stability. People will no longer accept the nightmare of the intensive ideological mobilisational campaigns of the past. A kind of new dynamism for the success of the 'four modernisations' seems to be a voluntary response from the people who welcome new opportunities for material progress and spiritual relaxation in their daily life. They endorse whole-heartedly both the new economic policies and the younger leaders in charge of daily policy execution. If the people and the government can continue to remain united in this new dynamism for progress in science and technology, the nation may be able to redeem itself for having wasted the last twenty years during which Mao erratically imposed on the country his commune system, 'Great Leap Forward', and the cruel cultural revolution. The new dynamism in production seems to come quite naturally from the people in enthusiastic response to the policies of a rational government now at the centre. This does not imply, however, that all is well in planning and policy making by the central or provincial leadership. Ambitious thrust, excessive campaigning or optimistic promises by the government often produce disappointments. In economic development, many decades of investment in education, transportation, public administration and enterprise management skill, etc., is critical for greater future success. China has not done so well in the past. Yet the people desire progress and cannot wait for the effects of long-term capital investment. It is, therefore, expected that, in planning, the people and their government will make mistakes in learning by doing. In short, the spontaneous dynamism for speedy development in all fields, in the wasteful aftermath of the cultural revolution, is understandable provided that occasional setbacks will not upset anyone.

1.3 DENG'S UNIQUE PREPARATION IN LEADERSHIP SUCCESSION

For the first time in the history of the communist world a country's leader has sought out individuals of different age groups to succeed him in leadership before his own departure from the other scene. Stalin and the East European Communist leaders did not do so, nor did Sukarno of Indonesia, Nehru of India, Park Chung-hee of South Korea and Marcos of the Philippines. It is also curious to note that all Chinese leaders (except perhaps Sun Yat-sen), that is Chiang Kai-shek, Lee Kuan-Yew and Mao Zedong, have each, during their lifetime, guided their followers implicitly toward leadership succession. But none acted in the same unselfish way as Deng. Deng himself refuses to occupy the official seat of power. He does so to impress upon his fellow colleagues to do likewise within the Communist Party (CCP). More research should be done at the appropriate future time to understand the actual inner politics of the CCP since the 3rd Session of the 11th Central Committee (CC) in 1978 when Deng's supporters won out against those who followed the then Premier Hua Guofeng. Not only did Deng himself decline to occupy the highest position officially, he was also able to persuade many others to retire. In addition to those who will succeed him immediately after his death, he has brought together many much younger leaders into high office to succeed his immediate successors. This provision will be described in detail. That Deng has done such an expert job with leadership succession is a unique tribute to his ingenuity and ability to act within the political system. Party reform itself has been a crucial factor in leadership transition. Intra-party unity in many communist states was achieved through purges, something which Deng skilfully avoided. Deng's succession is certainly an exception to communist rule. The transition from one-man helmsmanship under Deng to a form of collective leadership will be tested on its workability when Deng is no longer available to lead and arbitrate. The criteria by which Deng has chosen younger leaders seem to assure that a substantial degree of harmony will continue through the division of labour at the top level.

1.4 THE CHALLENGE OF ECONOMIC REFORM

This is the most pressing area for reform in view of continuing poverty in China as compared with Hong Kong, Taiwan and the other surrounding countries of South Korea, Japan, Malaysia and Singapore. China did follow the Soviet economic model at first and failed. It went on to experiment in Mao's own model of the commune and the Great Leap Forward in the late 1950s. This, too, failed. Instead of abandoning his revolutionary radicalism, Mao put the country under his personal domination from 1966 until his death in 1976. His uncontrolled cultural revolution disrupted the leadership and unleashed Lin Biao and Jiang Qing in a cruel power struggle. The common people paid an untold price and sacrificed a great deal in their economic well-being when production in many cities and factories was stopped, transportation interrupted, and civil government replaced. Economic reform today under Deng not only has replaced the 'decade of horror', but has also set down a new realistic order of priority in economic development: rural recovery and free marketing, urban enterprise responsibility autonomy, expansion of light industry, and rational planning in heavy industrial development. The story of rural economic recovery is a fascinating one in which initiative comes directly from the people. The expansion of rural initiative for overall agricultural prosperity has led to many other economic and commercial activities which had been forbidden under Mao and Hua.[6]

A second land reform to return land to the efficient tillers under Deng is a communist revolution in reverse. Presently many things are happening in rural China: dismantling of the commune, restoration of township government, elections in local self-government, restoration of rural commerce, investment, formation of commercial companies, population shift from farming to other jobs, and emergence of specialised rural family industries. There is an enormous potential for an expansion of rural light-industrial development provided the government is efficient and capable of supplying rural needs to satisfy people's economic creativity.[7] I shall highlight such changes in succeeding chapters. On the other hand, urban economic restructuring is, indeed, a follow-up on rural experiments by political leaders at the national level. It seems that incentive to work efficiently and enthusiastically is not a common trait in Marxist economics, whether in Russia or East Europe. Today China has changed this. Five years after rural responsibility farming had begun in 1979 the central government finally announced on 20 October 1984 urban production and enterprise decentralisation in decision making.[8]

1.5 THE CHALLENGE OF 'ONE COUNTRY, TWO SYSTEMS'

Hong Kong and Taiwan are, of course, Chinese territories. Their return to China is irreversible. There have been no international legal complications regarding either one of them since the Shanghai Communiqué between Beijing and Washington in 1972. The Japanese and the Russians have made no legal protest against Taiwan's return to China. However, the new challenge is an internal one that will test the possibility of coexistence among Taiwan, Hong Kong and the People's Republic of China (PRC) on Beijing's own formula: 'one country, two systems'. This promise has beeen written into the Sino-British Agreement in 1984. The formula is also intended to apply to the return of Taiwan. Much of Beijing's policy development toward Taiwan has long been known, but the policy remains unacceptable to the government of the Republic of China (ROC) on Taiwan. In short, the challenge of unification is a political and economic one. If the PRC proposition is accepted by Taiwan, for example, the latter will become a local government of the PRC despite all other favourable promises. Likewise, Hong Kong will definitely hope to become an 'un-interfered' free port at best under a central government which must still deal with many issues directly affecting Hong Kong's autonomy. The stationing of defence forces in Hong Kong, for example, is an obvious serious concern and controversial issue.

Will Beijing policy officials understand the various needs, including self-government, of the Chinese in Hong Kong? Can the central government help Hong Kong to be independent in its commercial relations with the outside world? How will the free flow of Hong Kong's experience affect the economic and political development inside China? Will Hong Kong be an asset or a liability to the central government in its impact after the return? Many similar questions and concerns can be raised about the unification with Taiwan, which is in all respects an independent state with a long working relation with many countries of the world. The political system which has emerged in Taiwan is a unique one. Through reforms and modifications the system is basically acceptable to the people on the island who do not feel at all eager to join the PRC. However, pressure for unification and from internal factors compel the government of both the PRC and the ROC to insist on their separate stands so far taken on unification. Chapter 7 will deal in detail with 'one country, two systems', especially the attached conditions of both sides on unification and the difficulties in finding reconciliation between them. The island of Taiwan is presently a major trading partner of the United States which it ranks as number five in volume of trade. The Taiwan Relations Act of the US Congress promises defensive arms supply to the island since the formal diplomatic severance between Washington and Taipei. These close relations bring Washington's measure of influence on the scene concerning the ultimate destiny of Taiwan. On the other hand, relations between the United States and the People's Republic of China will never be correct, let alone friendly, as long as the United States is angrily perceived as being interventionistic in China's internal affairs and as being a dishonest party to the joint Shanghai Communiqué of February of 1972, in which it pledged non-interference in the Chinese internal affairs in clear language: 'There is but one China, and Taiwan is a part of China ... ', 'unification is for the Chinese to describe'. US involvement will also be discussed in detail in view of Beijing's pledge to resolve the issue of unification before the end of the century.

1.6 THE CRISIS OF IDEOLOGICAL VOID

Since the beginning of the twentieth century, Chinese intellectuals and revolutionaries have been influenced by the foreign ideologies of liberty, equality, individualism, human rights, democracy and capitalism. But they were strongly affected by the victory of Marxist Communism in 1917 in the Soviet Union. After the failure of Kang Yu-wei's 'Hundred Day Reform' in 1898, all Chinese patriots came to embrace either the Western democratic ideology or the Marxian centralist one-party dictatorship. Both of these mutually antagonistic ideologies have now been implemented in China and failed. And both have been modified and adapted to the Chinese political and cultural environment. Chiang Kai-shek failed to implement Sun Yat-sen's 'Three Principles of the People' (nationalism, democracy, livelihood) in the mainland (1927–49). However, a modified Western democracy involving a one-party system in Taiwan has succeeded since 1949. Chiang Kai-Shek's formula was further liberalised and improved by his son, Chiang Ching-Kuo. Mao's ideological failure has been replaced by Deng's leadership with very little modification or change in the political system's intra-organisational structure. However, Deng has literally abandoned Mao's leftist revolutionary radicalism which was preached by the 'Gang of Four' under Mao's wife, Jiang Qing, in the later years of the cultural revolution. Jiang Qing and her collaborators were tried and are now in gaol. Mao's radicalism has been criticised but not totally condemned.

Mao Zedong earned for himself a deified position in the hearts of devotees and among his allies in the political power structure. Politically, it has not been easy for any new leader to condemn Mao in the same manner as N.S. Khrushchev had indicted Joseph Stalin in 1955. Deng has dealt with Mao's legacy skilfully in lowering him from the altar of worship. Therefore, Mao's mistakes from his radical ideology or Mao Zedong Thought could be rationally revised or ignored. In short, only lip service is today given to Mao's impractical writings and past leadership. Moreover, his concept of 'continuing revolution' or revolutionary immortality, condemnation of intellectuals, or his 'Great Leap Forward' are rejected. As political pragmatists, Deng and his followers uphold the Marxist political power structure and ignore certain tenets of Marxism. He has, in fact, reduced the entire tenets into four cardinal principles to justify new policy legitimacy and his 'Socialism with Chinese Characteristics'. What Deng's socialism really amounts to has to await implementation.

One American China specialist has said at a symposium on East Asia that 'Socialism is what the Chinese say it is'.[9] There is today in China what I call 'an ideological void' in contemporary politics. No one talks much about ideology. Many people quote from Marx, Lenin and Mao in their speeches or writings simply for form's sake. Deng's 'truth from practice' is a popular criterion to judge policy success or failure. But it is hardly adequate as an intellectual or theoretical proposition to be developed into a system of ideology. An ideology foundation will have to be structured to interpret the fundamental experiments: 'Socialism with Chinese Characteristics', 'Socialist Legality', 'Collective Leadership' and the abolition of lifetime tenure in office.

1.7 THE PROMISE OF GNP QUADRUPLING BY THE YEAR 2000

The entire thrust of the Chinese effort has been devoted to 'double the GNP twice' by the year 2000, using China's GNP of 1980 as the base. Several major policy documents will be examined and described to provide a fresh basis for the new economic planning and reform. I shall report on my case study of rural interviews and on my visit to Shenzhen Economic Special Zone in 1985. I have learned from several industrial cities in Manchuria (Da Qing Oilfield, Chang Chun, Shenyang, Dalian and Harbin, etc.) through interviewing factory leaders on decision-making practice in their enterprises. My visit to Nanhai county in rural China was most interesting. I discovered how local and country cadres from 1979 onward have stimulated and promoted the campaign for rural economic changes. The replacement of rural communes set up at Mao's insistence in 1958 was politically too dangerous for any cadre to advocate officially. There seemed to have been no national policy discussion on the fate of the communes until the peasants themselves slowly started dividing up land for more efficient farming. Without a national policy, the peasants had only the half-hearted support or acquiescence of some courageous commune cadres. The increase in working incentive for farmers suddenly demonstrated to officials at the highest level that the 'truth has come from practice'. Premier Zhao Ziyang and Vice-premier Wan Li in Sichuan and Anhui provinces further demonstrated their initiatives in policy leadership in the field of agricultural reform. Their success may be responsible for earning them the leadership at the national level. Today they are the two front leaders in national economic reform. The rural success encouraged experiment in new urban economic policy. Changes in various sectors were needed to gain incentive for production increase. The climax of urban economic restructuring occurred finally on 20 October 1984, when the central government adopted the policy of decision-making decentralisation to gain production and management efficiency.

At the 12th Party Congress in 1982, Deng promised the nation the redoubling of the country's GNP by the year 2000. Can this promise be kept, given constraining factors in the economy, in central leadership transition, and in the nation's emerging economic relations with foreign countries? For example, trade, investment, technology, transportation, energy expansion, and human resource development are but a few of the central factors that will determine whether redoubling of the economy will be possible. Current signs and indications seem to assure the fulfilment of the promise, which may even be surpassed. However, there are factors which are beyond anyone's control, such as global economic recession, trade decline, and reduction of foreign investment in China. What can be assured with certainty is the mobilisational dynamism and careful, rational planning so far undertaken by the Chinese government. The success of the Fifth Five-Year Plan (1980–5) and the cautious planning of the Sixth Five-Year Plan, which was recently passed in September, 1985, by the second CCP National Conference, are positive indications of a confident government determined to continue the current economic policies at home and to expand China's economic relations abroad.

1.8 THE IMPACT OF A NEW OPEN DOOR POLICY

China's door has been opened and closed several times: in 1842, 1899, and 1949. Each time when the door was either opened or closed, there were major implications. For example, after 2000 years of self-sufficiency and voluntary isolation, she was forced to stay open in 1899 under pressure from Secretary of State John Hay, presumably for the nation's own survival. This was a time when China had suffered half a century of foreign invasions from the West and Japan and was likely to be cut into 'Spheres of influence'. The foreign yoke of imperialism, as guaranteed by the unequal and humiliating treaties were not completely removed until after the Second World War. The term 'open door' of that period carried with it a very ugly connotation. The Chinese and Sun Yat-sen wanted to keep the door open on 'equal

terms under international law' after the Hsinhai Revolution of 1911.
This was rejected by the West and Japan. Chinese patriots and
progressive intellectuals, then, 'opened the back door' to Marxist
revolution after the Bolshevik victory in 1917. Chiang Kai-shek tried
to close the door against communism but failed. His defeat in 1949 led
Mao Zedong to close it tight against the West. He followed literarily
the Soviet model in building a strong, industrial and modern state.
Mao, too, failed and turned against 'revisionist Russia' in the 1960s.
Mao himself and his chief followers, Zhou Enlai and Deng Xiaoping,
surprised their countrymen and shocked the world by opening up the
country to the West in 1972. China today, only sixteen years after
President Nixon's first visit, is so open that it depends almost totally on
the Western nations and Japan for high technology, investment, trade,
and, in short, the critical succeess of Deng's four modernisations in
defence, agriculture, industry and science. What a zigzagging path full
of conflict in modern China's foreign relations! Presently, the Chinese
leadership is fully determined to keep the Chinese door open to the
rest of the world, including a new effort to reconcile her tense relations
with the Soviet Union. The most important long-term question to be
asked is what will be the ultimate consequences this time when the
Chinese themselves, having gone through the two revolutions of 1911
and 1949, have insisted on a non-aligned policy to keep China open to
the rest of the world? Obviously, the Chinese will acquire scientific
and technological skills, increase trade and other economic and
cultural relations, and develop friendly diplomatic relations for
self-interest and world peace. However, this is a world of global
ideological conflict between political totalitarianism and democracy.
It is a divided globe saturated with conflicts and competition between
two superpowers seeking to dominate and survive at the other's
expense. China is fully aware of this reality. It used to be a loyal
supporter of one superpower.

With the opening of China to the West, the intellectual demand for
freedom, young people's preference for the Western way of life,
partial restoration of the practice of religion, the impact of cultural
exchanges with Western nations and Japan, and many other contacts,
may sooner or later make their unexpected marks in influencing the
way of life in China. When economic mutual dependence and
politico-diplomatic relations with the Western nations are becoming
stronger and when a new generation of Chinese leaders are trained in
the West and will make their weight felt in future China, how can the
Chinese political system be kept insulated from the Western views of

those managers and diplomats who will be policy decision makers of the Chinese nation? It is in this long-term impact that we may see a different China emerge in future decades. In the concluding chapter, such related questions will be raised and explored again for the long-term understanding of China's road ahead.[10]

1.9 NEW ORIENTATION IN HISTORICAL PERSPECTIVES

How much is Deng's new political orientation going to change the nature of the current political Marxist line? How much will the economic development and the Western cultural influence affect the political style and the economic relations between individuals, families, and the central government's planning and its political power? Since the present political and intellectual life in Taiwan are much influenced by Taiwan's strong ties with the Western nations, it is, therefore, possible to expect the same kind of Western influence to permeate the Marxist government on mainland China. The case of Japan and India are additional examples that illustrate future trends under Western influences. Japan has achieved enormous economic wealth and a democratic political system since 1947. Nevertheless, the Japanese have preserved the major tenets of their own traditional culture. New wealth and democracy of Western origin in Japan seem to have reconciled well with the traditional lifestyle. India, like China itself, could not easily mobilise to rapidly acquire economic wealth and to bring the nation out of the traditional religious and linguistic conflicts, although it has been committed to a secular state with a democratic constitution since independence nearly forty years ago. My point is that all large nations with a long cultural heritage, such as India and China, do not change much in the short-run. The contemporary transformation in China would not seem to be able to substantially alter Chinese traditional culture. Cultural values in China were developed over several thousands of years. Western values, Marxian or non-Marxian, reached China in the twentieth century. This fact may be responsible for Deng's insistence on 'Socialism with Chinese characteristics'. Deng has to develop a modern state within the context of a Chinese historical perspective, having experienced the failure to create a communist state in the Russian style. Political indoctrination and election politics, for instance, do not really change the substance of traditional values. Taiwan's political system, for example, has not affected Chinese cultural values since the Second World War.

However, no government can resist the cry for democratic participation and the respect for human rights, although few non-Western nations can fully implement them successfully.[11] This common cry for democracy constitutes part of the essence of modernisation. The May 4th movement of 1919 in China succinctly pointed out the long-term political orientation, namely, democracy on the one hand and science on the other. They constituted seemingly the only long-term way to modernise China. The same 'democracy' and 'science' of 1919 remained valid in 1949 and in 1976 to persistently challenge both the Nationalist government and the communist government for their fulfilment.

Given this historical context and modern revolutionary expectation, it may not be difficult to speculate what Deng Xiaoping should do for China at the end of the four modernisations, namely, to build an independent, democratic, respected, modern industrial state capable of self-defence and willing to contribute to international peace and security. Ideological specification of whatever artificial brand remains merely a technique, a trade mark, an artificially devised intellectual mechanism to inspire unity and support at home and to attract foreign followers seeking a way toward the future. Deng, Mao and others have all been Chinese patriots first. They each sought political power to make strategic policy decisions, although Mao seemed to have pursued the vanity of power to satisfy his personal ego. Vanity and ego satisfaction usually lead to corruption of power and the downfall of the individual. More discussion on this will be included in the last chapter.

As a matter of historical perspective, what have the Chinese people and their leaders learned through their successive revolutions and the rise and fall of several leaders? Such questions surely can not be easily and adequately answered. They can, however, be approached indirectly. One may feel that the Chinese people, including the intellectuals, ought to realise that, like the Japanese and the Indians, they cannot eradicate their historical heritage through a cultural revolution. Any form of modernisation must recognise a nation's past legacy as a valuable experience and a powerful influence. Sun Yat-sen, for example, could not easily introduce into China a 'strange Western democratic political system' at the turn of the country. Chiang Kai-shek and his advisers did not know how and when to implement Sun's 'Three Principles of the People'. Mao and his followers vacillated between their support of the Nationalist Government between 1923–45, and the making of a revolution of their own which Mao led to victory in 1949. But Mao unwisely destroyed his early achievement before his death. Deng today profits from these valuable experiences as the single most powerful leader in China who is guiding the Chinese ship in a stormy ocean through peaceful reform. He wants peaceful reform not violent revolution.

Still, what do the Chinese intellectuals and average people themselves want in their national development? They honestly think about preserving their historical heritage and enjoy fair treatment at the hands of their own government. They do not want to be treated as 'stinking intellectuals' who desire to express views that are different from those of their government. They want eventually a democratic political system to channel popular and genuine participation. They prefer the system of rule of law which Deng calls 'Socialist legality'. They expect political equality for all citizens and individuals who shall resist any privileged party seeking to perpetuate class or political power. They want certain fundamental constitutional rights which no government or any leader in power can take away from them. It seems these are the long-term fundamental concerns that many Chinese today think about seriously. They have been taught a bitter lesson since 1911 and during the cultural revolution when mad Mao Zedong became a 'tyrannical human god'.

In short, the following chapters will deal explicitly or implicitly with the various issues raised in this introduction. It is a study of reflection which will inevitably hinge on my personal bias and preference. I shall allow my former experience and recent travels in China to guide me to formulate observations and judgements. The entire study may imply an effort to speculate constantly about how a different China may emerge through Deng's leadership and his policy of peaceful reform which he calls 'a second revolution'. And finally, it will be argued, explicitly and implicitly, that in the next thirty to fifty years China may have a good opportunity to emerge as a relatively 'open democracy with Chinese characteristics'. The dividing line between Sun's democracy of the 'Three Principles of the People' and Deng's 'Socialism with Chinese Characteristics' may be much blurred, if it does not disappear totally. Until then, the unification between Taiwan and the mainland will not be easily advanced, although both governments in Beijing and Taipei will continue to pledge effort for unification on their own separate terms. Any sign of Taiwan's moving away from the irreversible trend toward unification will be suicidal. It is useful for both sides of the Taiwan Strait to be reminded of the words in the famous Shanghai Communiqué of 1972 that 'there is but one China, and Taiwan is a part of China'. Non-political and non-negotiable contacts between the two governments may in time be considered unharmful to either side. Reaffirmation toward peaceful merger of the two under whatever future terms is a periodic necessity to prevent a dangerous drift of the two governments, and the search for mutually acceptable terms for unification is a useful practice.

1.10 MANY QUESTIONS BUT NO ANSWERS

Given the far-reaching prospect of Deng's reform consequences in various fields, the fact remains that every major reform is undertaken as an experiment which can be easily revised or abandoned. The ideological umbrella for reform legitimacy is still Marxism, although Marxism itself has been reduced to nothing more than the party's four official cardinal principles. Economic development is moving away further and further from Marxism in the name of 'socialism with Chinese Characteristics'. Does anyone know what these Chinese characteristics are? The failure of Mao's cultural revolution created a crisis of confidence in Marxist ideology and in the ability of the Chinese Communist Party to lead the nation. Can reform in time allow the Communist party to regain the full confidence of the people, especially from Chinese intellectuals who supported the revolution in 1940s and suffered under the new regime in the 1950s, 1960s and 1970s? Can reforms and innovations succeed without accepting some of the values of the capitalist countries and their methods for efficiency and policy making? Will there not be conflicts and crises in China between the four cardinal principles and the broad ideology of Western democracy? How can the four cardinal principles be implemented by the future leaders who will be influenced by their contacts with and knowledge of the non-communist world? What is a 'spiritual pollution' from the West, or Hong Kong, Taiwan, or Japan? Why have the people, young and old, been so easily influenced by the so-called 'spiritual pollution' in so short a time since the opening of the nation to the outside world? Will there not be more conflicts and cultural interactions with the Western world so long as China continues to expand its relations with the Western nations? How can the government fight against what it advocates on the one hand, and objects to, on the other, over the inevitable accompanying results deemed unacceptable?

What does 'Socialist legality' include, besides a few new pieces of legislation in recent years? For example, constitutional guarantees for fundamental human rights, basic political rights of participation and criticism, and freedom of the press and assembly, etc. are essential individual rights which must be enforced by the government on behalf of every citizen. Such rights are in conformity with the human rights charter of the United Nations. How can China avoid value conflicts of this sort in dealing with the foreign nations whose people are coming into individual contact with Chinese citizens in China and abroad?

Another set of unanswerable questions at this stage concerns the prospect of how far China will be reformed politically, especially in terms of political structure and process. For example, will there be a constitutional separation of powers between the party, the executive, the legislature and the judiciary? Can we assume that China will abandon the Soviet model of institutions and politics? Will there be open competition in the election process, such as an open system of nomination of candidates and campaign activities of different political parties? Can the Chinese legislative body acquire equality in policy making with the State Council? Can judicial process be free of political and ideological influence to apply law and punishment on the basis of the rule of law only? These kinds of questions have, perhaps, little significance now. They will, however, be likely to assume greater significance when Chinese society becomes more open and as China moves away from the Soviet model. Further questions can be asked. Will the Chinese political system emerge into a non-Western consultative polity which accepts power monopoly by one strong party, with non-adversarial participation granted to several minor political parties? Or will 'Socialist legality' be developed along the Japanese experience of one party dominance in the executive, with minor parties confronting the cabinet through legislative inquisition but unable to affect policy outcome?

Is it correct to assume that standard Western parliamentary democracy is alien not only to China but also to many other non-Western states? China has, in particular, a long political tradition of its own. And there is no such Westernised political culture in favour of standard Western democracy in China. Therefore, it is impractical to expect China to follow Western political development. It can also be observed that one-party government is common in East Asia in both communist and non-communist states, Korea, Taiwan, and even in Singapore, where single party rule remains a fact, although Japan has a few minor opposition parties in the Diet. These Japanese opposition parties have since 1947 never been able to form a single cabinet. Perhaps it is unfair to expect China to become a two-party or multi-party democracy. What kind of democracy do Chinese people want and what kind can they get is as yet an unanswerable question. For nearly eighty years since the revolution of 1911, Chinese revolutionaries and intellectuals have fought for political democracy and freedom. So far they have not succeeded. Perhaps they did not truly understand that Western parlimentary democracy cannot be transplanted to Chinese soil either from the USA or England. However, Democracy as a way of life and an ideal value concept can never die among Chinese intellectuals and revolutionaries until they truly know what democracy is and until China can independently institutionalise her own form of democracy. The Japanese, for example, developed their own version only after the Second World War. Perhaps, this is what Deng has in mind about China's 'Socialist democracy' in the future. Deng, too, may not know as yet what is to be the precise content and practice of his 'Socialist democracy'. Thus, it remains to be seen how a 'democracy with Chinese characteristics' is to be defined.

As the chief architect of the current reform, Deng must take all things into consideration. What he must insist upon includes what he must not say. Political necessity dictates what is to come about through experimental reform. There is a long list of major themes he always emphasises. It is, perhaps, very appropriate to summarise what he said at the September 1985, party conference. The highlights of his speech there included the progress already made and the task still ahead. He made an evaluation of the past seven years of reform achievement and offered an agenda of issues to stress in the coming decade. They include in summary as follows:[12]

1. *Present circumstances and reform.* 'Every one has seen that the last seven years have been the best and key significant period since 1949. We did two things during the difficult period: eliminate disorder and return to normal, and initiate the overall or comprehensive reform. For years we were victimised by emphasis on class struggle in neglect of production forces ... Now, on the basis of the four cardinal principles ... our result of success has been the struggle against leftist mistakes. Without the four cardinal principles we could not have preserved unity in the country. Our reform in rural areas stirred up three years of conflict since 1978 ... Since the Third Plenum of the Twelfth Congress emphasis has been concentrated on urban reform. On the basis of agricultural success, we have now launched urban comprehensive economic restructuring. Reforms have increased production forces, but also brought on a series of in-depth changes in our

economic, social and work methods and spiritual life. Reform is a socialist system's self-correction which, within certain limits, has brought a certain degree of revolutionary change. This change is a major event to prove that we have begun to discover a new road to construct Socialism with Chinese Characteristics...'

On the other hand, Deng quickly reaffirmed that the publicly owned sector of the economy will remain predominant. Everyone will enjoy better living standards with some improving faster than others. Concrete methods of economic restructuring still 'remain experimental'. He confidently said 'I believe whatever is in harmony with the interest of the majority of the people and receives their support will invariably succeed regardless of whatever difficulties lie ahead.'

2. *His confidence in the future success of the Seventh Economic Plan.* Seven per cent economic rate of increase annually is not too high. Faster growth creates too many management problems. Our main emphasis is on management skill, product quality and economic and social efficiency. If our economic structural reform can achieve regularised continuity, stability and harmonious development, we will, then, feel sure of reaching our growth goal fixed for the year 2000. The middle of next century will, then, see great changes when China makes a greater contribution to mankind. This is clearly an expression of cautious confidence in the future socialist economic prospect. Will the future still be a socialist phenomenon relevant to Marxist 'scientific prediction'?

3. *Development of 'Spiritual Civilization'.* Deng expressed disappointment in this area in spite of his acknowledgement of much work already done by the party, the central and local governments, and among the masses. He asserted socialist superiority over capitalism in developing productive capacity and in preventing greed, corruption and injustice. He complained: 'Although production has increased in recent years, diseases of feudalism and capitalism not only fail to be reduced to the most possible low level, many of the long disappeared evils since 1949 have now been resurrected ... Without emphasising spiritual construction, material civilisation will suffer ... and our revolution and construction cannot achieve victory.' Here lies China's dilemma: to choose between continuity of her socialist past, economic inefficiency and the evils hidden in capitalist efficiency in management and production. Deng emphasised reform and the fight against 'spiritual pollution' as the key path to exercise self-control and criticism. How well the party will set an example against economic

crimes, bureaucratic corruption and the misuse of authority
should become clear when the task of party reform completed in
1987 as targeted.

4. *Leadership transition and the need to study Marxism*: Deng
advised the younger leaders to faithfully continue the good and
dedicated revolutionary tradition of the older generation. He
warned them against 'false speech, vanity, misuse of public
authority for private gains and nepotism'. Continuity of party
policies depends on successful leadership transition and recruitment. Deng's policy emphasis includes 'national independence,
democracy and rule of law, open door policy toward the outside
world, and the economic growth and liveliness. These policies will
not change. The basis for these policies is our insistence on the
four cardinal principles. Otherwise, our society will be disorderly
without stability and unity, let alone reform and rejuvenation.'
His last emphasis in the speech was that all must 'study the theory
of Marxism... It is not indoctrination. Marxism is a compass to
action and a method to resolve new problems in accordance with
new circumstances.' In short, experiment brings about choices
which may require new changes and more reforms. Deng's grand
reform is, therefore, a revolution by peaceful methods. Much
depends on the end-products of the experiment. One can expect
China to be under this 'peaceful revolution' for many decades to
come, barring unexpected circumstances which may intervene
drastically in this process. 'From the time of the Opium War in the
1840s to the year 2040', Deng predicted in his speech, 'China will
have changed very much in 200 years', so that the country will
probably appear neither majestically imperialistic as in its distant
past, nor as a Western democracy as Sun Yat-sen expected through
his revolution of 1911, nor yet socialistically Marxian as the
communists expected to achieve in their revolution of 1949. China
will more than likely emerge in its rejuvenated cultural tradition
with modernised material circumstances and in accord with the
nature and conflict in a vastly expanded global community of
nations. China has to preserve its identity as all nations do. But it
cannot ignore the global forces which influence the destiny of all
mankind. The outcome will remain speculative until the result of
long-term reforms are visible. Deng's ideological commitment, or
the four cardinal principles, may not be able to control the future
forces for new reform to be initiated by the government and even
by the people themselves.

2 Deng's Return and Reform

2.1 HIS LEADERSHIP DIMENSION AND UNIQUENESS

If modern Chinese revolutionary leaders can be ranked on some fixed criterion for their contribution in the areas of freedom, equality, democracy, material progress, peace and political stability, Deng's achievement, in only a few years after Premier Hua Guofeng's removal, has been phenomenal. His accomplishment can be viewed not only in material progress, but also in the people's mood and confidence. His leadership as a reformer demonstrates in many dimensions its unique responses to various challenges. Although Deng was not a forefront leader in the communist revolution in China to be ranked with Chen Tu-hsiu, Mao Zedong and Zhou Enlai until 1978, he has achieved, in the last half dozen years, more than his predecessors for the average person in material progress, social stability, freedom for initiative, and in policy implementation of the four modernisa- tions. While Mao was a sentimental visionary and Zhou a consensus builder, Deng has been a courageous reformer and a confrontationist who persists to fight and fights to win. Previously, he was known to have given up a struggle easily. His policy views in the past were well known. Almost thirty years ago in one of his reports as the Communist Party Secretary-General, he said:[1]

> Ours is a land with a population of 600 million. To unite such vast population for the cause of building socialism is a glorious yet arduous task. To achieve this unity we must constantly consult and work with all the people. We must handle correctly internal contradictions among the people. We need to create a political situation in which we have both centralism and democracy, both discipline and flexibility, both unity of will and personal ease of mind and liveliness.

He was then fighting against Mao's attempt to introduce the rural commune system and 'Great Leap Forward' proposal. Deng realised long ago that China was too big to be totally controlled by a distant central government. The people must be allowed to do what they can for themselves. This is precisely what has happened in rural China during the last eight years when the farmers themselves went on to divide up the commune lands before the central government policy was even formulated. Deng is different from Mao who preferred to impose on the people what he thought was absolutely right and ideologically progressive. Deng is prepared, on the other hand, to consult and take advice from the people so as to 'have both centralism and democracy'. To combine discipline with flexibility under Deng today is to build unity with diversity. If more people are able to see him as a modern revolutionary with a traditional pragmatism, Deng's socialist democracy will easily be seen as a genuine substitute for the Communist utopia.

Deng is a unique leader in modern China in a number of unusual ways. For example, twice he was ousted and twice he wrote personal letters to Mao Zedong and Hua Guofeng to get himself back into a leadership position. Before he was reinstated in 1973, he had written to Mao for an opportunity to rededicate himself in service to the nation. Mao circulated his letters among top party leaders before his reinstatement.[2] While Zhou was hospitalised in 1974–5, Deng was effectively in charge of the military affairs (as Chief of Political Department of the PLA), the Party Affairs (as one of the Vice-chairmen of the party) and as the First Vice-premier of the State Council. He was the busiest politician and the third in the leadership hierarchy next to Mao and Zhou. He worked diligently in new policy orientation and in party rebuilding after Lin Biao's downfall. He was in confrontation and in conflict with the 'Gang of Four'.[3] He antagonised them so much as to cause his second downfall immediately after Zhou's death.

Deng wrote to Premier Hua immediately after Mao's death in September, 1976, for an opportunity to return to the government. Hua was cautious in handling his reply. But he wrote to Hua again. The support for Deng's return was so overwhelming that Hua had no choice but to reinstate him in 1977. The 'shared leadership' in the decision-making process since his reinstatement lasted fifteen months only, prior to the Third Session of the Eleventh Central Committee in late 1978. During the session Deng's policy on new political orientation and economic adjustment received the majority support. Although Hua's 'little leap forward' in the economic field was criticised and defeated, Hua himself remained as Premier and party chairman.

The uniqueness in Deng's leadership might have come from the fact that he is the only central leader who has travelled widely abroad since the 1920s. He has a living experience of several years in liberal-democratic France. He has travelled often since 1949 in many foreign countries. In particular, in the aftermath of destruction that took place during the cultural revolution, he went to Europe and to the United States in 1974 to speak to the emergency sessions of the United Nations. And as the 'strong man' of China he came as the state guest of the US government immediately after the formal opening of the diplomatic relations in 1978. Thus Deng, like Zhou before him, was privileged to know more about contemporary progress and living standards in other countries. These unique opportunities might have contributed to his new policy of reform and emphasis on the four modernisations which Zhou announced to the National People's Congress in January 1975. The Four Modernisations represent Deng's programme which is supported by the moderate groups within the party. The leftish faction was thus compelled in 1974 to carry out a new political campaign against the Zhou-Deng 'Confucian-nonrepentant' capitalists during Zhou's last year in hospital. This again illustrates that Deng is a confrontationist willing to pay any political price in order to reform the system and serve the country. Zhou, on the other hand, was a reconciliationist who was prepared to pay any price at personal cost as a crisis manager in order to rebuild inter-group consensus within the party and the government.

Another part of Deng's uniqueness is his preference for the organisational approach, being an institutionalist bureaucrat himself. As a party bureaucrat during the years of the Second World War, he often represented the party leadership on his various assignments within the 8th Route Army and later in the People's Liberation Army (PLA). In that capacity, he had to make decisions that not only represented a higher party authority but which also received the coordinated support of the military leaders. This experience as a horizontal and vertical intermediary authority gave him an institutionalised decision-making habit as well as an understanding of and acquaintance with the military commanders. This was especially true during the 1947–50 period when he virtually exercised top authority as party and military supreme leader marching along with the field commanders to cross the Yangtze River to liberate the Nanking––Shanghai region and to southwest China to sweep in victory the entire region all the way to the Vietnam and Burma border. These years of civil war helped his political power in the PLA and his personal relations with field commanders who later supported his return to government and party before and after Mao's death in 1976. This unique background is exceptionally useful in his 'helmsmanship' today in China without fear of military disloyalty. It was this close relationship between Deng and the PLA leaders that made former Premier Hua's struggle to retain central leadership difficult, because the military had a major voice in the politiburo of the party. Since Deng has the support of the armed force – the barrel of the gun – he has political power.

Still another unique feature in Deng's leadership has been his appearance not to have formally organised any faction of his own in the party, the bureaucracy or the army. He was well-known to all factions in the party hierarchy. Deng was much like Zhou in this respect within the government bureaucracy as well. He had loyal friends and subordinates everywhere but was above formal factional alliances. In his fight to return to government after Mao's death, he received support from nearly all quarters because of what he had stood for and his ability and influence within the power structure in the party, the army and the government. More than Zhou, Deng had intimate working experience with all echelons of leaders vertically and horizontally in both regional and in central government units. His sharp mind, quick tongue and administrative talent have been well-known since the early 1950s when he was promoted from the southwest region of the country to become both finance minister of Zhou's cabinet and the party's secretary-general. He remained as party secretary-general for more than twenty years until his removal in 1966 at the start of the cultural revolution. In short, no one in the People's Republic of China had such a broad administrative experience as he. Even Mao or Zhou never had the experience and close contact below the central leadership level. Given broad experience and administrative capacity, he would have been ideal to succeed Zhou, had it not been for the 'Gang of Four' who surrounded Mao and persuaded him to remove Deng in favour of the little-known Hua Guofeng, as acting premier at first. His removal by Mao was universally though silently disapproved. The whole nation was angered and, therefore, acted in violent retaliation on 5 April 1976, in Beijing at Tiananmen Square where they avenged Zhou and Deng.

One other unique trait in Deng's leadership is his absolute control over the hierarchy after his victory against Hua. The new political circumstances since then have allowed Deng to be the first and definitely the last voice in all major policies. He is the final arbiter of all things, like Mao, but without being surrounded by a personality cult. In practice, he chooses to delegate decision-making authority to others in accordance with their respective institutional capacity. Much of his time is reserved in thinking about problems, strategies, personnel, policy goals and institutional coordination. In short, his position is supreme and unique in the entire communist world. Mao did not have such a political and decision-making environment. He had to fight against the majority in the party or divide them up in order to prevail. He had to fight laboriously for the implementation of his commune and the 'great leap' in the late 1950s. He also had to rely on purging and cruelty to eliminate those who were against his policies. Zhou, on the other hand, never really made major and independent policy decisions on his own. He merely expertly participated in the decision-making process and was responsible in implementing policy decisions made elsewhere. In contrast Deng overrode decisions already made and known to the public. In 1984, Deng suddenly announced at a press interview that China would have to station a certain number of troops in Hong Kong after its return in 1997. This stand contradicted several high officials who had long stated that China would not dispatch troops to Hong Kong for purposes of defence in view of the fact that Hong Kong would be allowed to exist as an autonomous region of China after 1997. This example illustrates'a potential source of embarrassment if Deng in future repeats the exercise of such supreme authority. On the other hand, it is clear that Deng, by his volition and by political necessity, has chosen not to occupy a formal institutional position in the government and the party in order to impress other leaders to accept retirement in the transfer of power. Deng has been far more concerned about bureaucratic and systematic decision-making through formal institutional infrastructure. Thus, Lord Acton's dictum that 'power corrupts and absolute power corrupts absolutely' may not be applicable to Deng. It remains to be seen how Deng will conduct himself in future years. It is clear Deng himself refuses to become another Mao, but health and mental capacity often work against the best interests.

How did Deng achieve this unique leadership position? There are a few important factors which suggest explanation. First of all, it was a matter of destiny that Deng's experience and positions before the cultural revolution had given him unique advantages over many other well-known purged politicians, such as Peng Zhen, the former Mayor of Beijing, and Chen Yun, the former chairman of Economic Planning Commission. Secondly, Deng's age qualifies him as a younger and well-experienced statesman who is from the old generation that experienced the famous Long March. He can best command the loyalty and respect from those younger than he. Thirdly, Deng was

purged as the 'Number 2 Capitalist Roader' next to Liu Shaoqi, the
then real bureaucratic head of the party and the head of the state and
also designated by Mao to succeed himself. But Liu died too soon.
Fourthly, Deng was highly praised for his policy of restoring the
purged colleagues to their personal honour, to former or new positions
in the government, by overturning the unfair accusations of the
cultural revolution. Deng did so as a matter of necessity to control the
party and political power for the good of the state. The moderates, and
other anti-Jiang Qing and anti-Lin Biao senior leaders were returned
to positions of responsibility at the expense of the radical leftists.
Deng's 'de-purge' policy received nationwide acclamation because
many millions of former leaders and cadres were waiting and eligible to
be rehabilitated. He rectified the abuse and damage done to the
civilian population during the cultural revolution through monetary
compensation. Such compensation by the government or return of
confiscated property to the owners was appreciated. As a result of
correcting the wrong deeds of the government of the past, Deng
benefited from public acclamation concerning his statesmanship.
Fifthly, his struggle against the leftists and their influences within the
government, the party and the army earned for him gratitude of many
individuals and groups who, like Deng himself, had suffered various
kinds of humiliation and mistreatment from Mao's followers during
the cultural revolution. The climax of Deng's courage and justice
against the followers of Lin Biao and Jiang Qing was finally highlighted
in the televised court trials. These trials further exposed the hated
individuals through the media coverage. By reversing the result of the
cultural revolution, he actually ended the era of Mao and launched the
era of Deng. Finally, Deng's popularity and statesmanship as an old
revolutionary resulted from his new policies to save the economy, to
benefit the people, and to retain political power for the Communist
Party to finally make good their revolutionary promise to build a
strong industrial state. His programme of four modernisations was the
answer which Deng had called for publicly through Zhou Enlai's last
speech to the National People's Congress in January 1975. Deng was then
already in confrontation with the Gang of Four twenty-one months before
Mao's death and Jiang Qing's arrest in October 1976. Taken together,
these factors helped to transform politics and to distinguish Deng, the
pragmatist, from Mao, the radical leftist, during and after the cultural
revolution.

Deng's return to power in 1977 was made inevitable by the then
political circumstances. He was so well-known for having drawn up the
blueprint of the four modernisations which was well-publicised and

received nationally. Secondly, Deng's close association with Zhou as fellow pragmatists in their political and policy views and Zhou's open preference for Deng to succeed him to resist the radical leftists were also major factors in Deng's popularity and leadership image. After his return to leadership in 1973 as Vice-premier, party vice-chairman, and commissar of the political department of the PLA, he was not only in daily charge of all three areas administratively but also began to implement reforms within the three branches. For example, in his speech to the PLA leaders above the level of regiment in 1975, he told them forthrightly that

> our practice has always been the party in control of the gun, not the gun in control of the party. This tradition was interrupted by Lin Biao as defence minister since 1959 and especially during his later years. Now the good tradition is gone, military budget is too large ... training for battlefield is inadequate. Chairman Mao lately has suggested reforms in the armed forces. The size of the army must be reduced; tradition restored. There is much work to be done in the three headquarters of the staff division, the political division and the logistics division.[4]

He then warned the audience that those who insisted on practising factionalism would not be employed or promoted. Military discipline must be restored. Work efficiency would be promoted.

In March 1975, addressing a group of party leaders in charge of industrial management at the provincial and city level, he told the cadres of the need to complete the four modernisations within twenty-five years. The success depended, he said, on having more railroad and energy supply. Everywhere he went, Deng spoke of the four modernisations, on the need of a strong and committed party leadership, on the struggle against factionalism at the workplace, on the need to de-purge abused leaders and cadres, and on restoration of institutions and accountability of individual responsibility. Economic recovery and further expansion were constantly in his mind. He often emphasised the need for political stability and unity.[5] On industrial expansion strategy, Deng was able in 1975 to insist on first having a blueprint of development targets: (1) making agriculture the foundation of industry by modernising agricultural expansion first; (2) importing new technology and newer equipment from abroad by the joint contract method with foreign governments and companies. China should rapidly develop export trade in order to accumulate foreign currency to purchase what China did not have; (3) the need to build up scientific research; (4) enterprise reorganisation to utilise management science and skill; (5) enhancing the quality of products to assure market expansion abroad; (6) stressing the personnel system and organisational efficiency in work accountability; and (7) allowing wage discrepancy to reward efficient workers. These seven guidelines of 1974 were basic and still constitute part of the reform cornerstone. In short, before his downfall for the second time in January 1976, Deng had launched his four modernisations campaign. His determination to return to power after Mao's death was based on his desire to again continue his reform work for a modernised China by the year 2000. This goal has now included a new target to 'redouble the GNP by year 2000'.

The dimension of his leadership is wide and inclusive. His goal is to create material progress and spiritual advancement in the quality of life. Besides the living standard, the cultural, moral and recreational activities of the people have also been much stressed in Chinese media campaign. Educational expansion, for example, is the key to industrial technology and human resource training. He has set the key concepts or criteria for reform, according to his many speeches in recent years:

1. *Avoid ideological entanglement*: 'work more, speak less'.
2. *Speed up leadership transition*: leaders and cadres must be 'young, knowledgeable, revolutionary, and with specialised skill or capabilities'.
3. *On political reform*: follow the socialist path, insist on communist leadership, practice democratic centralism, and continue with Marxism, Leninism and the Thought of Mao (the four cardinal principles).
4. *On immediate goals*: economic expansion, unification with Taiwan, and preservation of world peace.
5. *On urban economic restructuring*: enterprise autonomy, wage differentiation, bonus incentives, separation of government from economics, emphasis on worker's participation in enterprise decision-making, and implementation of new tax systems.
6. *On party reform*: emphasis on the disciplinary approach at all levels, institutionalisation of central collective leadership via the secretariat, abolition of party chairmanship, institution of retirement system at all levels with full material compensation, elimination of leftists or followers of the leaders of cultural revolution.

To better understand the dimensions and uniqueness of Deng's leadership it is necessary to discuss what he has actually done about the leadership succession. How has he dealt with the tenets of Mao Zedong's Thought, Marxism, and Leninism in the context of his reform? How can he support and reconcile the four cardinal principles? Whether Deng and his followers can operate without their own revised or new and fresh ideological foundation is worth exploring. It is true that no popular interest exists at this stage for having a strong ideological commitment. Most people in China are tired of and disgusted with ideological argument or debate. Their minds need a rest. The population wants material progress and · opportunity to advance personally. Life without ideology and with less politics is better and more satisfying. However, in the long run there is likely to be a serious conflict between material and spiritual progress on the one hand and the four cardinal principles on the other. Unless these principles are revised or disregarded, they must be in accord with future new reality of Chinese socialism which itself must be ideologically reconciled with the new political, cultural, social and economic relations that will be in existence by the end of the year 2000 or later. Finally, it would be interesting to explore the new implications from Deng's grand experiment in various fields, especially the likely future domination by the new industrial elite *vis-à-vis* the younger generation of party leaders.

2.2 THE UPHILL STRUGGLE AFTER MAO'S DEATH

Trained throughout his life in dialectical thinking, Deng clearly gave a lot of his time during his downfall to analysing dialectically what had gone wrong since the eighth party congress in 1956. He read a great deal in those years of 'reform and study'. This was, perhaps, the best time in life when he could calmly and peacefully formulate judgement and conclusions on mistakes of the past and problems in China's future. His daughter's recent work confirms what her father went through in those years of study, work, rest and thinking about future reform.[6]

Deng has never been and is not now a 'capitalist roader'. His philosophical commitment to a Marxian society appears irreversible, although his readiness to adapt and to reform is unquestionable. He was always open to alternative methods to achieving practical success. It is, perhaps, helpful to paraphrase Deng's current goals and strategies for his socialist China as follows: (1) a socialist economy with many non-socialist subdivisions or capitalistic components; (2) an

advanced stage of elective socialist democracy with top-level centralism; (3) a modernised country in terms of wealth, science, defence and
a relative equality of material and spiritual life for all citizens; (4) a
socialist legal system defined as rule of law without class privileges; (5)
collective leadership in government and within the Communist party in
conjunction with other minor political parties through the institutionalised mechanism of CPPCC (Chinese People's Political Consultative
Conference); (6) a political or ideological commitment to the four
cardinal principles of communist leadership, a socialist path, people's
democratic centralism, Marxism, Leninism, and the Thought of Mao;
(7) the party's need to regain popular support through rapid
improvement in rural economic reform and industrially diversified
development; (8) urban economic decentralisation to assure production efficiency and completion; (9) upgrading of and respect for
intellectuals to regain their faith in the Communist party and its
leadership: (10) thorough reform of the Communist party to lead
the country into the 21st century in peaceful reconstruction; (11)
abandonment of ideologically futile arguments to liberate the creative
intellectual power of the people and leaders; (12) domestic policy
experiments in all fields when necessary, such as the system of
responsibility farming, etc.; (13) 'socialism in one country', to
cooperate with and aid socialist movements abroad, and to maintain
China's independence for world peace through contacts with the two
superpowers. These thirteen categories of goals and strategies may not
exhaust what is in Deng's mind as a reformer or as the remaker of
China in a different mould from what Mao and the Russians had hoped
for. Mao seemed to want a China in permanent revolution, while the
Russians wanted a weaker and dependent China subordinate to the
Soviet domination. Deng clearly hopes to build a modernised China
which is proud of its heritage, capable of self-defence, respected by all
nations and eager to make a positive contribution to world peace.

When he returned to power in 1977, he was faced with a formidable
situation in which Hua Guofeng was the premier whose legitimacy to
leadership derived from Mao's decree. Hua could not lead any fight
against Mao's ideological leftism. Instead, he had to hoist higher
Mao's flag of leadership to help himself retain power and to inspire
other Mao followers. Hua could not do less than to work harder to
unite his supporters and Mao's devotees to consolidate his own
leadership position against Deng's moderate faction.

After the Tiananmen Square Riot on 5 April 1976, Mao immediately made Hua the Premier from his position of acting Premier. After

Mao's death on 6 September Hua was able to get himself elected by the Politburo to be chairman of the party to succeed Mao and Chairman of the powerful Military Affairs Committee of the Communist party. This was a position from which Mao dominated the armed forces. It is the same position Deng holds today. Secondly the majority of the members in the Politburo were still Maoist. Hua had resisted strongly and artfully Deng's return to power. As mentioned earlier, Deng himself wrote to Hua to indicate his wishes to serve the country and the party. Hua did his best to postpone Deng's return in order to better fortify his own defence. However, pressure came from many directions demanding his return. Several strong military leaders also urged his resumption of power, including Deng's close friend Xu Shiyou of the Guangzhou military command. Vice premier Li Xiannian, now president of the country, and defence minister Yi Jianying, 'the king maker after Mao's death', were the strong voices of the moderate faction on Deng's behalf. The media and the public eagerly expected his resumption of leadership in some major posts in the party and in the government.

Meanwhile, the Gang of Four sat in goal. But those who had been close associates of Jiang Qing were still in high posts. Some of them were members of the highest policy-making body, the politburo. Others were in the State Council or cabinet as ministers and vice premiers. And a few high military commanders had also been strong supporters of Jiang Qing, including Chen Xilian, the Beijing military district commander. These factional leaders had lost their chiefs since the arrest of the Gang of Four through joint efforts of Hua and the defence minister, Yi Jianying, and Wang Tong Xing who had been closest to Mao as director of the party central office. In short, Hua was in a very precarious position. On the one hand, he clearly needed the support from all anti-moderate forces against Deng. However, he had to arrest the Gang of Four who were Deng's arch enemies. Hua could not hold on to his leadership without the support of moderate Li Xiannian, Yi Jianying and several military commanders. Without a strong base of political power of his own in the party and the government, Hua eventually gave up in 1977 and Deng came back to power in July 1977.

It is easy to understand the lack of leadership stability in Beijing when Mao died. The Gang of Four made a bid for power. They wanted Zhang Chunqiao to be the premier. Jiang Qing hoped to become the party chief. Even Wang Hung Wen expected to be the head of state. It was rumoured that Wang Hung Wen had had his official photo made as head of state long in advance in preparation for the leadership takeover. The arrest on the Gang of Four quickly silenced many rumours. Some Mao followers resented Mao's wife, Jiang Qing, and helped Hua retain his leadership longer than he deserved. Wang Tong Xing was the strongest among those loyal to Mao only. It was, in fact, Mao's 8341-strong security force, the palace guards, who made the arrest of the Gang of Four in October.[7] The alliance between Wang Tong Xing and Hua Guofeng made Deng's return more difficult. This and many other complicated factors were responsible for explaining why Deng did not come return to power immediately after Mao's death. These same factors in party factional struggle were responsible for Hua's election to become the Chairman of the Communist party and the Premier. Illegally he had been made Premier by Mao's handwritten edict, not by election of the politburo or the Central Committee of the party. Chairman Mao, the cause of all conflicts toward the end of his life, was himself unwilling and unable to trust anyone around him – not Deng, not Jiang Qing nor Zhang Chunqiao. He chose Hua as acting premier instead of the 'presumed automatic promotion' of Deng as premier upon Zhou Enlai's death. Presumably, Mao chose Hua either as a transitionary caretaker or for a test period to try his ability. However, after the 5 April violence at the Tiananmen Square, Mao nervously and quickly enpowered Hua as Premier to strengthen his rising leadership. Mao expressed his fear and suspicion of everyone else by writing to Hua the following: 'when you are in charge, I am at ease'. Without being closely identified as a Maoist, Hua slowly gained the support of all those who had been Mao's devotees, including Jiang Qing's followers. Such was the environment when Deng attempted to return to power.

Once in power, Deng patiently watched Hua's own 'little leap forward' fail. He observed Hua's lack of sensitivity by trying to imitate Mao's style; while Deng's own motto was 'speak less and work more'. Slowly but steadily, individual Mao followers were forced to leave their posts. The media and the public began to criticise indirectly the policies of the cultural revolution. 'Democracy Wall' in Changan Road vehemently condemned the corruption in the government through 'Big Letter Pao' in the Democracy Wall. Several military leaders were removed for their close association with the Gang of Four, including Chen Xilian, the Beijing Military District Commander.

In late 1978, at the Third Plenum Session of the Eleventh Party Congress, Deng's supporters finally achieved a majority in the party leadership, while Hua Guofeng remained as premier with less and less actual power over policy making of his own government. Deng won the struggle without advancing himself into higher offices. He remained as Vice-premier until his official retirement from government, but not from his important post in the party as chairman of the Military Affairs Committee.[8] Deng's success resulted from several major steps. First of all, he speeded up the rehabilitation process to bring back to leadership many well-known victims of the cultural revolution. For example, Chen Yun had been chairman of state planning commission since the early 1950s. Peng Zhen was the powerful mayor of Beijing before his purge in early 1960s as a close ally of Liu Shaoqi. General Wang Zhen and Field Marshall Luo Ruiqing were well-known leaders of the People's Liberation Army. Other leaders, including Yang Dezhi, Keng Biao, Wan Li, and most important of all, Hu Yaobang, were all back in power shortly after Deng's own rehabilitation for the second time in 1977. His second major action was to remove those who 'helicoptered' themselves to the membership of the political bureau as benefactors of the cultural revolution. They had been close allies of Jiang Qing or 'unconditional yes men' of chairman Mao. After the removal of Wu De, the mayor of Beijing, Chen Yongqui, the hero of Dachai, Ji Dengkui, a vice-premier and Wang Dong Xing, a party vice chairman, Hua's position in the political bureau was drastically weakened, while Deng's supporters grew more numerous. It was, however, a zigzag struggle. Some of the members in the political bureau did not want to be closely identified with a power struggle. For example, General Li Desheng, the commander of the Zhenyang military district and a benefactor of the cultural revolution, and Deng's own early close ally, General Xu Shiyou, objected to campaigns against Mao. Even Li Xiannian and Yi Jianying felt that Hua Guofeng could be preserved to join the moderate new leadership under Deng. However, by the Fifth Plenum of the Eleventh Congress in 1979, Hua's position in the political bureau was much weakened. His resignation from the premiership and party chairmanship was expected but he fought to delay it again.

On the other hand, Deng advocated party collective leadership against Mao's era of 'deified helmsmanship'. He suggested the abolition of party chairmanship in the new draft party consitution in favour of restoration of the party secretariat which Mao abolished during the cultural revolution. Deng also gained from nationwide TV broadcasting the open trial of the Gang of Four to fully discredit the 'tyrants' of the leftist radicals. The final most critical reason for Deng's political victory was his ability to instigate a re-evaluation of Mao's place in the communist revolutionary movement. Without this major step, the moderate pragmatist Deng and his followers could have had many more difficulties ahead in ousting Hua.

Implementation of the four modernisations required a drastic change of attitude toward a realistic evaluation of the past mistakes made by Mao both in policy and in ideology. A liberation of mind from Mao's ideology of the cultural revolution was essential in opening up the country to foreign science and technology, management methods, and capital investment. Readjustments and reform in China's rural and urban economic development required removal of the rigid central control and egalitarian ideology. Without an evaluation of Mao's achievements and mistakes, it was almost impossible to unite, under Deng, millions of party cadres and hundreds of top-level Maoists in the government and the armed forces. An evaluation of Mao's place in the revolutionary struggle was unavoidable in order to remove Hua's Maoist claim to leadership. Mao's personality cult, for example, helped Hua to consolidate his position and to unite Mao's blind followers. As expected, at the time of the party's Sixth Plenum of the Eleventh Congress in June 1981, the evaluation of Mao's record and the resignation of Hua as premier came about simultaneously.

The unanimously approved official party document on Mao was titled 'The Resolution of the Central Committee of the Chinese Communist Party on some Historical Problems Since 1949'[9]. This document, indeed, was a review of all major intra-party conflicts and factionalism, with emphasis on Mao's policy mistakes in two decades, 1956–76. It was a document allowing Deng to advance rapidly his modernisation and reform. In it, Mao's policy failure in the late 1950s and during the cultural revolution was bitterly described. The document also reviewed China's overall revolutionary circumstances under Sun Yat-sen and described how the Communist Party was born and taken into alliance with the Nationalist party prior to 1927. Mao was credited with great leadership during the first twenty-eight years before victory in 1949 (1921–49), especially his role in setting up the Soviet base in Jiang Xi, during the long march and his creative contribution as a theoretician, a strategist, and a reform leader in Yanan shortly before the victory of the Second World War. The document also credited the communist victory in 1949 as a victory over feudalism and imperialistic foreign capitalism as well as a victory for national 'true independence and unity' under proletarian 'democratic centralism' for socialist construction in a new pledge for a classless society. It further hailed the success in economic rehabilitation, rural land reform, and successful urban socialist construction during the first Five-year Plan (1952–6). The document complained that Mao departed from and compromised the party's correct position on economic, political and social development as adopted at the Eighth Congress in 1956. The nation in 1954 began its orderly constitutional practice of the 'New People's Democracy' and successfully persuaded the intellectuals in the early 1950s to join in national development. However, Mao personally initiated the 'catastrophic failure' plan of economic development since 1957 against the loyal and patient advice of Liu Shaoqi, Zhou Enlai, Chen Yun, Deng Xiaoping, Zhu De and others who collectively tried to persuade Mao to agree to and to adopt, for example, Chen Yun's proposal on economic planning on the basis of actual reality. In the interest of the country and with a concern for the well-being of the masses, Deng Xiaoping's proposal on reform of industrial enterprises, improvement over enterprise management and worker's participation in enterprise decision making was ignored by Mao. Zhu De's suggestion on the need to diversify cottage industry and the need for a multiple management approach toward agriculture and Deng Zihwei's urgent recommendation for the adoption of a farming responsibility system were also rejected by Mao in the late 1950s. All these critical proposals for adjustment and reform in the late 1950s could have been adopted had it not been for Mao's opposition in favour of his own commune and the 'great leap' policy. The document admits that the party under Mao's leadership mistakenly classified many loyal intellectuals within and outside the party as 'anti-regime rightists' and subjected them to unjustifiable humiliation and purge. Mao's radical leftist subjectivism, blindness, arrogance and the unrealistic expectation of very high agricultural and industrial production were indefensible. The failure of Mao after the Lu-shan conference in July 1959 to reverse his fatal mistakes of the 'commune' and the 'leap' was compounded by his mobilisation within the party to oppose comrade Peng Dehuai and other so-called 'rightists'. Mao arrogantly insisted on his subjectivism to cause political and economic sacrifice and suffering by the masses. Fortunately, later at the party's Central Working Conference in January 1962, some of Mao's political and economic policy mistakes were adjusted or partially corrected. The majority of those wrongly accused by Mao at the Lu-shan conference were rehabilitated. However, Mao persisted in wrongly expanding 'the class conflict' which again caused in 1964–5 many cadres to suffer. Mao's subjective ideological criticism was again intensified against intellectuals in 1964-5. He failed to appreciate the party's effort to bring the economy back on the right course toward modernisation in industry and defence. The mistakes of the anti-rightist movement and economic catastrophe during the ten-year period, 1956-66, should mainly fall on Mao's shoulders. His personal dictatorship seriously damaged the party's democratic centralism. 'Personality cult was not corrected ... these mistakes led eventually to the outbreak of the cultural revolution.[10]

The document correctly summarised Mao's worst behaviour which contradicted Mao's own writing during the cultural revolution, 1966–76. He personally led the 'ten years of horror' on the false accusation that the party, the army, the government and the cultural sphere had been infiltrated by 'a great number of capitalist representatives and anti-revolutionary revisionists'. They had penetrated, he insisted, all levels of the government and organisation. Mao further insisted, the document says, that there was no other way but to mobilise the masses to 'openly and completely' uncover them in order to regain political power by the proletarian class. Events proved that Mao himself violated the precepts of Marxism and misjudged the existing reality. The document repudiates Mao's charges as follows: (1) there were no facts to prove the takeover of the country by the capitalists and the revisionists; (2) the cultural revolution purged those who were actually the leading cadres of the party and in the country; (3) only in name did the cultural revolution rely on the masses. It, in fact, deviated from the masses and the party; (4) events proved that the cultural revolution was not and could not in any sense be called a revolution or social progress. It was not 'a struggle against enemy'. It was a 'self-distortion and confusion'. The cultural revolution itself had 'neither economic nor political basis. It could not propose any constructive policies. It merely created serious disorder and destruction ... It brought for the party, the country and the citizens of all nationalities internal calamities.'[11]

The document against Mao further specifies how Premier Zhou Enlai worked to preserve order and unity and how the Lin Biao and Jiang Qing factions plotted against Zhou and against each other. It described how Mao vacillated and failed to support Deng after Zhou's death and failed again after the 5 April 1976 revolutionary incident at the Tiananmen Square. The rest of the document turns to Deng's struggle to rehabilitate many leaders and cadres since 1977 and the failure of Hua Guofeng to create his new leadership after Mao's death. Instead, Hua followed closely in almost every respect Mao's footsteps, especially in his support for Mao's Dachai agricultural policy and a tendency to create a personality cult of his own. The document describes the need for Deng's effort to restore the party leadership, the correct role of Marxism-Leninism and Mao Zedong Thought as the guiding signposts in 'socialist construction with Chinese characteristics'. In short, the document concludes that Mao's contribution to the communist revolution up to 1976 was far greater than his mistakes. And Mao's Thought shall remain to guide the party. It ends with a call for unity to develop a modernised strong nation.

Having evaluated Mao's place in revolutionary history, criticised Hua's leadership failure, and publicly tried Jiang Quing and her cohort, Deng was now able to convince more colleagues and the people of his genuine devotion to go a long way in reforming the political system, the party internal leadership structure, and the economic changes. He had, by 1981, broken down the political resistance within the party and in the army to criticism of Mao. The next major concentration for Deng was to choose his own successors to Hua as party chairman and as new premier. Deng himself could have easily retained and occupied the major posts, the practice in nearly all other communist countries. But he deviated from the usual practice in favour of what can be called a personal sacrifice for genuine 'peaceful revolution' under his own control.

Deng himself was approaching the age of eighty when Hua resigned in 1981. No one was as strong politically or in as good health from among his own generation. Old Marshall Yi Jianying was closest in prestige and reputation to Deng's stature. But he had been suffering from ill health. Deng would have lost a great deal of prestige and leadership capacity had he himself remained officially in the top posts of the party and the government. He would not have been viewed as such a great reformer and been so well respected had he not reached out for younger leaders to divide up Hua's leadership role as party chairman and premier. As a pragmatist, Deng chose successors not on the basis of ideology, but on the merit of efficiency and ability to succeed, to innovate, to experiment and to share political leadership with others. Thus he selected Zhao Ziyang as 'premier apparent' months before Hua's resignation (as vice-premier in charge of daily administration routine). On the other hand, he selected Hu Yaobang as party chairman temporarily, pending the revision of the party constitution to abolish the post of chairman in favour of restoration of the post of party secretary-general which, in fact, becomes the highest party post.[12] Mao abolished the post of the secretary-general at the 9th Party Congress in 1969, a post Deng himself had occupied during 1954–66.

One of Deng's major reform proposals has been the restoration of 'party collective leadership' as reaffirmed at the Eighth Party Congress in 1956. But Mao as chairman ignored the past practice of collective decision making. Mao's personality cult grew out of his chairmanship that gathered the prestige and power in the hands of the single occupant of the post. The secretary-generalship is a chief administration post only, at least in theory. Its occupant is 'one and the first among equals'. It is, therefore, far more difficult for the secretary-general to usurp the shared leadership roles of his fellow secretaries of the secretariat. At the Twelfth Party Congress in 1982 Hu Yaobang became the secretary-general. What do we know about Deng's chief successors? What are their major qualifications and their relations with Deng? Are they acceptable to the rest of the party? Can they lead the nation effectively after Deng's departure? How do they share power with Deng on the one hand, and with other fellow decision-making contributors on the other? It is impossible to answer precisely all these questions at this time. With regards to Hu Yaobang and Zhao Ziyang, it appears by now that, after six years of actual exercise of power since Hua's resignation in 1981, they each have acquired a sufficient amount of administrative skill and experience to have met the approval of the nation and Deng's satisfaction. Hu worked closely with Deng in the 1950s and 1960s as an organisational leader of the party's Youth League. He joined the party as a young boy and experienced the Long March. He was assigned to various party and military posts before the cultural revolution. Mao purged him in the 1960s. Deng rehabilitated him in 1977. He seems to be a leader with an open mind and a spontaneous frankness. He is ideologically well-informed on Marxism-Leninism and Mao Zedong Thought. Thus he was the 'official party theoretician' who proved eager to implement changes and reform and to share power with others.

Deng rehabilitated Hu only one month after his own last return to power, as a partner in the struggle to regain leadership in order to implement the four modernisations. Deng may have had Hu in mind in 1977 as his successor, but Hu, in fact, was merely one of Deng's several close associates. They included Zhao Ziyang, Wan Li and others. Hu has had more party experience than Wan Li and others. Thus, Hu is more familiar with party work in contrast to those who have been better acquainted with government work. For example, Hu, at one time, was a director of the organisation department of the Eighth Route Army, later a political director of a branch campus of the Anti-Japanese War College, a political commissar of the 18th Army Corps at a still later date, and First Secretary of the Communist Youth

League in the 1950s. He also worked in Deng's home province in Northern Sichuan. In the 1960s he was once the Acting First Secretary of Shaanxi Province, a Secretary of the Northwestern Bureau of the party and Deputy Secretary-General of the Chinese Academy of Science. He remained longest on the top post for fourteen years in the Youth League. Thus, Hu had closer working experience with Deng when both were in Sichuan in the early 1950s and also in Beijing in the late 1950s. Deng knew Hu also through close private friendship as a bridge-playing partner. In 1975 when Deng was back in power during Zhou's premiership, Hu became Deng's very close intimate. Hu's greatest assets, which no one else seemed to possess, include his organisational ability, propaganda experience in the cultural field, and his working knowledge of non-communist thought through the United Front organisations. Finally but most important of all, Hu has achieved very great skill and knowledge in interpreting Marxism-Leninism and Mao Zedong Thought. Hu's own political power base includes the rank and file leaders of the Youth League and its mass membership. Presently, the party favours choosing top leaders from those with strong League background. In comparison with others around Deng, Hu has the best credentials as party leader and enjoys Deng's best confidence.[13]

In his early years, Hu did not receive much formal education. However, he was always an eager learner. Indeed, he acquired a solid foundation in working knowledge and tested ability. As a political-organisational leader his knowledge and experience include: (1) a good foundation in history, literature and ability to write, especially on Chinese history and Chinese classic literature which are often cited in his speeches; (2) his communication skills demonstrate logical consistency in written manuscript and richness in content, although he may not be a inspiring speaker because of his shrill voice; (3) his administrative ability has an accumulated advantage of many decades in the party, the army and in the Youth League which is almost as long as Deng himself in similar capacities with the party. Since 1977 he has helped Deng enormously as the party's organisation department director and later as propaganda department director to defeat the followers of Mao and Jiang Qing. Hu communicates best with younger people. As a person, Hu is very frank and courteous, unlike Deng who is direct and confrontational. Hu is also deeply respectful of intellectuals who see a great difference between Hu and Mao in their disposition toward intellectuals. He is also an efficient and persistent leader who demands quick implementation of policies in spite of overwhelming difficulties.

But he is a faction-oriented reformer who, since the early 1980s, has made major appointments largely from his own followers. One of his traits is his impromptu and often sentimental remarks that receive unfavourable media reaction, one of the reasons for his removal in 1987.

Since his return to power, Hu has helped Deng speed up his rehabilitation programme and has participated in the reform policy formulation and execution. It was important to Deng when Hu replaced Guo Yufeng as the Organisation Department director of the party in late 1977. Hu's faithful execution of Deng's policy to return loyal cadres to positions of power in the party and government weakened Hua Guofeng's leadership at all levels, including the army. The second most important contribution from Hu was his persistent effort to formulate a theoretical basis for Deng's pragmatic policy. Deng's realism needed a well-supported and accepted criterion to 'test truth from practice'. Hu persuaded the *Kuang-ming Daily* and several party school publications to publish professor Hu Fuming's philosophical article in 1978 which advocated 'practice as the only test of truth'. The party's theoretical journal, *Red Flag*, under Hua's control, refused to discuss and publish professor Hu Fuming's article on truth criterion. The Party's propaganda department under Zhang Pinghua as its director stonewalled the theoretical debate. It was, indeed, Hu's effort to convert the black-and-white cat speech into a broad theoretical foundation that justified Deng's policy of reform. Thirdly, Hu was influential also in encouraging students and underground papers and publications to speak up via the 'Democracy Wall' in Beijing. This practice for a period of two years (1979–80) attacked some of Mao Zedong's Thought and the followers of Mao while Hua was still the head of the party and the government. Pressures were being built up gradually before the Third Plenum of the Eleventh Party Congress in late 1978. It was at this meeting that Deng's followers opened their attack against Hua and his supporters. The Deng–Hu pragmatists achieved a majority at this meeting for the first time. Shortly after the Third Plenum, Hu became the director of the Party's propaganda department to replace Hua's man, Zhang Pinghua. In short, Hu became Deng's right-hand strategist and fighter against Hua Guofeng and other Maoists after his own rehabilitation in 1977.

The second most important 'heir apparent' as premier was Zhao Ziyang, now Secretary-General. Zhao is from the North central China province of Henan. He was born in 1919 and, is therefore, four years younger than Hu. Zhao had remained a local party cadre in his home province during the war years of Japanese aggression. He became influential only when he followed the liberation army in its move southward in 1948–49. Zhao was merely a party local functionary at this time. Shortly after reaching Guangdong, Zhao became one of the provincial party secretaries. He was later promoted to the position of first secretary at the young age of forty-five. During the cultural revolution, he was purged. In 1973, Premier Zhou rehabilitated him. He was appointed to a post of regional party secretary in Inner Mongolia. Shortly thereafter Zhao was returned to his former post as first party secretary in Guangdong province and director of the Guangdong provincial revolutionary committee (equivalent of the post of Governor). His continuing success in Guangdong convinced the leadership in Beijing that he would be the best administrator to be sent to Sichuan province where for years, in addition to poor government leadership, terrible famine and poor harvests had plagued the population. Sichuan has always been known as 'the richest state under heaven', yet starvation remained continuous for years. The people lost initiative in production and in self-help. A reformer was needed.

Zhao came to Sichuan to change the plight of living, to courageously reform and innovate. While there, he was the First Party Secretary of the Province and simultaneously the chairman of the Provincial Revolutionary committee (the provincial government set up to replace regular government during the cultural revolution). Soon Zhao was also made the political head of Chengdu Military District. Thus he became the most powerful leader in Sichuan and the Southwestern region of China. With such overwhelming authority, he began to reform Mao's commune system of production and distribution. He broke up the commune land and distributed it to individuals, families and to small production teams. They could freely produce whatever they thought best according to traditional farming experience. The farmers could keep for themselves any amount of surplus over what had to be handed over to the state on a quota basis. The commune's own brigade, production team and the commune administration itself were thus rendered redundant and without power over production. The farm people welcomed Zhao's reform overwhelmingly. Their initiative and incentive to work soared. Increases in production multiplied. Zhao also encouraged the rural population to resume traditional marketing among themselves. People could exchange or sell for the first time any goods without any restriction from government regulations. Zhao himself went from village to village to investigate and suggest what the people could do best for themselves. He also permitted urban small shop owners to open their own little business in self-help. In only a few years between 1975–8, Zhao's new reform policy had produced great positive results. There was no more starvation in Sichuan. People's income increased. New jobs multiplied and absorbed the surplus labour in both rural and urban areas. Economic activities diversified and multiplied. There was other new innovation and new momentum as a result of a new profit-making incentive on the part of the people. In short, Governor Zhao created a 'Sichuan model' of economic reform. His experience became known nationwide. In addition, Sichuan is Deng's home province. Deng could not help hear about the miracle-like reform success. The whole nation should now benefit from such a success in the aftermath of the commune's catastrophic failure.

Deng and Zhao had very little direct working experience together. Their paths did not cross until after the cultural revolution. However, Zhao was an expert in economic reform in the late 1970s and Deng needed such leaders to execute his policy of four modernisations. Zhao is a self-taught innovative leader who 'learned by doing'.

In 1976, while Deng was out of office and stayed in Guangdong, Zhao joined Deng's cause in common opposition against the Gang of Four who were then strong in Beijing. When the Deng-Hu group in 1978 publicly declared their 'Truth through Practice', some supported it while it was opposed by others. Many remained non-committal as an indirect expression of approval. Zhao, however, enthusiastically advocated it, and so entered the leadership core of Deng's camp. With his economic expertise and reform experience, Zhao is best suited today to translate Deng's four modernisations into policy execution. Besides, Zhao is an impressive and confident individual who handles the media and media people expertly. He thinks fast and is good at public relations. He is also known for his skill at reconciling conflicts in the decision-making process and in handling personnel issues. Zhao has been highly praised by colleagues and bureaucratic followers as an efficient and effective administrator. He appears to have some of the unique qualities of former premier Zhou Enlai. Therefore, Deng and Zhao today share a division of leadership, with each enjoying an exclusive sphere of control. For example, Deng is the final arbiter of policy conflict and chief innovator of policy measures and directions. Zhao remains in daily close charge of party bureaucracy and party control of ideology and personnel policy-making. Zhao, on the other hand, is the supreme administrator and innovator of programme planning. This leadership structure is bound to govern smoothly until Deng's departure. Hu is no longer on the top but may rise again.

On the other hand, Zhao, like Enlai before him, is in immediate daily contact with a much larger bureaucracy. Zhao is better known throughout the country. He maintains a closer relation with the masses in general. His popularity is rising. In style, Zhao is a polished and impressive leader. Since his takeover of the premiership in 1980, much success in economic and social reform has been achieved. Within the party circle Zhao has been highly praised for his sense of stability and his quick mind. He is also quite prudent and capable in public relations and in diplomatic visits abroad. Like Zhou, Zhao has travelled very widely, recently to some forty countries on state visits. He has built global understanding of China and made an acquaintance with many contemporary world leaders. He is, in addition, appearing younger than his age. Nothing seemed to encourage him in his top leadership ambitions. He seems to have shown no desire to succeed Deng and to have concentrated only on economic decision-making power in his office. Around him are several young rising stars, including Li Peng and Tian Jiyun as vice premiers who are competing to succeed Zhao's premiership in early 1988.

In 1985 a party conference was held in Beijing to restructure the party's top leadership.[14] At this time 131 senior veteran top level leaders resigned. A half dozen members of the Political Bureau had also resigned a week earlier. They included, for example, Marshall Yi Jianying, and Madame Zhou Enlai and Wang Zhen. These resignations created a grand opportunity for the conference to elect about 179 young leaders during the week-long session. This was an extraordinary party meeting to accomplish an extraordinary recruitment task. As reported, fifty-six seats of the Central Committee and thirty-four on its alternative body were filled. Fifty-six older individual colleagues were elected to the party's Central Advisory Commission and thirty-three to the Central Commission for Discipline. This smooth transition in leadership was an achievement of unusual persuasion on the part of Deng and Hu. This was another large measure against lifelong tenure as practised in nearly all other communist states. The conference was presided over by Hu Yaobang. It was itself clear evidence of Hu's leadership role next only to Deng. During the conference, a total of ten seats were designated for new occupancy on the Political Bureau. Such a large-scale election has drastically lowered the average age of the central leadership. The first generation veterans are practically all gone. Their seemingly voluntary resignation has avoided the impression of a purge. The retired leaders, however, still can help around in other advisory capacities. Deng and Hu do not push them away from Beijing. They still retain their official automobile, government residence and all other benefits as if they were still in office. Mao did not want to deal with colleagues in this way. Deng must be credited for such an accomplishment. One report indicated that China is 'left more thoroughly prepared than ever in its modern history to transfer power when an aging top politician leaves the scene'.[15] With the election of several well-known younger leaders, the second-tier group will succeed Deng's successors toward the end of this century. The result of this leadership transition has been credited to Deng's hard work in three years since the Twelfth Party Congress in 1982. Among the elected in September 1985, the following attract special attention:[16]

1. Hu Qili, age fifty-eight, a new member of the political bureau, groomed to succeed Hu Yaobang (they are not related). Young Hu is also a member of the Central Secretariat and an efficient organiser. Deng considers him the 'talent for Secretary-General'. He was a student leader of Beita in 1948–51, a former high official in the Youth League, was purged during the cultural revolution, and became mayor of Tianjin upon rehabilitation in 1978, standing Committee member of Politburo in 1987.
2. Li Peng, age fifty-nine, educated in the Soviet Union, presently also a vice premier with special responsibility (since July 1985) to develop educational expansion and reform to meet the modernisation needs in coming decades. He was adopted by the late premier Zhou. At the recent party conference he was promoted to be a member of the Secretariat and the Political Bureau. Li is an engineer by training in the Soviet Union in the 1950s. He is considered an expert on energy development. His parents were revolutionaries and were killed. He grew up for some years in Hong Kong before it was occupied by Japan after the Pearl Harbour incident. In 1985, Li accompanied President Li Xiannian on a state visit to the United States. He was made a member of Party Central Committee only in 1982 and acting Premier after Zhao in 1987.
3. Tian Jiyun, age fifty-eight, a vice-premier for several years, a protégé of Premier Zhao Ziyang since their days in Sichuan province in the middle 1970s, thus a contender for Zhao's premiership some day. He is now also a member of the Political Bureau and the Secretariat. Tian has the Sichuan experience as a

rural reform expert. He was one of the authors to draft the urban economic restructuring package in 1984.

4. Wu Xueqian, age sixty-five, foreign minister since 1982, a Hu Yaobang confidant. This year he was promoted to be a member of the Political Bureau.

5. Qiao Shi, age sixty-three, a new face in top leadership. In 1985 he was made a member of the Political Bureau and the Secretariat. There is very little known about his distant or recent past. In 1987 became a member of the Standing Committee of Politburo.

6. Yao Yilin, age seventy, has been one of the four vice-premiers and until now an alternate member of the Political Bureau. He has been known as an economic expert on oil development. Yao is a confidant of President Li Xiannian of the Republic. In 1987 become a member of the Standing Committee of Politburo.

7. Hao Jianxiu, age fifty-two, the only woman among the eight to be promoted to the Secretariat.

8. Wang Zhaoguo, age forty-six, a former car factory manager, the youngest among the eight. He is now a member of the Secretariat.

In short, from 1977 to 1985, Deng has fought all the way to create and stabilise a pragmatic leadership in the party and government. It can be said that he has succeeded well in peaceful leadership reform. Mao could not do this without a blood bath. Deng has done it with popular acclamation. There lies the difference between an ideological visionary and a pragmatic realist. One leader's failure created the circumstances politically and ideologically for another to succeed. Deng came back to power at the right time when the abused nation was waiting for such a leader to emerge. Hua Guofeng was not prepared nor experienced enough to initiate what Deng had long prepared to do if the opportunity should come, which it finally did. Could Deng's sucessors afford to do less than Deng? In January 1987 Deng removed Hu in order to balance off resistance from the leftists to save his continuing reform.

2.3 DENG'S 'FOUR CARDINAL PRINCIPLES' AND NEED FOR POPULAR SUPPORT

Before Mao's death, Zhou and Deng had acquired their popular approval and support throughout the country. This was repeatedly expressed by the common citizens and those who resented Mao and his wife during the cultural revolution and during the succession struggle immediately after Zhou's death on 8 January 1976. The people were bitter and sad when the Gang of Four did not allow the media to be more fully used during the mourning for Zhou. They were stunned when Deng was not made Zhou's successor. Most citizens in China were happy three months later when the people in Beijing expressed their mourning for Zhou on the memorial day at the Tiananmen Square which led to Jiang Qing's angry decision to suppress such spontaneous shows of emotion and respect for Zhou. Thus, on 5 April 1976, violence occurred.

Zhou and Deng have shared a common cause against the Gang of Four. Deng also inherited Zhou's legacy of popularity to add to his own. Without this popularity throughout the country, Deng could not easily and realistically dream of a return to leadership. He knew well the country and people were on his side in the leadership struggle. He understood, of course, that more was at stake than his personal cause. The supporters of Jiang Qing, Lin Biao and Hua Guofeng within the party, the army and the government knew also the outrage of the people against them. Deng's task was to fight the Maoists, the Huaists, and the followers of Jiang Qing and Lin Biao. He had to win the majority support of the party, army and those who would make political decisions. But how to win support was still a problem and a major crisis for Deng, in addition to strengthening his own popular support. To broaden the party's support, he declared his Four Cardinal Principles once back in power. Furthermore, to redeem the party Deng had to reform the party which had been radicalised and controlled by his political enemies. He had to consolidate the armed forces under the command of the party and within his personal control. However, the military was dangerously divided ideologically between those supporting Jiang Qing and those loyal to the Lin Biao faction or devoted to the defence of Mao's legacy. Deng had worked with all these factions and divisions at every level of government, party and the army. As a political pragmatist, he mended their conflicts, divided his enemies, and won them over to his point of view. This immediate political crisis for unity under him required Deng to pledge his loyalty to Marxism, party leadership, the socialist path, and proletarian democratic centralism. In the long run, these four principles will also help him retain all the necessary support to build a 'New Socialism with Chinese Characteristics'. Therefore, he had to assure those in the party, the army and the government that he would not abandon any of the fundamental tenets of the communist revolution.

In the realm of ideology, Deng himself has always been a Marxist revolutionary. He could not possibly abandon any single one of the four cardinal principles, especially the leadership of the party and Mao Zedong Thought in order to silence his opponents who are still doubtful of his ideological commitment. In the long run, his reform would no doubt work only at the expense of his ideological rivals. Thus Deng had to reasure them that a new capitalist China would not emerge. Moreover, Deng himself might not know the long-term ideological implication of his reform or 'peaceful revolution'. Where will China be ideologically twenty or thirty years from now as a result of Deng's experiment in reform? How will Deng's 'reform experiment' end in terms of changes in the political system and a new economic entity? It is quite possible that Deng himself could not tell in 1978 shortly after his victory at the Third Plenum of the Eleventh Party Congress. It is also possible that Deng did not wish to anticipate ideological development. The future can be left to future generations to decide that issue. He only needed to be sure that whatever he did was right and necessary at the time. Therefore, ideologically in both the short and the long run, Deng's insistence on the four cardinal principles has been realistic and expedient. These principles summarised well what all Marxists can agree upon and want to follow or achieve. It is within these guiding principles that a new ideological framework can emerge as 'truth from practice'. This stand as taken in late 1978 by Deng and his associations has provided them with the freedom of choice to experiment in 'Socialism with Chinese Characteristics'. Within the scope of these four cardinal principles, they can promote also new policies to carry out their other concrete pledges which include (1) socialist legality; (2) collective leadership; and (3) a united front with other political parties through the CPPCC (Chinese People's Political Consultative Conference, which has existed since 1949 but largely as window dressing). What is the extent of practice of the rule of law as suggested by 'socialist legality'? At what level of practice will Deng's 'collective leadership' be implemented? What are the 'characteristics' of his 'Chinese Socialism'? There are no precise answers, but one can speculate that this is precisely what Deng intends now in order to provide definitive alterations in future years. It may be quite possible that by the year 2000 AD China's economic and cultural relations with Japan, North America and West Europe will have become so close that ideological and political reform will occur with ease. A richer middle-class society will emerge eventually. We can, then, determine ideologically the new guidelines for 'Socialism with Chinese Characteristics'.

For immediate domestic political necessity against factional leadership struggles in China today, the four cardinal principles have been officially supported by the party through its propaganda department and government controlled media. The public cannot compromise it at all. The official basis for political unity comes from Marxism-Leninism and Mao Zedong Thought. In short, Deng's four cardinal principles have performed well satisfying the immediate or short-term needs of the reformers. Following the official line, the four principles can be easily summarised.

Insistence on the four cardinal principles (socialist path, people's democratic centralism, communist party leadership, and Marxism--Leninism–Mao Zedong Thought) is perceived politically as a fundamental necessity to assure the success of the four modernisations (in agriculture, industry, defence, and in science and technology). The argument of the official party line 'on primary conditions' is to provide a basis for political education to guide the whole nation toward socialist revolution. Without unity of the party on rededication to these 'high sounding' and 'guiding' principles, confusion, defeatism and unexpected new conflicts may emerge within the party and disorient the masses. Deng seems sincere in his commitment to these four principles. His power would have been at risk if he had lost party support and if he had suggested any strange revolutionary ideology which none could understand. Deng had to reaffirm his dedication to the four principles before party reform is achieved. Changes in ideology must wait for new experience in coming decades. As a pragmatist, Deng certainly was not prepared to declare, for example, in 1978 that Marxism, being more than one hundred years old, cannot be expected be solve China's problems.[17] Ideology cannot be abandoned overnight. Any shift to new ideology is, by the same token, difficult to accept. Deng knows only too well the urgency to reform from past failures. He does not need to worry about the ideology of his reform experiment. He only needed to announce the basis and goal of his reform policy. The broad goal that all wanted to hear and strive to achieve included, for example, better living standards for all citizens, rural and urban economic reforms, party unity, school reform, and importation of Western and Japanese investment and technology. The four cardinal principles is a strategy, politically and ideologically, to assure and unite the nation and meet an immediate need at the current stage of development.

Deng has reaffirmed the advantages of socialism over capitalism despite the failures of misguided Maoist leadership in the economic and ideological spheres in Mao's last twenty years. Why did Deng insist on communist party leadership? Many people in China today accept that 'without the communist party, there could not be the revolutionary victory of 1949'. Party leadership is the beginning of everything in China. No communist wishes to lose power. Party leadership, for the foreseeable future, is to be a fact of life and a necessity for reform. There cannot possibly be the emergence of a new alternative party capable of competition with the communist. Why, then, did Deng insist on 'Democratic Centralism'? It is meant to be a proletarian dictatorship against only those opposed to the regime of the working class, although the workers have little to say on policy initiative of whatever sort. The enemy of the people turned out to be Maoist communists, including Lin Biao, Jiang Qing and a few others. The fourth principle perceives Marxism–Leninism–Mao Zedong Thought as the 'guiding compass for action'. Why did communists Lin Biao and Jiang Qing violate the 'guiding compass' themselves? China under Deng has reaffirmed officially its philosophical faith in Marxism and also declared its inapplicability in many respects. Until the time when new experiment leads to new theory, there is no need for ideological debate in the coming decades. For the foreseeable future, China will insist on being governed ideologically by the forces radiating from the four cardinal principles.[18]

Marxist ideologists in China insist that the socialist path is the inevitable path of human history in China and for all nations. It will finally replace capitalism. The Chinese communist party officially does not share the view that capitalism has worked better economically than socialism. They accept, however, that science and technology in certain capitalist countries have made greater advances since the end of the Second World War. Overall, Marxists believe that capitalists and capitalism have done poorly and have become weaker. Economic development in leading Western countries and Japan peaked in the 1950s and 1960s. All of these countries since 1970s and 1980s have declined in their economic rate of production, and their future is bleak. Therefore only socialism can save China. Sun Yat-sen tried in his revolution to save China by following the capitalist path but failed. Obviously the Chinese media and party theoreticians considered the commune and the great leap as Mao's personal mistakes and his deviation from classical Marxism. Many Chinese propaganda specialists in the media have related the economic failure since 1949 to Chinese feudalism of the past and to foreign exploitation during the preceding one hundred years before communist victory in 1949. China could not, therefore, advance on equal footing with other countries in the world.[19] Such an argument is really very unconvincing and narrow-minded. These propaganda experts have failed to take into analysis the economic success in Hong Kong, Taiwan, Singapore, South Korea and Malaysia. None of these Asian nations and half nations has the blessings of natural resources as China has, nor the internal unity of democratic dictatorship which China achieved under the communists. There is no apology sufficient enough to explain the failure of the Soviet model of political economy in China since 1949. The British did not make much investment in Hong Kong. Hong Kong has prospered due to efficient management and people's working incentive for profit. Singapore had neither raw materials of any kind nor independence from British colonialism before full sovereignty in 1965. It has proudly achieved the second highest standard of living in all of Asia, next only to that of Japan.

In short, the four cardinal principles are of political necessity. They are superficial policy guiding premises without ideological depth. The four principles are politically necessary for the leadership to disarm internal resistance. At the propaganda level, these principles help build unity and permit the government-controlled media to indoctrinate the public in the view that communism shall win out at last, that only socialism can guarantee a decent living for all citizens in relative equality, that socialist democracy and legality is superior to Western rule of law and capitalist democracy, and that China can be strong only through the practice of socialism. These may be perceived as the genuine faith and belief of the communist leadership in China. And indeed, the current leadership has accomplished many great feats toward a more open and free society under these four principles. The irony of it all is that the four principles have not won all the intellectuals and the former victims of the Maoist dictatorship. Experience tells the people what to believe. The experiment to develop 'Socialism with Chinese Characteristics' will inevitably need to meet the people's expectations.

2.4 IDEOLOGICAL VOID AND SOCIALIST DEMOCRACY

It can be amply demonstrated that in China today there exists an ideological void which is necessary to allow freedom to experiment with democracy. Since the death of Mao and the elimination of the Jiang Qing group in 1976, only Premier Hua and followers have attempted to preserve Mao's ideological front but failed. Nearly every intellectual or moderate politician in China today is reluctant to talk about Marxism or Maoism. People have lost interest in politics and ideology entirely. Upon his return to power, Deng declared in 1977 'speak less and work more'. In his conversation with other high level comrades even before his return to power, he insisted that if 'Mao had been right ideologically, it is a contradiction for the party to rehabilitate me. Furthermore we cannot, then, declare the 5 April incident in Tiananmen square in 1976 a correct and revolutionary one.'[20] In the field of ideology, Deng insists that no one can be always right and consistent, 'not Marx, not Lenin ... Chairman Mao never said he himself was always right'.[21] Ideology, Deng believes, can be misused and misinterpreted. For example, Deng argued that Lin Biao abused Mao's thought. Worse than Lin Biao, Zhang Chunqiao revised Mao's thought to suit his own need. In short, ideology can be easily twisted. On the eve of the 3rd Plenum of the CCP's 11th Congress in December 1978, Deng insisted in his speech on 'thought liberation' from ideological misinterpretation of Marxism and Mao Zedong Thought. Deng said:[22]

Liberation of thought, open-mindedness and emphasis of practice are essential for unity in forward achievement ... when our minds are open we can, therefore, properly interpret Marxism and Mao Zedong Thought as guiding instruction to solve our inherited problems and decide on new issues ... many comrades are close-minded. They live in thought paralysis or semi-paralysis.

Deng attributed this thought paralysis to disruption by the Gang of Four, by the destruction of democratic centralism in the party, by development of the bureaucracy, and the lack of disciplinary criterion. When thought is paralysed into a formula, many strange phenomena will occur. For example, Deng complained that 'party leadership' was misinterpreted as 'party in charge of all things' –party and government unwisely became one. It seems to Deng that ideology can become a constraint, a yoke or chain to prevent vitality, creativeness and adaptation to reality. Thus, in order to change and experiment, Deng wants ideological truth to emerge from practice. With this attitude toward ideology, he advocated the four cardinal principles and left all other ideological issues to future adaptation and innovation.

Deng's ideological commitment to experimental socialism is unshakable. But he would not allow the need for ideological abstraction to disrupt the need for policy flexibility. Ideology does not change easily. Policy, however, must derive from certain particular circumstances which themselves can change overnight. We can easily understand current ideological premises through reading the revised party constitution at the Twelfth Party Congress. The policy goals and structural changes in the constitution reflect 'thought liberation' as advocated by Deng in 1977.

Deng and Hu have been party organisational bureaucrats. They believe that the party constitution of each given period of time must be revised to highlight certain work emphasis. Ideological dogmatism, personality cult, and radical leftism were eliminated in the new 1982 constitution. The new policy line of Marxism, new guidelines on new organisational changes must, at this stage of development, emphasise 'socialist democracy' and 'improved socialist legality'. One of the features of the new constitution is its restoration of intra-party democracy and its pledge of cooperation with minor parties and other non-party individuals in future policy-making. Contrary to the Ninth, Tenth and Eleventh Congresses, the Twelfth Congress wiped out the leftist mistakes, while it restored the good tradition of the Seventh and Eighth Congress experience of 1945 and 1956. Another feature of the party's new constitution is to raise four qualifications for membership recruitment: more education, youthfulness, professional specialisation, and revolutionary rededication.[23] To achieve these goals, the constitution advocates emphasis on discipline, retirement of senior officers, creation of a party advisory commission and expansion of disciplinary inspection. Thirdly, the new constitution insists on genuine practice of democratic centralism to assure normal political life within the party for the purpose of unity and command. No one can seek a personality cult for self-glorification. To achieve it, the new constitution has abolished party chairmanship in favour of a central secretariat which consists of a large number of equal colleagues who are responsible for collective administration decision making in pursuit of policy decisions made by the political bureau which itself now consists of a younger and larger membership since the restructuring in September 1985.[24]

It is critical for the party to redeem itself after the popular crisis of confidence that arose after the havoc of the cultural revolution. Besides, many problems have internally plagued the party's strength and its leadership image. Hu Yaobang in his report to the 12th Congress in 1982 enumerated a few of these internal problems. They are: weak and ineffective leadership, cadres' lack of a sense of responsibility in their work, bureaucratic corruption, abuse of power to further their personal interests and 'seeking privileges to live in style ... getting involved in corruption, embezzlement and other serious malpractices in the economic fields'.[25] Much reform and consolidation remain to be done yet, especially in areas of discipline concerning economic crimes committed by party members and their relatives. In July 1985, for example, it became open knowledge that the highest party and government authorities in Hainan Island conspired for a long time in automobile purchase and resale for profit-making in violation of the law. Party reform was expected to be completed step-by-step by the end of 1986. Without reform in party leadership, unity and rejuvenation, the party cannot lead the nation toward the hope for accomplishment of the four modernisations.

On the positive side, it must be observed that the removal of ideological entanglement has itself been a universally welcome departure from the days of the cultural revolution. The current de-emphasis on ideological debate gives the current reform leadership a freer hand to experiment in socialist democracy, collective leadership and socialist legality without justifying ideologically whatever policy measure is taken to meet the reform need. The current ideological void does not, however, imply an abandonment of Marxism and Mao Zedong Thought. It simply postpones to a proper future time the revision of the ideological front which will be an after event without failure. The four cardinal principles will likely be reviewed or replaced to meet ideological consistency with new reality under future leadership. On the other hand, a new interpretation of Marxism and Mao Zedong Thought now would inevitably open a new battlefield of debate and legitimacy. Without an ideological confrontation, Deng's leadership can easily condemn the leftist adventurism of Mao's fatal ideology. The Lin Biaoists, the Jiang Qingists, and the Huaists have all been criticised or tried by the court for their abuse and misinterpretation of Mao Zedong Thought. Therefore, technically there is an advantage to be gained from an ideological void. Future ideology may condemn classical Marxism and Mao Zedong Thought as they stand today.

There is, however, a future necessity for ideological clarity when the four cardinal principles (Communist Party leadership, people's democratic dictatorship, the socialist path, and Marxism–Leninism and Mao Zedong Thought) shall be no longer adequate to harmonise and synthesise the new reality with old Marxism and Mao Zedong Thought. When that time does come, a new interpretation of Marxism will emerge. Future criticism against Mao and Maoism will likely be more condemnatory when his devotees shall have long gone 'to see Marxism in heaven'. Presently, the pragmatists will continue to maximise their freedom at ideological expense. In short, it is difficult to forecast what will emerge ideologically through peaceful transformation. Decades from now China may become very democratic by parliamentary or Western standards and remain socialist only in name. Or it will reimpose more non-democractic practices. With current de-emphasis on ideological rigidity, the void will become less noticeable or relevant to the general public. Intellectual rationalism and bureaucratic meritocracy may fill this void as the new criteria for reward and punishment. In short, genuine democracy and rationalism in the name of socialism may emerge in the long run.

2.5 REFORM EXPERIMENT AND FUTURE CHALLENGE

Deng Xiaoping and Chen Yun are the most senior leaders since the retirement of Marshall Yi Jianying in 1985. Their entire life history since the 1920s has been filled with experiments and challenges. Success or failure in the past symbolised their party's idealism and mistakes which brought for the Chinese People many memories between hope and despair. As an objective observer of the communist movement in China, one is forced to conclude that in domestic policies the Communist party leadership seemed blind on many fronts. In the area of land policy alone, for example, there were the following: Autumn Harvest Uprising in 1927; Land Reform in Northwestern China without substantial improvement of the rural living standard; land to the tillers in 1949–52, land confiscation from the family tillers in 1955–7, and the commune disaster of 1958–79. These zigzag changes in land policy for whatever reasons brought enormous instability and suffering in the rural economy. Perhaps, this land policy of the Communist party under Mao Zedong's grandfatherly leadership is enough to explain why the Chinese standard of living today is one of the lowest in the world, although much better than at any time in past history. It is particularly useful to view Deng's new land policy since 1979 in this historical perspective. The abolition of the rural commune and the implementation of 'responsibility farming' by family or individuals on long-term contract with the state is an innovation unprecedented in Chinese land policy history. It is a policy of popular demand. People love the land. Maoists did not seem to know this or disregarded the people's wishes in order to experiment with the Soviet land model in China. In restrospect, the people may ask why the Communist Party divided land in their favour in 1952 but took it away only a few years later. At long last, the government has realised it is better to give land to the farmers who can produce more than they did under the commune. No nation wants to starve. The Chinese people for the last thirty-five years have struggled just to avoid starvation. The experience seemed to remind Chen Yun to warn his fellow comrades not to neglect food production. In his September 1985, speech he stated:[26] 'One billion people must have food and clothes. This must be one of our greatest concerns. It is also one of political problems. "Chaos emerges from lack of food". We must not belittle food issue.'

Land policy failure of the past is an example indicative of other failures elsewhere, such as urban economic mistakes, disregard for higher education, political purges of fellow comrades, condemnation of intellectuals as 'stinking number 9' and blind imitation of the Soviet model of socialism. In view of all these mistakes, Deng's grand peaceful reform takes great significance in the Chinese revolutionary history after 1911. It is a new revolution in peaceful experiment. Circumstances have afforded Deng the grandest opportunity to launch this wholesale reform. However, it is also the man who expanded the opportunity in order not to just correct past mistakes, but to inaugurate new fundamental changes in the Chinese political and economic system. Courage for foresight aided by revolutionary experience has made the post-Mao era an era of communist redemption in the systematic overhauling reform which Deng himself has called 'a second revolution'. This is why the challenge is very difficult to overcome because too much is at stake in building a strong and modernised China. These are multiple kinds of challenges in this peaceful revolution. To name just a few, they may include:

1. A rigorous test for the communist leadership after Deng;
2. An introduction of collective party leadership in unity to pursue the four modernisations and to resist the rise of a personality cult;
3. The development of form and content of 'socialist democracy and legality' through institutional device and procedure;
4. A drastic increase in national gross income and people's standard of living to meet and control the popular revolution of expectation;
5. The creation of more jobs and educational opportunities for young Chinese whether the four modernisations succeed or fail. Young people cannot remain unemployed without creating disorder;
6. The prevention of party and government bureaucratic corruptions of all possible sorts, especially the economic crimes by the privileged few;
7. The retention of popular support in favour of continuing reform experiment against political instability and ideological revolt or struggle;
8. An improvement in democratic, elective popular participation in government, such as allowance for relative expansion of freedom of speech, the press, assembly, etc.

There are also external challenges that may come from uncertainties, confusions, threats and trade competition in the international arena. The following may be illustrative of an unending list of issues:

1. Political relations with major powers and Asian neighbours to test China's peaceful intention against war of any sort, revolutionary or imperialistic;
2. Foreign investment and foreign markets in China and their impact on China resulting domestically from economic and trade interaction with the rest of the world;
3. The external conflicts and pressures against Chinese choices in the handling of Taiwan and Hong Kong in future decades;
4. The crisis of unification with Taiwan and Beijing's ability to implement the Sino-British treaty over Hong Kong after 1997 on the latter's autonomy as prescribed in the treaty of 1984.

While Deng is on the political scene, these problems may not even exist or assume any great significance. Looking beyond him and even beyond his immediate successors, however, many unexpected difficulties may occur. Deng's reform experiment has been under way only a few years. Much remains to be institutionalised, routinised, revised or changed. On the positive side, Deng remains physically healthy. He has anticipated many of the problems just cited. For example, party reform is under way and has progressed as planned. New, young and dedicated cadres equipped with greater professional skill, better educational background, and a vigorous revolutionary spirit are being placed vertically at all levels of the party. The economic growth is moving ahead better than expected, especially in rural development where people are much more able to organise themselves with only minor assistance from the government. Intellectuals are much appreciated and better paid than in the past. Thus, the capacity to sustain challenge has been more than sufficient.

For the first time since the revolution of 1911, the Chinese people are promised a definable long period of peace in economic development. Civil war, warlordism, and foreign aggression are all out of the question. The government under Deng provides rational guidelines to allow the people to work and experiment for their own material benefit. The people welcome such an opportunity which should have come to them in the early 1950s. When the government retreats, the people are able to take care of the interest of the country and those of their own. In short, China is a nation on the move today. Ironically, the greater the improvement in the people's living standard, the faster their expectation rises. This is the common challenge for all Third World nations. In order to build a new nation both materially and spiritually Deng must accept the Chinese cultural heritage, not the foreign utopian model of democratic socialism. But only a modernised open and democratic society is capable of meeting global challenges and the internal demand for freedom and equality in the long run. Democracy cannot be accomplished in one or two generations. However, faithful dedication and liberal experiment must be maintained without any interruption. Deng appears willing and capable of contributing to such a strong foundation. Otherwise, his effort is but another short-term experiment in peaceful reform, which may end with his departure.

An account of Deng's success in reform during the last several years since his return in 1977 looks, indeed, impressive. For example, he has removed and discredited the Gang of Four, Hua Guofeng and his associates, the major blind followers of Mao from within the party, the army and the government. Above all, he has successfully and artfully criticised and evaluated Mao in order to unite the party, the army and the masses against the personality cult. A giant step was taken in September 1985 in placing the third tier leaders at all levels in the party.[27] Rapid economic development is under way in both rural and urban areas. In short, Deng, as an experienced fighter and shrewd planner, has carried out his 'grand reform' step by step and stage by stage through persuasion and with dignity for all in the process of leadership transformation. Deng himself has provided much counsel on the goals of his reform through speeches at different times. At the Twelfth Party Congress in 1982, he said:[28]

Since the Third Plenary Session of the Eleventh Central Committee in December 1978, the party has returned to its correct policies in the economic, political, cultural and other fields and, in addition, ... our party today has attained a much deeper understanding of the laws governing China's socialist construction, acquired much more experience and become more conscious and determined in implementing correct principles. We have every reason to believe that the correct programme to be decided at this congress will create a new situation in all fields of socialist modernisation and bring prosperity to our party, our socialist cause, our country and the people of all our nationalities.

In carrying out our modernisation programme we must proceed from Chinese realities. Both in revolution and in construction, we should also learn from foreign countries and draw on their experience. But the mechanical copying and application of foreign experience and models will get us nowhere. We have had many lessons in this respect. We must integrate the universal truth of Marxism with concrete realities of China, blaze a path of our own and build socialism with Chinese characteristics – that is the basic conclusion we have reached after summing up long historical experience.

Having confidently staked out a new course for socialism with Chinese characteristics, Deng repeatedly asserted China's independence, self-reliance, and willingness to 'unswervingly follow a policy of opening to the outside world'. There are three major tasks Deng has repeatedly insisted on accomplishing in the current decade, namely, to step up socialist modernisation, to work toward national unification and to oppose hegemonism in the preservation of world peace. Economic construction, however, is at the core of his plan.

3 New Political Orientation and Economic Development

In the nineteenth century, Karl Marx was clearly the most revolutionary political economist. His *Communist Manifesto* argued scientifically that means of production and private ownership determine the economic relationship between the ruling elite and the exploited. The state, he claimed, is an instrument in the hands of the rich to exploit the poor, and the most advanced countries industrially should first have a violent revolution by the working class. All such claims are now debatable because events did not occur as he predicted. His followers in subsequent generations had to reinterpret his ideology. Lenin, Stalin, and Mao Zedong all made their revisions and reinterpretations to meet their own immediate national circumstances. But none so far has succeeded in creating a classless society to get rid of the state as an 'instrument of exploitation'.

Before 1917, no intellectuals and revolutionaries in China had known anything at all about Marxism or communism. China was governed by various warlords and remained a divided state. Lenin skilfully interpreted 'colonialism and imperialism' as an inevitable expansion of Western capitalism into the poor exploited countries. A world communism united against Western imperialism everywhere was necessary and inevitable. This propaganda sounded extremely pleasant to a few Chinese intellectuals and disappointed revolutionaries who had followed enthusiastically Sun Yat-sen's democratic revolution of 1911. Thus, China soon became an arena for two revolutions which joined in 1923 and split in 1927. Neither the democratic revolution of the Western model nor the Communist revolution of the Soviet Union style has succeeded in China in carrying out its promises to the masses. Both are today still struggling to deny full validity and legitimacy to the claim of the other. The Kuomintang Party failed between 1927 and 1949 while on the mainland, Mao's own Communist revolution deviated from its course and failed in Mao's own lifetime. At the end of his cultural revolution, Mao left behind a nation divided between factions within the Communist Party. His lifetime comrades had been purged and humiliated by millions. The country was in a poor state of agricultural and industrial development. At the time of Mao's death, after a quarter of a century under communism, the Chinese people were still suffering from one of the lowest living standards in Asia. Those who had been purged by Mao and Jiang Qing's faction could not easily be reinstated because Mao's radical followers were still in charge in 1976–8.

Deng Xiaoping was too young to know much about communism and the Soviet Revolution in 1917. He was only thirteen years old living in land-locked Sichuan. Upon his return from a study tour in France in 1926, and by way of the Soviet Union, he became a loyal follower of Mao. (He was even purged once in the early 1930s because of his loyalty to Mao.[1]) He rose in power and leadership during the Second World War and the civil war years in the late 1940s. By 1954, Deng was considered the fourth most powerful leader in Beijing, next to Mao, Liu Shaoqi and Zhou Enlai. Even Mao himself often cited Deng as the most capable leader on party affairs and in leadership. However, Deng and many comrades of Deng's calibre in high leadership roles were purged in the 1960s. Even through Deng himself publicly admitted his mistakes, he could not escape Mao's heavy axe of humiliation – twice. All of these loyal followers were stunned by Mao's leftist radicalism and his erroneous economic policies since the 1950s. During Mao's last ten years he did not even follow his own writings. Mao brought anarchy and disorder to the whole country. He terminated education and closed all schools. He destroyed the party as the best institutionalised source of leadership for stability and control. Civilian government was replaced by Revolutionary Rebel Committees at all levels except Zhou Enlai's premiership. Mao's madness was clearly incomprehensible to many experienced, moderate, and pragmatic leaders who had been with Mao for decades before and after 1949.

Mao died after Liu Shaoqi. Liu had been considered Mao's original chosen successor. Zhou Enlai passed away eight months before Mao's own death. The only person, most qualified and suitably available, was Deng Xiaoping as already arranged at the time of Zhou's death in 1976. But Mao reversed the decision and removed Deng again as vice premier after having rehabilitated him from the first purge only two years earlier. Thus, after Mao's death, the struggle between the Gang of Four under Jiang Qing and Premier Hua Guofeng further delayed Deng's return to power which was universally awaited when Hua sought to consolidate his position in the party and the government.

What were Deng's choices after his return in 1977? Should he follow party chairman and Premier Hua Guofeng who was designated by Mao and replaced Deng when Zhou died? Besides, Hua himself had chosen to follow Mao's policies and Mao's style of leadership. Therefore, new conflicts between Hua and those who urged Deng's rehabilitation were unavoidable. Besides, Hua was an unknown provincial party leader who helicoptered to highest central leadership purely by Mao's handwritten decree in disregard of the party's central committeee and its powerful political bureau. If returned to power it would appear that Deng had little choice but to continue to dismantle Mao's erroneous policies of the cultural revolution. He had to, first of all, restore the party's correct leadership vertically and horizontally throughout the country. Unity within the party, however, was critically far more important before any restoration of the purged leaders was to be initiated at all. A new reform of the party itself was unavoidable.

Secondly, the army, as Mao's instrument of the cultural revolution, was practically in charge of everything after Mao's death, although itself factionalised and divided even before Lin Biao's downfall in 1971. Now 'the barrel of the gun' in 1976–8 controlled the party, not the other way around as Mao's theory has always insisted on. Careful reform within the armed forces was, therefore, equally unavoidable.

But it was still politically suicidal or at least dangerous for anyone to criticise Mao directly or unskilfully before the followers and the influence of the Gang of Four were removed from politics and the party leadership. For Deng the new strategy of struggle for reform against Mao's mistakes and his erroneous policies had to be accomplished in Mao's own name. Much blame could be assigned to those who deserved being condemned as 'betrayers of Mao'. The followers of Deng made clear the differences between 'minor mistakes' of Mao and his 'great accomplishments' as the revolutionary helmsman. This was artfully done technically as well as honestly in using Mao's godly image in politics. And Mao Zedong Thought was used against Mao himself and those diehard blind Mao followers. Such, in short, was the political reality of the leadership and policy struggle between the premier and party chairman Hua Guofeng and Deng Xiaoping, together with the fight among their respective followers between 1977 and 1978. Sixteen months after Deng's return he won. He skilfully achieved this decision-making majority in the party in December 1978. To further discredit Mao's and Hua's policies, Deng and his supporters finally came to evaluate Mao's place in revolutionary history at the 6th Plenum of the 11th Congress in 1981.

Why did Deng and his followers have to struggle so diligently and with such determination? Because they are devoted pragmatic communists who have been eager to realistically and successfully pursue their own four modernisations as long-drawn up by Deng and formally announced by Premier Zhou in January 1975 to the National People's Congress. They realised then that Mao had led the party into ideological myth and ended in a revolutionary failure. Their socialist revolution and the Communist party had suffered from Mao's tyranny and atrocities. There are several crises of confidence in the party, in the government, and in Marxism itself. These pragmatic purposes of socialist revolution could not be achieved without a series of thorough reforms. China could not become an industrial modern state capable of self-defence and economic development without a relentless pursuit of the four modernisations before the end of this century. Deng and his followers do not believe in Mao's theory of 'continuous revolution' and his personality cult. They want to get on with the task of national construction without 'class struggle' which, to them, has been fully achieved by 1956 when all anti-communist groups had largely been eliminated. They did not believe in Mao's commune system for rural China. Nor did they support or understand Mao's Great Leap Forward movement. They failed to see why Mao had to continuously punish China's intellectuals since the 1960s. In short, they had disagreed with but had not resisted Mao in the late 1950s and early 1960s before Mao purged them after 1966. In policy choice they are now benefiting from Mao's failure. As moderate and pragmatic and tested battle field leaders they have been capable revolutionaries since 1949 and are now eager to build a new and modernised state in fulfilment of their original revolution. In addition, the promise of Mao's 'New People's Democracy' did not succeed. Mao violated the party's institutionalised 'collective leadership'. 'Democratic centralism' within the party and the nation, according to the 1954 constitution in China, was ignored. Mao and his supporters in the cultural revolution partially ruined the revolution, which Deng and his followers wanted to save by peaceful reform. They hoped to introduce socialist democracy and socialist legality. They wanted to turn the country toward the Western nations for science and technology without abandoning the original purpose of the communist revolution in China. However, new experiments were necessary since the old and the Maoist methods had failed.

'Socialism with Chinese Characteristics' has emerged as the central ideology. It does not have well-defined philosophical depth nor independent variables to form a coherent school of thought. 'Socialism with Chinese Characteristics', however has a wide appeal to most Chinese today. Politically, it is being built up on the basis of Marxism and Mao Zedong Thought. Institutionally, it returns to an organisational model of Communist party's infrastructure and its leadership theory. But the interpretation of Marxism itself is now with flexibility adapted to 'Chinese characteristics' which itself derives from a political tradition of at least 3000 years. Deng is neither conservative nor liberal. He is a 'cat-and-mouse' theorist who is after pragmatic results by whatever means so long as the result meets popular demand and revolutionary purpose. If the demand and support from the masses change, so must be the purpose of the revolution. Revolution should not be made in the vacuum of needs and approval.

If socialism strictly means the public ownership of means of production and public distribution of goods and services, Deng's 'new socialism' falls short of this standard definition. However, his new socialism is little different from Sun Yat-sen's third principle of the people, namely, 'the principle of the livelihood of the people' which advocates the following:

1. Constraints against the expansion of private capital ownership;
2. The development of publicly owned national capital for the public interest;
3. Land distributed to the tillers against exploitation by rural landowners;
4. Large enterprises, such as railroad and telecommunications, banking and so forth, which are considered too large an investment for private ownership and too important to be left in private hand, should be in the hand of the public; and
5. A progressive tax system should be employed to carry out the objectives of the above-mentioned 'mixed economy'.

Sun Yat-Sen emphasised the well-being of the entire population against the evils of private capitalism. Today, Deng advocates a series of policies similar to Sun's revolutionary goals of 1911. For example, he broke up the commune practice to contract land out to the tillers for long terms of production freedom and for the farmers' own enrichment, however, they were not given legal ownership of the land. Deng introduced a new tax system in the early 1980s to encourage production and to prevent excessive private profit. Since 1984 the People's Republic of China has begun to experiment with decentralisation of state-owned large enterprises to adopt the management experience of private capitalism. In short, 'Socialism with Chinese Characteristics' can be any successful experiment in the decades to come. Much of this in the economic and industrial fields will be discussed in later chapters.

Politically speaking, 'Chinese characteristics' could include reference to Chinese authoritarian institutions and traditional leadership roles, in addition to rights of the people as guaranteed by the state constitution which may or may not fully embrace the protection of civil liberties. However, the demand for political participation in the process of governing was not a 'Chinese characteristic' in the ancient past, for example. Thus, much depends politically on future developments as well as past traditions. Deng is not really committed to any ideological specifics. Practice success will provide ways for his theory reconstruction. Flexible and realistic interpretation of Marxism and Mao Zedong Thought will continue to guide daily policy actions of the government and its leaders. It is in this mood of flexible adaptation, that China's newspaper has announced that Marxism is more than one hundred years old and can not be expected to resolve China's problems today.[2] What, then, is most relevant to resolve China's current economic problems? The answer is, no doubt that of Western technology and foreign capital investment if the four modernisations drive is to have any hope of success. This devotion to economic development compels the new leadership to keep the country open to the outside world. China has also developed several Economic Special Zones to attract foreign investment. In 1984 it announced the opening of fourteen additional coastal cities for foreign investment and trade. An elaborate system of new law dealing with foreign economic affairs has been legislated to arbitrate conflicts and to facilitate business transactions in China. In short, a change in ideology, the necessity of political and economic modernisations are the compelling reasons for drastic reform under Deng because reform alone may save the Marxist regime from a crisis of confidence.

As a reformer in 'peaceful revolution', Deng has been, since the 3rd Plenum of the Eleventh Congress in December 1978, in a winning position. He decides policies on the basis of his experience of the last sixty years. He has been in a unique leadership position against challenges to his reform measures. By virtue of his experience as past party secretary-general, finance minister, economic planner, a regional supreme leader in Southwest China, a party leader within the armed forces, a vice-premier (acting during Zhao's absence), and, most important of all, the author of the blueprint for the four modernisations, he finds in the party or the government no one who can claim to be his equal in policy leadership and in party politics. Thus, today he enjoys the support of his many senior colleagues, Peng Zhen, Chen Yun, Li Xiannian and Yi Jianying. One of Deng's reform measures was for himself as leader not to occupy any institutional top position either in the party or the government. Therefore, he can easily persuade his follow colleagues to be equally unselfish and to convince the citizens on the basis of his dedication to the future of the nation. As a result, he has been in a much better position than Mao, Zhou and Liu Shaoqi, to exercise personal leadership.

3.1 THE SCOPE OF DENG'S REFORM AND THE REASON FOR IT

Having achieved his leadership of reform in 1978, he has been under a variety of pressures to be responsible to his colleagues and to the entire nation, to the communist party and to his own future place in Chinese history. First of all, he has to reconcile many conflicting issues under a new peaceful revolutionary environment. Chinese history has recorded many reformers of the past. Some succeeded well enough to extend the longevity of the dynasty for hundreds of years, such as Liu Xiao of the East Han Dynasty. Others failed, such as Prime Minister Wang An-shih of the Sung Dynasty. There were modern reformers such as Kang Yu-wei and Liang Chi-chao who hoped to create a rejuvenated modern Manchu Empire by combining the Confucian state with the Japanese success of the Restoration of 1868. Deng did not, of course, wish to abandon the socialist revolution. Nor could he tolerate any more chaos and disorder resulting from Mao's cultural revolution. He wanted to provide order and normal life through 'peaceful revolution', a revolution of experiment in reform throughout the polity.

His reform movement is different from Mao's mobilisation campaigns of the past which each time had to target 'innocent victims'. Deng's approach is constructive and non-accusative. For example, he removed his opponents with grace and with care of their interests. After retirement or transfer in post, he provides them with the same services and privileges as they would have received. As a confrontationist leader of repute, he wasted no time in his planning for reforms as soon as he was restored to power even in 1974. Much of what he has been able to implement since 1978 had been spoken of or planned well before his second removal from leadership in January 1976. Before making a brief comment on what he had said before Mao's death, it is appropriate to relate his reforms to popular beliefs in traditional Chinese political culture. He is, indeed, a traditionalist with a socialist outlook.

Traditional political culture speaks well for the reasons of successful dynastic renewal and political institutional rejuvenation. In China's three thousand years of well-recorded history, popular support was indispensable for any successful reform, or for a change of dynasty. Chinese traditional leadership of the imperial dynasty did not have an institutionalised adversarial supervision against royal abuse of power. This fact did not imply, at all, a lack of imposing constraints on the exercise of power by opposition factions or by popular expression. Morally, all emperors had to impose self-constraints according to their training in the Confucian tradition of an imperial moral code of ethics and conduct. For example, an emperor should treat ministers with courtesy in order to be reciprocated with absolute loyalty from them. Mao violated this fine tradition in his treatment of fellow revolutionaries in their policy and human relations. Ancient Chinese political culture even justified tyrannicide on the basis of popular revolt against immoral imperial conduct. Emperor Qie and Emperor Zhou were so condemned for their misdeeds by popular approval during the Zhou Dynasty. Another popular saying which was often used to justify rebellion or revolution was as follows: 'Heaven hears what the people hear. Heaven sees what the people see.' It placed popular judgement firmly at the centre of education of imperial conduct. If the emperor acted against public judgement, his dynasty would not last long. Chinese traditional popular moral approval did not imply popular sovereignty in the institutionalized or elective sense. However, such popularism often was used by revolutionaries to try to establish their own dynasties. Even after the intrusion of foreign political culture, all contemporary Chinese leaders are still convinced of the need of popular support for their political success. But Mao manipulated the masses. He fed them with his dirty propaganda and utopian romanticism. The masses knew how to judge Mao. Deng Xiaoping, Zhou Enlai and other mistreated victims of Mao's abusive leadership have been perceived popularly as champions of the people. Today Deng acts with benefit from such popular support in the post-Mao, era.

Deng and his reform colleagues know of such support from the entire national constituency. In the past, the 'silent majority', the people, did not have an independent press to express their protest against the Mao regime in their demand for a better future. One of the popular demands was the improvement of material life, especially in the rural conditions for 80 per cent of the population. Their specific pressing need, in particular, has been food supply. They would work harder in the field if they could keep a larger portion of their product.

Rural restlessness has always been the major cause of dynastic overthrow, or leadership downfall. Deng remembers, it seems, one of the traditional cultural axioms: 'people are the foundation of a state. And food is the minimal necessity for survival' [author's translation]. Under Mao, there was simply not enough food to prevent starvation in some parts of China. This starvation seemed to have caused popular demand for the reform of Mao's commune system. By comparison, China's living standard, after thirty years of communist rule, was so low as to be direct evidence of misrule. Deng knew this. He did not attribute the low standard of living to socialism, which to him is by far a superior system of production and management to the evils of capitalism. Mao's own economic wrong policy was, indeed, responsible for it, in addition to the decade-long destruction of the cultural revolution. Furthermore, intellectuals could not speak and write under Mao. By 1976, no one wanted to accept independent responsibility in their posts for fear of purges against innovation or deviation. In the end, a system of unproductiveness or stagnation emerged. Thus, Deng's reform was indispensable if the Communist Party or Marxism was to survive in China at all. It is from this perspective that Deng is comparable to an ancient dynastic reformer providing restoration as well as peaceful change. Ancient Chinese political culture had a 'theory for change' which literally means 'in desperation, one must change; and such change will always be helpful'. Burdened by the need for change from Mao's failure, Deng was in some sense, desperate for drastic reform of the system. Official Chinese press and party policy did not want to declare Mao's misrule of twenty years, 1956–76. Research clearly reveals Mao's deviation from the collective leadership of the party which was reaffirmed at its 8th Congress in 1956.

How did the Communist political system perform during that twenty years? Deng and other victims of the cultural revolution knew it better than anyone else. They could see it more thoroughly from inside the party, the government, the army, the press, and the decision-making process. It seems the Western contemporary systems theory can best examine and explain how the communist political system under Mao functioned poorly against the interest of the people. First of all, it must be pointed out that the political system could have functioned more democratically and efficiently if Mao had not intercepted its natural course of development and rational evolution. Mao did not recognise the limits to a system's boundary. As a political system, it invaded the territory of private life and cultural autonomy too much. It eliminated religion as the 'opium of the people'. 'Politics in command of everything' was one of Mao's preferred slogans. No autonomous social forces were tolerated, including the family institution and its integrity as a cherished living experience, traditional forces of social controls, and the independent intellectual life. Secondly, Mao's political system itself was not made up of autonomous parts or units which were also mutually dependent in the system's performance. The hierarchy of the internal relations among those of Mao's political system ruined the need for mutual dependability. For example, the National People's Congress (NPC) in practice was inferior to the state council, although in theory the NPC represented the people. The state council obeyed the party's decisions even though the former was in theory responsible to the NPC which appointed the council to execute policies at the former's pleasure. Functionally speaking, there was no division of power and responsibility possible to perform rationally, efficiently and accountably. Democratic centralism was not well practised. It produced irresponsibility, unaccountability and escapism. Thirdly, under the system the legislature, the NPC, could only represent the majority of the people, or respond to their needs or demands. How could it, then, receive their support? The NPC existed in the vacuum of power and leadership. The majority of people could not but treat it with apathy and despair if not sarcasm. The press was without independence to discover popular views on anything at all. It was a voice of the party unilaterally to create popular response by official inducement. For example, Mao's purge of the intellectuals in 1957 began with the colourful invitation as follows: 'Let a hundred flowers blossom; let a thousand thoughts contend.' At first, most intellectuals were reluctant to open their mouth. But more inducements came in the press. Many were later trapped in voicing their rather frank criticisms of communist rule. In the end, those who dared to speak and write were condemned as rightists and were purged with various degrees of humiliation and losses. When the president of Beijing University spoke out and wrote to Mao, as an economist, against Mao's policy on population growth, he was purged. Only some twenty years later, Deng rehabilitated his reputation and made this well-known population expert professor emeritus. Such examples as this cost the communist regime much public confidence. The whole population was locked up silently from within and the country was sealed off from the rest of the world. In the end, a bitter price had to be paid for such bad policies. Perhaps, Mao alone was not totally responsible for all the wrong things. On this, Deng's leadership has made a proper response in the document concerning some historical problems at the Sixth Plenum of the 11th Congress.[3] In short, Deng's overhauling of the political system results in saving it by improving it. If socialism is to survive and govern the nation, it has to meet popular demands from indigenous traditional political culture and from newly adapted modern foreign political culture. As the highest voice to initiate reform measures on every fact, Deng must speak up in all areas for proper changes. He is, in fact, making his own revolution today. The *Selected Works of Deng Xiaoping*, 1975–82, includes most of his major policy statements. The next few pages highlight only a few examples.[4]

The content of Deng's speeches followed the curve of the rise and fall in his career relevant to his duties at each given time. For example, as party secretary-general for twenty years, the only important speech he made was his black and white cat speech. He said nothing when he lived in oblivion. As vice-premier and chief of the army his policy speeches covered a wide range of topics. During the first seventeen months of his last rehabilitation, he was most careful not to frighten his political opponents by speaking out too loudly. At the end of the Eleventh Party Congress in July 1977, he declared 'speak less and work more'. After the Third Plenum of the 11th Congress, Deng openly spoke on many reform ideas. Some of them had been expressed before but not treated with the same authenticity as policy guides.

On rural policy, he slowly guided the government on specific measures. For example, as late as May 1980, he insisted on rural 'collective economy' and the 'production team' as the 'main economic units' although the country was already expanding 'farm output quotas on a household basis'. He stressed the need to 'expand the productive forces and thereby create conditions for the further development of collectivisation' at a higher mechanisation and a higher management level. He wanted a diversified rural economy to lead to specialised production teams and an increase in rural income. He spoke out against certain fears that 'the pace of socialist transformation had been too rapid ... [But] the main problem in rural work is still that people's thinking is not sufficiently emancipated concerning both organisational forms and production suitability for each specific locality'. Contrary to Mao's practice, Deng emphasised the need to 'take into account the wishes of the people. We must not propagate one method and require all localities to adopt it.'[5]

Whatever Deng says counts heavily because he is today the most wanted national leader China has had since the revolution of 1911. Yuan Shih-kai, Chiang Kai-shek and Mao Zedong were each very powerful. However, their exercise of power was checked by the environment against which they had to struggle. Deng has conquered the adverse environment created by his political opponents. He is the strongest modern leader in the sense that most people in China support his reform. They benefit from his success, and share his hopes for a modernised industrial nation by the year 2000. He is strong because he is guided by rational choice and an understanding of non-political expertise of modern technology and science. Under his leadership there are no personal selfish ideological objectives. As such he is enjoying an enthusiastic national support which none of his predecessors ever had. When he spoke of policies on readjustments, political stability and unity, he had only the future of the four modernisations in mind, because he had won most of the political battles already. A content summary of one such speech may highlight what was central in his mind.[6]

1. 'In economic policy making, we must draw correct lessons from the past thirty-one years as comrade Chen Yun draws on his personal experience in handling economic problem in the past. Now he is able to serve as our guide in this field for a long time. We continue to support his proposal for economic readjustment as adopted in April 1979, but not to implement it well until recently when unanimous understanding of it is now possible. To readjust, we will curtail some of our construction projects in some areas to support growth in agriculture, light industry and the production of daily necessities, along with development of energy resources and transportation and undertakings in science, education, public health and culture. In all these areas, we must improve management... professional and technical skills of production workers and office staff, efficiency and initiative and inventiveness. Without curtailment in some areas, we will not be able to ensure the steady growth of the economy. Our economy has all along been plagued with serious disproportions stemming from the historical conditions before the liberation and our protracted over-ambitious drive for success after the First Five-Year Plan (1952–6) ... damage of the ten years by the cultural revolution, failures in 1977–8 ... By the time of the Third Plenum (December 1978), all these had created imbalances in finance, credit and material supplies as well as between foreign exchange receipts and payments. Changing these things is to correct the leftist errors. Too much currency has been issued and prices have steadily risen.'

2. 'Capital construction must be cut in certain areas. Cut-backs in production or switches to new areas of production, amalgamation between enterprises, suspension or closure of operations are simply needed for readjustment. To achieve proper balance among various sectors of the economy, including defence and administrative expenses, are important to "shake off the fetters of erroneous leftist policies that have hampered our work over the years"'.

3. 'A lot of work has to be done before the people in the whole country can achieve unity of understanding. We must make clear to the people why further readjustment is imperative, what problems may arise in the process and what we hope to achieve by it. This way, the people will understand the necessity for further readjustment ... Then, they will give us their support. ... We should continue to try to break away from stereotypes, whether old or new, and gain a clear and accurate understanding of China's actual conditions as well as the interrelation among various factors in our economic activities.'

4. 'It is true that in the thirty-one years since 1949 we have made quite a few mistakes ... Nevertheless, through our endeavours over these years the number of industrial and transport enterprises has grown to nearly 400,000, and the value of the fixed assets of state enterprises has increased nearly twenty-one times as compared with early post-liberation days. We have trained large numbers of skilled workers and nearly ten million specialists and established a fairly comprehensive industrial system and economic system. The life of the whole people is far better than it was before liberation. Compared with some major developing countries, China has achieved greater progress and a faster rate of growth ... We are sure to make steady progress toward our modernisation goals provided we do the following: heed the principles laid down for economic work, improve the party's leadership, bring into play the superiority of the socialist system, and the people's initiative and creativity, utilise our abundant natural resources more rationally, make our work conform increasingly to actual conditions, constantly sum up new experience, avoid new shortcomings and errors and, if any should occur, correct them in good time. Our future is bright. In this sense, our readjustment means a step forward, not backward.'

5. 'The Third Plenum called for all party members to "emancipate their minds, use their heads, seek truth from facts, unite in looking ahead, study new situations and solve new problems" ... We have

worked out a series of policies and carried out many reforms with marked success. Since April 1979, we have called for economic readjustment, restructuring, consolidation and improvement. The masses and cadres support these correct party policies. But they fear these to be changed again. These will not be changed, or only the implementation measures, not the policies, can be shifted.'

6. 'We must firmly maintain the four cardinal principles – namely, keeping to the socialist road, upholding the people's democratic dictatorahip, upholding leadership by the communist party and Marxism–Leninism–Mao Zedong Thought. No one should be allowed to undermine these principles ... The core of the four cardinal principles is upholding the leadership by the communist party. We have said many times that without the leadership by the party a big country like China would be torn by strife and incapable of accomplishing anything. Whether inside or outside the party, all tendencies towards weakening, breaking away from, opposing or liquidating leadership by the party must be criticised. ... Leadership by the party is the key to the succcss of the four modernisations and of current readjustment.'

7. 'The work style of a political party in power has a direct bearing upon its very survival. We must strictly implement the guiding principles for inner-party political life and strive unremittingly to correct all bad trends. In particular, we must oppose the erroneous, two-faced attitude of those who feign compliance with the line, principles and policies ... while actually opposing them. Reform of the system, of the party and of state leadership must be carried out in an orderly fashion.

8. 'We should continue to develop socialist democracy and improve socialist legal system ... There are still inadequacies in our democratic system, so it is necessary to draw up a whole series of laws, decrees and regulations to institutionalise democracy and give it legal sanction. Socialist democracy and socialist legality are inseparable. Democracy without socialist legality, without the party's leadership and without discipline and order is definitely not socialist democracy. On the contrary, that sort of democracy would only plunge our country once again into anarchy and make it harder to truly democratise the life of the country, develop the economy and raise the people's standard of living.'

9. Democratic centralism and collective leadership 'should be genuinely practised in inner-party life as well as in the country's political life.'[7] It is also necessary to take firm action against all

violations of discipline in the party, army and government organisations. Discipline and legality were strongly emphasised by Deng as a requirement for all organisations in the government, in the army, 'in enterprises and schools as well as among the people as a whole'. He resolutely stressed that 'anarchism and violations of law and discipline must be resolutely opposed and checked'.

10. To build up a well-structured, rational system of institutions seems to be Deng's way of preventing deviation from the normal course of decision making. Here he advocates efforts against the 'over concentration of power'. He asked that 'systematic measures should be adopted to institute a retirement system of life tenure for leading cadres'. To prevent protest and opposition, Deng suggested 'appropriate arrangements be made for the political status of the retired cadres, for their material benefits and so on'. This policy has been in progress up to 1986. Mass retirement by members of the political bureau, the central committee, and the advisory and disciplinary commissions took place in September 1985, as announced at a party conference to allow Deng and Hu Yaobang to choose some 200 new and younger cadres to fill the vacant posts. On party recruitment he proposed a four-fold criterion for new cadres. They must: be young, well-educated, with professional managerial knowledge, and be revolutionary.

11. He complained that 'at present many [government] units are over staffed ... Some enterprises may cease operation partly or wholly'. Training of new and more capable workers and officials is a part of an economic efficiency policy which requires the retirement or transfer or retraining of workers.

12. As proposed by comrade Chen Yun and Comrade Zhao Ziyang the government should 'make readjustment our main job, with reform subordinate to readjustment so as to serve it and not to impede it. The pace of reform should be slowed a little, but that does not mean a change in direction'.

13. 'In modernising China's agriculture we should not copy the Western countries like the Soviet Union but should proceed along our own path, in keeping with specific conditions in Socialist China.'

14. The number of industrial enterprises experimenting with extended decision making powers by the end of 1980 had reached 6000 which produced an aggregate output value of 60 per cent of the national total, an indication of finding a better way to deal with

factory autonomy in production, and decision making long before the official announcement on 20 October 1984, to restructure through management decentralisation. 'The purpose is to expand work incentive, production efficiency and enterprise initiative in reform through adjustment.'

15. Deng is very concerned about new avenues of employment for millions of new job seekers annually. To expand such job opportunities, China has opened several 'special economic zones' in the southeast coastal region. These new economic zones are also subordinated to the domestic economic readjustment program in process. These economic zones are not permitted to compromise 'national independence and self-reliance'. In his 1984 grand tour of these Special Zones, Deng unconditionally endorsed the irreversible continuation of importing foreign capital, technology and management efficiency through these special zone experiments in coming years.

16. He continued to advocate the emancipation of the mind and the necessity of party self-criticism. But he qualified criticism of Mao Zedong by looking at Mao's 'contributions as primary and his mistakes as secondary. This is in accord with facts, and cannot be doubted or denied. And his mistakes absolutely cannot be attributed to his personal character ... Mao Zedong thought remains our guiding ideology. We must adhere to it and develop it in the light of specific conditions.' This policy statement was crucial before the coming 6th Plenum of the 11th Party Congress in June 1981. At that Plenum Mao's place in history was evaluated as Deng anticipated.

17. A new area of policy stress has been in 'socialist high culture' or 'spiritual civilisation' *vis-à-vis* 'Material civilization' as a result of the four modernisations. Deng asked 'how can we educate the younger generation and lead our country and people in building socialism if we ourselves are unarmed ideologically?' The recent resistance against 'spiritual pollution' coming from the outside was an episode of some future significance as it may occur in a more challenging manner. Deng called on the people 'to continue to criticise and oppose surviving feudal influences on ideology and politics both inside and outside the communist party ... We should criticise and oppose the tendency to worship capitalism and to advocate bourgeois liberalisation. We should criticise and oppose the decadent bourgeois idea of doing everything solely for profit, seeking advantage at the expense of others and always putting

money first'. What resources Deng's followers will, in the distant future, appeal to in order to reject capitalist morality should be observed with great interest in the future. The revolutionary spirit and dedication disappears now slowly but steadily as the 'Long March spirit recedes into history'.

18. Deng is very concerned about political stability and unity which is essential to current economic readjustment and future growth. He emphasised the need to fight against 'the remnants of the Gang of Four' and other new economic crimes in violation of regulations by even very high officials in secure places. He suggested that to eradicate these crimes we must 'not use campaigns and mobilisations of the past as means but to depend on new laws and more detailed regulations and other educational methods'.

19. Finally, he cautioned that 'while persisting [in] our effort to develop socialist democracy, we call on all our party members and our people to maintain strict vigilance against anti-party, anti-socialist and criminal activities and to take firm action against them ... Marxist theory and objective reality have taught us again and again that only when the people ... enjoy a high degree of democracy can dictatorship be effectively exercised over the tiny minority who are our enemies ... It is in complete conformity with the desire of the people and the needs of socialist modernisation to use the repressive power of the state apparatus to attack the counter-revolutionary saboteurs, anti-party and anti-socialist elements.'

This summary of his speech given on 25 December 1980, reveals Deng as the supreme leader in complete charge of the reform movement while Hua Guofeng was still not out of office yet. It is clear that Deng's primary emphasis is to succeed in his four modernisations by the year 2000. All other necessary measures are subordinate to this highest objective. Unity and stability are essential for economic growth and to induce foreign investment in China. Socialist legality and democracy, collective leadership and party reform are necessary means and channels through which a new socialism or 'democratic socialism of Marxist style' may truly emerge in China. Since this above-quoted long speech, eight years have gone by during which Deng's reforms and readjustment in the economic field have been largely successful. His greatest accomplishment, however, seems to have been in the area of party reform and institutionalisation of his own leadership succession by Hu Yaobang or Zhao Ziyang and other young ones collectively.

Deng has spoken up in nearly all other areas, including reforms in the army, in education, etc. A brief summary of a few of them may reveal the following:

1. While still vice-premier and the most likely sucessor to Zhou and Mao, Deng spoke out on 25 January 1975, about consolidation in the People's Liberation Army (PLA). The major policy statements he made include: (1) 'with this army of ours, the party commands the gun, and not vice versa... However, it was thrown into considerable chaos after Lin Biao was put in charge of army work in 1959, and especially in the later period under him... We must reduce the size of it, confront the problem of over staffing and restore the army's fine traditions. The Headquarters of the General Staff, the General Political Department and the General Logistics Department bear major responsibility. They should be the first to be consolidated. We must set things right in the armed forces in accordance with Comrade Mao Zedong's instruction on stability and unity... Future appointment and promotion will deal with those heavily involved in factional activities or cling stubbornly to factional ways; (2) Deng re-emphasised Mao's past insistence on military discipline of the 'three main rules and eight points for attention';[8] (3) 'There can be no mistake about the principles I have just mentioned in terms of military consolidation, stability and unity, and the implementation of party policies. We must restore party spirit, eliminate factionalism and improve efficiency and discipline.' What he mentioned as future policy guides began to be implemented only after his third return to leadership in 1978 and in 1984 with the reduction of one million in size.

2. On 5 March 1975, Deng spoke of building up 'an independent, comprehensive industrial and economic system by 1980' as the first step, and as the second step by 2000 to turn China into a 'powerful socialist country with modern agriculture, industry, national defence and science and technology'. Deng challenged his political enemies who 'only dare to make revolution but not to promote production'. He warned of China's weak transportation system, especially the inadequate railroad system. Again later in this speech he attacked factionalism and said 'persons engaged in factionalism should be re-educated and their leaders opposed... If they correct their mistakes, then we will let by-gones be by-gones, but if they refuse to mend their ways, they will be sternly dealt with.'

3. In his speech to a group of central party cadres on 4 July 1975, he cited Mao's three emphases: (1) study theory and prevent revisionism, (2) work toward stability and unity, and (3) promote economy and production. He quoted Mao in saying that not only the army, but the party also must be consolidated, especially at the level of leading cadres within the party and in the party's style at all levels throughout the country. Toward the end of the speech, he emphasised the long-standing formula in internal party rectification: 'Unity – criticism – unity.' Such party reform work did not truly begin on a massive scale until after the 12th Party Congress in 1982. And a three-year period was assigned, 1983–6, to complete party reform.[9]

4. Minor political parties in China played a major role in early 1950s and were purged severely at other times. However, as an institutionalised entity to help serve as a link between the communist party on the one hand and the intellectuals and the masses on the other, the Chinese People's Political Consultative Conference (CPPCC) was always maintained to meet and to discuss events. Deng's new leadership has further pledged to work permanently in co-existence and cooperation with the CPPCC. It has been periodically elected or nominated at various levels of its existence since 1949. The National People's Congress (NPC) and its corresponding counterparts of the CPPCC have formally and constitutionally served as the central legislative arm of the government. On 15 June 1979, Deng pledged quite strongly to work with these political parties in the decades to come, as follows:[10] 'To realise the four modernisations, it is essential to promote socialist democracy and strengthen the socialist legal system. The CPPCC is an important organisation for promoting people's democracy and maintaining contacts with people in different walks of life. To achieve China's socialist modernisation it continues to be necessary for the participants in the CPPCC to hold consultations and discussions on the nation's general principles, its political life and the social and economic questions related to modernisation. It is still necessary for them to exercise supervision over each other and over the enforcement of the constitution and law. We must give scope to the free airing of views and make full use of all talents ... so that the government can benefit from them, promptly discover and correct its own shortcomings and mistakes and push forward all phases of our work.'

It appears that the CPPCC has a supportive and modified role to play in helping the Communist Party and those who may influence the general public one way or the other. Deng, for example, quite specifically suggested to the CPPCC to concern itself with the return of Taiwan in the years to come. The major importance of it all is Deng's view of restoring some supervisory and constructive role for the body to play to generate national unity. On the theoretical level. Deng's institutionalisation of the non-communist intellectuals into the political system is a good tradition. This vehicle of participation and transmission of policy information to the non communist people is itself a unique Chinese practice. Other communist countries do not have such a practice, nor such a historical heritage. The government is guiding this political institutional development into non-adversarial institutional minor entity. Deng's speech on 24 May 1977, further delineated his position on intellectuals and other parties in China. It appears all these existing minor parties are to be kept and their future role in political participation and in socialist democracy can be shifted flexibly as the Communist party sees fit. However, research by political scientists on this subject should yield some definitive result in future decades. Deng pledged again in his 1980 speech to the Chinese intellectuals the following:[11]

> We must create within the party an atmosphere of respect for knowledge and respect for trained personnel. The erroneous attitude of not respecting intellectuals must be opposed. All work, be it mental or manual, is labour. Those who engage in mental work are also workers. As time goes by, it will become increasingly hard to differentiate between mental and manual labour... Great importance should be attached to knowledge and to those who engage in mental labour. And they should be recognised as workers.

In China, past tradition has always respected intellectuals who were most interested in and concerned about politics and their participation in it. Since 1911, most intellectuals have been involved in politics, and in the revolutions of their own time. They were organised by 1949, for example, into nine political parties on the eve of the Communist victory. In the 1960s Mao discredited them and called them 'stinking number 9 in social hierarchy'. Deng needs intellectuals today for their advanced training in the educational fields. The success of his four modernisations depends on their support. His new political orientation will ineviatably increase their political decision-making power whether they are members of the CPPCC or not. Many of them, as a socially elite class, will most likely remain politically neutral or aloof. But intellectually they are a powerful elite.

As the leaders of this revolutionary reform, Deng has so far been relatively silent on fundamental human rights. His socialist democracy and legality have not been well explored. He must some day speak out on basic human rights and the political protection for their enjoyment. Freedom of speech, assembly, press, and religion do not seem to impress Deng deeply at this moment. He does not emphasise political equality or the right of political opposition to communist party control of political affairs and policy making. Nor does Deng seem to anticipate certain inevitable consequences from the success of his four modernisations. A system of stability and open dialogue must prevail to accommodate to economic progress and natural changes among economic interest groups which will multiply in view of material improvement. In short, at this stage of political, social, economic and ideological developments in China, Deng has ushered in a new era of change and growth. He does not have yet a new ideology of his own to stand on. He must, therefore, simultaneously defend and oppose certain portions of Marxism-Leninism and Mao Zedong Thought because he depends fundamentally on them all for the legitimacy of his reform movement.

What Hu Yaobang repeated in his report to the Twelfth Party Congress had been previously said by Deng. As his successor, Zhou is carrying out in policy implementation what he has emphasised. This is the new basis for China's new political orientation and new economic development which has ushered in new opportunities as well as new constraints. As a new era, it is more rational, and far more acceptable to the Chinese masses than those of Mao's revolutionary romanticism.[12]

3.2 THE NEW ECONOMIC DEVELOPMENT STRATEGY

Given Mao's failure in his economic policy and the resultant poverty of China *vis-à-vis* the relative prosperity and higher living standards of her neighbours, new economic policy emphases were worked out by 1975 under Zhou-Deng and summarised in Zhou Enlai's January speech on the four modernisations of his government. Seven years later, Hu Yaobang's Report to the 12th Party Congress on 1 September 1982, gave more detailed emphases to policy priority choices in economic development. These include his new critical emphases on (1) rural economic recovery through a new land policy and (2) on light industrial development against Mao's emphasis on heavy industry. After a quarter of a century of Mao's socialism China did finally learn the mistakes in theoretical application of Marxism-Leninism without fully understanding the different objective conditions between China and the Soviet Union or other Marxist states. Mao's favoured strategy of priority for heavy industry at the expense of first expanding light consumer industry was a death-blow to Mao's wishful thinking. The ignorance of the consumer leadership on incentives for production efficiency, its blindness toward a sophisticated use of the theory of price, theory of taxation, a socialist commodity economy, flexible currency management, etc., were fundamental causes of China's failure in economic constructions between 1949 and 1979. Incentives and commodity theory have been largely responsible for the growth in wealth and prosperity in the West.

Since Deng's return to his reform leadership, China has begun to question her blind application of Marxist economic theory which is more than one hundred years old. A new soul-searching examination over the past economic productive strategy has helped to usher in new strategic priorities in various areas, including new proportional control between capital accumulation and consumption production, and a new balance between agricultural productivity and need for rural prosperity. Out of these new strategies there has emerged a series of new economic policy programmes as instruments of reform. Some of the highlights in theory, strategy and policy changes are to be touched upon in the following summary.

First of all, in theoretical debate Chinese economists have only partially admitted the inapplicability of certain aspects of Marxist economic theory. They have offered many 'valid reasons' for their economic failures and called for new needs to study the nature and the characteristics of economic objective conditions from country to country, the differences of stages in socialist economic development, and the long- or short-term goals of a socialist economy. All such theoretical analyses have been advanced within the very 'theoretical misconceptions of Marxism and Leninism themselves'. However, such soul-searching evaluation of economic failures has generously provided the Chinese leadership a full justification for the necessity of changing their theoretical interpretation of Marxism in order to initiate many very different new economic development programmes. In practical terms, socialist economists in China have liberated

Chinese economic planning from the past theoretical rigidity of Marxism. The Chinese leaders are now able to more effectively and successfully combine their own new theory and new practice. Their theorists do not concede to capitalist theorists that Marxism is now, in fact, extremely inadequate, archaic and must be thoroughly revised in order to be reconciled with global economic reality. It is no longer a refuge to hide behind classical Marxism. However, China's economic theorists have not yet gone this far, so for the purpose of practical understanding of the changes in China we need to appreciate the Chinese theoretical reinterpretation of Marxism today.

One of the most astute Chinese economists has been Professor Xue Muqiao, a teacher and an adviser on rural economy in China all his life, especially during the time as vice-chairman of the State Planning Commisssion and Director of the State Statistical Bureau in the 1950s and 1960s. He has written:[13]

> China's socialist revolution has entered a new historical era. The Third Plenary Session of the Party's Eleventh Central Committee set forth the task of shifting the focus of the party's work to socialist modernisation and building a powerful socialist state by the end of this century ... The Party Central Committee has called on theoreticians to provide guidance for practical workers. Thus we who work in the theoretical field are asked to contribute to the country's four modernisations in our own way.

Both as a theoretician and a practitioner, Xue's study has been guided by his own three emphases: (1) integration of theory with practice; (2) concrete analysis of the contradictions in a socialist society; and (3) the study of socialist relations of production as a process. Socialism in China has been a new system in the country's three thousand years of history. Actual conditions in China are very different from both capitalist and socialist countries elsewhere. Theoreticians in China today have the task of studying, discovering and applying 'the laws of the socialist economy to solve theoretical and practical questions of economic construction'. They admit their 'total dependence on Marx and Lenin', concerning the laws of transition from capitalism to communism through socialism. However, the new emphasis in China today stresses the role of 'Marxist classics as guides only to discover new laws for Chinese socialist economy' because socialism never actually existed in China. Xue insists 'we must never take what is said by Marx, Engels and Lenin in their works as dogma or as panacea'. With a backward or pre-capitalistic economy, China's transition to socialism and communism has to be one with Chinese characteristics. Contradictions and conflicts are present in all things; they 'permeate the course of development of each thing from beginning to end', Mao once said. Chinese theoreticians today focus on more suitable solutions to contradictions between economic production and the role of the state. As a lower phase of transition to communism, socialism is itself an imperfect socio-economic formation. Therefore, 'socialist ownership by the whole nation' is in itself imperfect and 'in need of improvement'. When economic relations of production and productive forces *vis-à-vis* the power of the state are in very bad contradiction, reform becomes inevitable. Transitory conflicts and contradictions will require a long time before the realisation of communism. The adaptable system of 'production and distribution of goods and services in China will be subject to review and change' for a long time to come. New theory and new laws of change will have to be discovered to govern the process of change. Seeking truth from practice is, therefore, quite accurate in guiding future reforms. The period of transition may last 'several hundred years'. Socialist ownership may include for a long time various types, including personal, household or private ones and group (or collective) and state ones. This variety of ownership will likely be protected for a long time in China during the rapid increase in productive force and increase in GNP. Today's new desire for stability and production incentives is in total contradiction to the time when the Gang of Four were in control who argued in favour of rapid change in relations of production in correspondence with the growth of productive forces. Today such radical debate for continual change in the social relations of production is no longer acceptable. Even transition itself, although an imperfect situation, requires a longer period of stability in social relations in order to gain first a greater growth in economic production. China prefers to move 'toward a socialist state step by step'. The country was basically feudalistic with little modern capitalistic growth in 1949. More than 80 per cent of the population subsisted on farming. The country went through land reform and cooperative movement in rural areas. A mistake was made in emphasising growth in heavy industry at the expense of rural population. It was 'indeed necessary to obtain some funds from the peasants, but they cannot be expected to contribute too much'.[14] By 1957, the theoreticians in China contended that the nation had completed the necessary degree toward socialist economic transformation. There cannot be an advanced stage of socialist ownership unless modernisation in technology and mechanisation has changed the productive forces. The system of distribution must follow the principles of 'to each according to his work'. Therefore, wage and salary differentiation must be maintained. Bonuses and other rewards for efficiency must be used to increase production. Egalitarianism has no claim in the present stage of economy.

Chinese economic theorists today openly distinguish the differences between the 'free capitalist economy' of the 1880s when Marx discovered his objective laws governing economic development and Lenin's theory to supplement Marx's theoretical inadequacy when Lenin related 'monopoly capitalism' to 'Western imperialism' as 'the highest stage of capitalism' which Marx did not anticipate. Sixty years later after Lenin, the capitalist countries have 'made fresh advances' and many new situations and problems have appeared which Lenin himself did not or could not anticipate in the 1920s. In the 1980s, Chinese theoreticians openly admit:[15]

> As capitalist society has not run its course, we cannot say that we have arrived at a complete understanding of the laws of capitalist economic growth ... Socialism is a new social system with a brief history. It has only been thirty years since the socialist revolution in China and we have not accumulated sufficient experience in our social practice. Since we had an extremely backward economy to start with and our present socialist relations of production are far from mature, we have many difficulties in studying the laws of socialist economic development.

Such a disclaimer in theoretical absolutism provides an unrestrained liberty for socialist economic experiment in China. She can now emphasise both growth and efficiency on the one hand, and seek new theory and truth 'from practice' on the other. There appears to be a long period when economic theorists will, through careful research on socio-economic conditions characteristic of China, derive and discover new laws governing 'Socialism with Chinese characteristics'. They must test new principles, new policies and plans to deal with Chinese realities before a new theory will ultimately emerge. Marxism and Leninism will simply remain as references to guide Chinese thinking. As China experiments in reforms and in economic growth, successes and failures are both expected. And experience will be drawn from both. In a sense, Deng and his close colleagues have put Marxism and Mao Zedong Thought to a severe test. If any part does not bring about the expected success, it will be cast out and ignored theoretically.

Practical experience becomes the central guiding in China's modernisation drive under the 'new socialism'. This does not mean that the reform leaders share enthusiastically the capitalist views and theory of economic means of production, or on relations between production and the growth in productive forces. China will probably end up in having a 'mixed economy' for a long period of time. It will recognise simultaneous co-existence of individual ownership, collective ownership and state ownership. In management and production incentives, China is likely to adopt freely any advantages of the capitalist economy, including a tax system, wage differentials, and currency management. In the name of egalitarianism and working-class interest during the past thirty years, people in rural China were cruelly exploited by government policy through a regulated low-price system for agricultural products and compulsory quota sale to the state. On the other hand, industrial products for consumption were priced high and were in short supply. Therefore, rural China became more poverty stricken relative to urban areas. In addition, the failure to realise the need to first develop the rural economy and light industry before concentration on heavy industries was the root of the economic disaster for the thirty years of communist rule. Marxian dogmatism and Mao's revolutionary radicalism were at the heart of the leadership failure. Ideological politics came to interfere with economic rationalism and the advantages of a market economy.

All these mistakes, now viewed in retrospect, were due to blind imitation of the Soviet economic model and blindness to Chinese objective economic conditions as of 1949. Mao's own commune system and the Great Leap forward in the late 1950s and his cultural revolution during the last ten years of his life further intensified the economic crisis. In addition the Soviet withdrawal of its aid programme in 1960 created new anxiety in China. The nightmare of the past thirty years has finally led to the new strategy for China's economic development after 1979.

The new strategy was adopted at a work conference in April 1979 to reform the economy in a fourfold approach, namely, 'readjusting, restructuring, consolidating and improving' the economy as a whole. Changes were to be implemented step by step within the limits of the nation's own resources. Readjustment was given a period of five years before other measures were to be taken. After the third Plenum in December 1978, various urban adjustment measures and rural changes were introduced, especially with emphasis on the responsibility system in farming and urban remuneration in relation to production increases. Many new areas of incentive were encouraged in rural production and private marketing, such as the increase in the size of private plots, and sideline occupations. The government drastically increased the price for grain purchases from the farmers. All these measures were aimed at raising the living conditions of the rural population. Likewise, experiments in factory management responsibility began in early 1980. The precise problems for the new strategy to correct were summarised by economist Ma Hong as follows:[16]

> China's economic development has been very unstable, with sudden ups and downs and major swings in direction. Economic results have been relatively poor and have had a tendency to decline. Thus the growth in national strength has been fairly slow and the people have not derived much in terms of material benefits. These are the major problems in our economic development since the founding of the People's Republic.

Due to political or economic policy changes the growth rate remained unstable in both agriculture and industry. For example, the annual agricultural growth rate was 14.1 per cent between 1949 and 1952, but declined to 4.5 per cent 1954–57. Due to Mao's commune failure, agricultural growth declined further by 4.3 per cent between 1958 and 1962. Then it registered a growth rate of 11.1 per cent from 1963–5. The annual growth in the industrial area during the corresponding periods was 34.8 per cent, 18 per cent, 3.8 per cent, and 17.9 per cent. Such fluctuation in growth rate is clearly a reflection of poor management and irrational policy changes. In the construction industry, for example there was always a marked decline in economic results, as measured in per hundred yuan of fixed assets from 1957 to 1976. Industrial enterprises under the ownership of the state (or the whole people) declined for the same time period by 48.8 per cent from 23.6 yuan in 1957 to 12.1 yuan in 1976. Statistics concerning such shocking failures are quite readily available in China today.[17] Due to such 'ups and down' in agricultural and industrial production, which resulted in the overall downfall of economic gains, the growth rate of national income had frequent tendencies to decline. For example, during the First Five-Year Plan, the average national rate of increase was 8.9 per cent according to Chinese statistics. However, national income declined by 31 per cent during the Second Five Year Plan period. During the rest of the years from 1963 to 1965, and thereafter the average increase rate was 14.5 per cent, 8.4 per cent or 5.6 per cent for the different planned periods. Such fluctuations were inevitably attributed to political instability and the ideological struggle within the Communist Party. Unlike elsewhere in Asia, the people's living standard in China did not improve much or improved unevenly from region to region and between urban workers and rural farmers. White collar officials did not have salary increases for decades while the national income went through many irregular ups and downs. The management system in both rural commune and urban enterprises simply destroyed any desire or incentive on the part of the working people to increase productivity. False statistics were reported by cadres for their job security and political survival. Slogans were shouted and self-criticisms were organised. But often they were artificially performed to meet political regulations and party discipline.

On the other hand, until the beginning of Deng's opening of China to the outside world, China was a locked up system in stagnation without much hope of catching up with and competing with other Asian neighbours in economic development. Foreign capital investment in China was ideologically unacceptable. International trade expansion would have violated Mao's ideological stand and belief in self-reliance. Western and Japanese technology and management skill could not enter China. Radical Maoist factions and their influences permeated every level of the communist party and the government units. Therefore, it was impossible to deviate from the ignorance and stupidity of ideological rigidity. Because of this, Deng's pragmatist vision since the Eighth Party Congress in 1956 and Zhou Enlai's crisis management after Mao's cultural revolution in 1966 wanted to differ quietly from Mao's approach to modernisation and economic development. But the Dengs and the Zhous and their moderate followers could not do anything until Mao neared his death, and until after most of them had been purged and abused. Some died during the secret confinement. With such chaos and disorder during Mao's time, it is easy to appreciate the urgency of Deng's return to leadership in 1973 to implement his four modernisations. A new strategy for economic reform has been, therefore, indispensable to get the country moving forward, if China is to join the ranks of modern industrial states.

In order to appreciate the need for a new economic development strategy, it is helpful to summarise the erroneous practice of the past in economic development as follows:[18]

1. The violation of economic laws in seeking the impossible high targets in production. Inefficiency and waste were disguised by falsification of statistics. In reality, the production output declined;

2. The eagerness to expand new construction projects and new capital formation, and the failure to take care of existing projects and enterprises through efficient management innovation and new technology;
3. The failure to produce consumer goods because of the emphasis on production in heavy industrial sectors, such as steel and mechanical equipments, which were over-produced and remained in warehouses to idle;
4. For two decades the foolish commune system stagnated rural economy to reduce the living standards of the rural population, while the central government failed to invest in consumer goods production and in adequate or other essential consumption needs. And the failure to develop sideline jobs and income to improve living standard by their own effort.
5. The official policy promoting domestic capital formation by refusal to allow people to spend on consumption. Many consumer goods were simply not available.
6. The lack of patience in allowing a gradual and healthy transformation of production from private individual and collective ownership to state ownership. The Maoist leadership unrealistically stepped up the pace of public ownership which caused waste and loss in productivity as has been statistically revealed:[19]

> We rashly transformed collective ownership into ownership by the whole people, and hastily neglected the role of the individual economy in cities and towns. In 1952 there were 8.83 million self-employed labourers in cities and towns; this number declined 1.04 million in 1957 and by 1975 only 240,000 were left. An over centralised system of economic management was also carried out within the sector owned by the whole people.

Such a rash policy had to be reversed after the adoption of the new economic strategy under Deng. Today, cities and towns are undergoing a reverse transformation and are becoming richer. The people like this new development which permits them to help themselves.

7. An erroneous self-isolation policy against the outside world denied China the benefit of knowledge, trade, and an understanding of global realities. A false sense of pride, self-reliance and independence prevented the nation from the natural contact of normal relations among states. Mao's sense of revolutionary mission and purity was a deadly self-delusion.

8. Mao's primitive concept of population policy brought about a burden of one billion people which need jobs, education, housing, transportation, etc.
9. The damaging policy of land reform and cruel class struggle allowed the government itself quickly to become the new master-exploiter and the entire country was put under centrally guided bureaucratic control and management. That the new rural policy under Deng has brought peasant prosperity is itself a proof of the past ignorance of the Communist leadership. The future of China still depends on further rural prosperity through peasant hard work to contribute to the wealth of the nation. Any visitor to rural China can see for himself that the peasants can be very innovative in self-help. They can contribute enormously to the building of a light consumer industry if the central government can properly guide and help them with credits, information, marketing, transportation, and a constructive price system.
10. The fabrication of class contradiction and anti-intellectualism under Mao's personal insistence from time to time since 1957 was totally unnecessary.
11. There was also China's failure to understand the role of education as the foundation for creating science and technology. Without much investment in pure science research no nation can make its own technology. Today, as a stop-gap at least, China has to borrow and import technology from abroad.

These eleven areas of negligence contributed to a result of an unsound economic cycle of 'high speed, high capital formation, low efficiency and low consumption', as pointed out by economist Ma Hung. Since 1978, the new economic strategy of 'readjusting, restructuring, consolidating and improving' contains both changes in policy goals and in methods of implementation. The new policy goals include the need to satisfy the material and cultural desires of the people, an emphasis on economic efficiency, greater production in consumer goods, a strong and healthy agriculture prior to concentration on heavy industry, and an emphasis on the importance of transportation, energy supply and education. To accomplish these goals requires time and careful planning. Before an undue rush to reform, there must be readjustment. Future production increases will depend on reorganising or restructuring the existing economy. China's economy is now open to influence from the outside world. Positive policy for foreign investment in China and for two-way trade expansion represents a permanent commitment in China's open door policy. Another shift is the policy of decentralisation in enterprise decision making to allow each production unit to build its own efficiency and accountability for better economic result and profit. The new strategy will see to it that the national economy is essentially dominated by those industries under national ownership; collective ownership and individual ownership are merely supplementary. The underlying assumption is that socialist ownership and capitalist planning are inherently superior to capitalist anarchy.

In short, China's new economic growth strategy moves slowly but steadily from adjustment to reform. Gradually the nation will be able to restructure itself for the improvement of the economy. The rate of economic growth will remain stable, instead of fluctuating as in the past, in order to minimise inflation and overheating by a high rate of growth. The economy will not slow down because of readily available measures for stability in its growth speed. Such a new strategy will eventually reach a stage in the economy as former Premier Zhao Ziyang said repeatedly that China will 'blaze a new trail' in developing its socialist economy. The long-term success of reform will require continuous effort on three fronts of the economy: (1) the rationalisation of the economic structure uninterfered with by non-economic irrational factors; (2) an organisational set up of enterprise to maximise production, marketing and management efficiency free of political heavy handedness; and (3) finally, an economic system of management to increase managerial accountability and success. In rural economic development the new strategy entails such implementation measures as suggested in Hu Yaobang's report: expansion in the decision-making power of the rural population, restoration of private plots, individual and family sideline production and village marketing, contractual system of responsibility farming, fair pricing of farm products by the state purchasing agency, and diversification of rural economic and occupational development.[20] The government has completed successfully the short-term goals called for by the new strategy during the Sixth Five-Year Plan period (1981–5) in readjusting, restructuring, consolidating and improving as expected. The 7th Five-Year Plan (1986–90) has been a fresh and real take-off stage for technological advance, rational reform of enterprises, energy development and transportation expansion, It is expected under the new strategy that 'the 1990s will witness an all around upsurge in China's economy which will definitely grow at a much faster rate than in the 1980s ... They [the people] will see a bright future more clearly and will be inspired to work with greater drive to usher in the new period of vigorous economic growth.'[21] It now appears that China is concentrating on control of inflation, economic stability, new expansion in banking institutions, finance and credit balance, prevention of trade imbalance and means of long-term stability. During the past several years, concentration on long-term goals include: (1) emphasis on key urgent development projects; (2) a greater effort to improve the people's living standards; (3) upholding the dominating position of the state owned portion of the economy while diversifying economic forms of production; (4) proper supervision over the leading role of the planned sector of the economy while encouraging the supplementary role of market regulation; and (5) preservation of the basic policy of economic self-reliance while encouraging foreign investment and borrowing or purchasing foreign technology. These various emphases and approaches have been maintained when the Seventh Five-Year Plan began in 1986. So far it seems to be impossible to control economic fluctuations during this period of massive reform.

One of the most important documents on reform measures of the economic restructuring was adopted on 20 October 1984, at the Third Plenum of the Twelfth Party Central Committee.[22] This was a document on policy implementation which sought to institutionalise the economic structural foundation to meet the greater challenge of growth in nine basic areas – for example, the training of party cadres, the industrial and human resource training, and the development of a strong and capable managerial class to man the some 40,000 enterprises currently under reform toward efficient and responsible autonomy. Overheating of the economy in 1985–6, Hu Yaobang's resignation affecting adversely foreign capital inflow in 1987, and new crisis in declining food production in 1987–8 seem to illustrate many inevitable problems associated with massive economic changes. There may be future unexpected problems in the 1990s to affect adversely the economic steady growth.

4 Broad Implementation of the New Economic Strategy

This chapter will focus on macro-implementation of the new economic strategy since the Third Plenum of the Eleventh Party Congress in late 1978. The period of major readjustment is near its completion. Restructuring, consolidation and improvement are being carried out simultaneously during the Sixth Five-year Plan (1981–5). (The discovery of the impact from rural economic decontrol, relaxation of politics and the fresh start toward rapid economic diversification and expansion has generated additional optimism toward urban economic reform both in scope and depth. In a sense, pressure for rapid urban economic reform is to acommodate the rural expansion and to bridge the increasing mutual dependence between the rural and the urban sectors of the growing economy. Unlike the lock-up rural policy under Mao, Deng's policy is to free 80 per cent of the population and let them follow their own destiny as being better for growth. The government has helped them recover from region to region, while the government itself has fully concentrated on urban heavy industrial reform for greater expansion.) Today, partial economic freedom in rural China has brought new vitality and strength to the entire economy. This chapter will touch upon a few major reform documents as a means to implement broadly the new economic strategy.

4.1 ECONOMIC STRUCTURAL REFORM

One of the most important documents on structural reform was adopted on 20 October 1984 at the Third Plenum of the 12th Party Central committee. It is a major implementation document which provides categorical delineation of reform specifics. Broadly speaking, it seeks to achieve the following very specific goals:[1] (1) to secure 'a dynamic socialist economic structure'; (2) to invigorate enterprises as 'the key to restructuring the national economy'; (3) to devise a planning system for 'developing a socialist commodity economy'; (4) to establish a 'rational price system'; (5) to separate government from enterprise functions to allow the enterprise to perform its proper economic functions; (6) to create various forms of economic responsibility system and to implement the principle of distribution of reward according to one's work; (7) to develop diverse economic forms to expand foreign and domestic economic and technological exchanges; (8) to promote a new generation of cadres and a contingent of managerial personnel for the future economy; and finally (9) to strengthen party leadership in the reform process and its success.

This document has clearly pointed out a continuing task of economic reform with very specific targets. If all the goals are to be reached in the Seventh Five-Year Plan period as generally expected in 1990, the Chinese economy will then have truly reached a stage of infra-structural completion. It will likely become, then, an institutionalised stable system with a rational economic decision-making regularity. The system will likely be able to resist fluctuations and rash changes. However, if political instability and unexpected economic disasters should occur in the next decade after Deng's departure, it will be difficult to anticipate what dramatic new shifts may take place. The October document has declared that, first of all, the growing rural economic prosperity and success now require much greater economic interaction with urban industrial centres. Rural agricultural demands have made urban economic reform urgent in order to meet 'the growing forces of production'. The present general defects of urban economic structure include: no clear distinction between functions of the government and those of the industrial enterprises, bureaucratic barriers between government departments and among geographic regions, excessive and rigid control of enterprises by the Communist Party, lack of well-planned attention to market commodity production, lack of understanding between the law of value and the government regulatory philosophy of the free market. These defects have plagued enterprises and caused them to suffer from their lack of decision-making power. Enterprise personnel have followed for some thirty years the practice of 'eating from the same big pot'. No initiative, enthusiasm and creativity in enterprises can be expected unless decision-making power is granted to them. The document says 'we must emancipate our minds more, follow our own road and build a socialist economic structure with Chinese Characteristics that is full of vigour and vitality so as to promote the growth of the forces of production. This is the fundamental objective of our present reform'. This reform is expected also 'to advance social stability' and the growth of state revenue and living standards.

Urban enterprise is designated by planning to bear 'the chief and direct responsibility for industrial production and construction and commodity circulation'. China presently has over one million urban enterprises which are divided into industrial, building, transport, commercial and service fields. They employ a total of 80 million workers. The tax and other profits from industrial enterprises alone amount to 80 per cent of government revenue. Having such importance, they must have 'great vitality' to lead the economy. This vitality can only be built in two ways: it needs to be free from unnecessary state control and an organised internal vitality needs to exist between the management leadership and the workers and staff. An enterprise must have power 'to adopt flexible and diversified forms of operation; to plan its production, supply and marketing; to keep and to budget funds it is entitled to retain; to appoint, remove, employ or elect its own personnel according to relevant regulations; to decide on how to recruit and use its work forces, and on wages and rewards; to set the prices of its products within the limits prescribed by the state'[2]. Each enterprise must be an independent entity as both a producer and a dealer of its commodity. The strength and vitality will come from internal human relations and organisational managerial efficiency from which it derives essentially the initiative, wisdom and creativeness of its workers. When workers' initiative is linked to their material benefits, urban workers will respond as rural farmers have in their recent experiment. Wages and special rewards must be 'given to each according to his work'. This will increase production and promote modernisation, which is the 'inevitable trend of history and the wish of the people'. The workers and staff of any enterprise must learn to produce what the country needs and what they themselves want. All units must be represented in the decision-making process of their enterprise through their own elected representatives. The unity of an enterprise's leadership and the interest of its staff and workers will be ensured by the laws of the state. In short, enterprise reform itself will be carried out step by step in relation to the whole national economy. Nationwide, the reform should be completed before 1990. Another major innovation proposed by the document is the device on the 'planning system for a socialist commodity economy'. The rationalisation for a socialist commodity economy has won an ideological battle over the merits between a planned economy and a commodity economy. No one knows the extent to which the socialist law of value should be applied to avoid the total anarchy of the market economy of capitalism. Socialism itself certainly has serious problems with egalitarianism. Public ownership of the means of production under socialism guarantees the state control over the national economy. Through government planning, the 'supplementary economy' dealing with important but non-essential articles and services should be left to the market forces for their regulation. Lines must be drawn between the scope of 'socialist command economy' and the market 'commodity economy'. China is clearly determined to incorporate both of them into its future economic development. The justification provided by the document is that China can combine 'at one uniformity and flexibility'. Dealing with reform implementation, account must be taken of the vast size of the country, her regional diversity, its huge population, the lack of transportation, inadequacy of micro-information for any detailed planning, and the uneven economic and cultural differences in various parts of the nation. Recent reform experience indicates the necessity to 'stimulate commodity production and exchange'. It is now realised that it is impossible for the central government to incorporate all the local details into a giant national plan. Any such effort would create new difficulties through misinformation and top heavy bureaucratisation. Implementation of a detailed national plan by administrative orders, rather than through natural market conditions, can be very inefficient. The document warns 'we must be realistic and admit that for a long time to come, our national economic plans on the whole can only be rough and elastic and that we can do no more than, by striking an overall balance in planning, ... exercise effective control over major issues while allowing flexibility on minor ones.'[3]

From this document, one can easily see that China will, for a long time to come, have a socialist planned commodity economy. Part of this economy will be based on public ownership as a form of state capitalism. A significant private ownership of this commodity economy seems indispensable in the early stage in the economic development. This appears the best way to reduce bureaucratic inefficiency and to reduce the size of state 'mandatory planning'. As a flexibly planned commodity economy, greater flexibility will carefully be confined to 'production for rural market exchange' which will include farm and sideline products, small articles, repair services, and retail trade.)

China is also faced with the need for a rational price system. There is much confusion in the current irrational pricing regulations which must be reformed if enterprises are to operate on a rational pricing system of their products. The leadership realises now that 'pricing is the most effective means of regulation, and rational prices constitute an important condition for ensuring a dynamic yet not chaotic economy'. The major irrational pricing in China currently includes; unfair price ratios among different commodities, inadequate price differentials for a given product with diverse quality, ridiculous price differences between farm goods sold cheaper in the open market and the same goods sold with higher price to the government. The government must drastically reform its own irrational centralised price control. The key emphasis of reform is to reduce the scope of uniform price as set by the state and expand the scope of floating prices as dictated by the market forces. Prices must be allowed to reflect constant changes in the law of supply and demand. The future reformed new price system must protect the interest of the individuals and their market sector in their living standard. The government seems prepared to deal with a new price system in relation to a new tax system and an expanded banking practice. For rapid adjustment macro-economic development, government regulation and growth trend must be taken together for pricing consideration. As the economy becomes freer and more flexible, the price system itself will become more sensitive and important as a regulating instrument.

One of the areas designated for serious reform is the separation of government interference from the rational and effective operation of the enterprises. This will affect the role of the party. It will require an enormous decentralisation of decision-making power as well as a hands-off tendency on the part of political cadres who are assigned to the enterprises. They will be likely to concentrate their activities in the future on morale building, recreation programmes, and other cultural matters. Such reform will probably bring about greater responsibility and freedom to managers and staff of the enterprises to innovate, and to create a new vigorous team spirit for production in competition with other related enterprises. The role of the government should be limited to formulating national production strategy, development plans, principles and policy for economic and social development. It is the function of the government at all levels to deal with transportation, resource development, energy supply, technology and other utility supplies. For profit or for loss, the government can leave enterprises to manage their own production, marketing, purchasing, bonus distribution competition or cooperation with other related enterprises, for survival or against bankruptcy.

The 1984 document is also eager to introduce various forms of a 'contracted responsibility system' into urban economic development. The responsibility system which has proved successful in rural practice should similarly work in the urban situation. It is possible to specify explicitly 'work post' and 'duties of each worker' of staff member through 'contracted jobs'. Thus, it will be easy to hold workers accountable in their merit evaluation for their wages and rewards. Material compensation can follow strictly according to work well done with initiative, creativeness and enthusiasm. This urban 'responsibility system' is to be a combination of responsibility, authority and benefit achieved in the interest of the state, the collective (enterprise), and the individual himself. However, it is unlikely that urban enterprises will follow any particular single model of responsibility system, in view of the major differences from enterprise to enterprise. Leadership will come from 'a systems manager' who will assume full responsibility. Party organisations within any enterprise are required to support the manager in his exercise of 'unified authority over production and management'. Under the unified command of an enterprise management, a system of 'enterprise democracy' must be implemented through the help of party organisations within the enterprise. Within an enterprise 'the workers are masters' and can exercise mutual criticism and encourage creativity. The new enterprise reform is to be strict in following a reward system of 'more work more pay, and less work less pay'. Differences in wage-scales will be sharply recognised between mental and manual work, and between skilled and unskilled work. A new wage system will be enacted. Egalitarian thinking in the socialist wage system is now considered incompatible with scientific Marxism.

Emphasis in urban reform is also given to the development of more 'diversified economic forms and various methods of management'. This thrust is linked to pledges to bring in more foreign economic and technological exchange on the basis of economic independence, self-reliance, equality and mutual benefit. Non-public and non-collectively owned segments of the new 'individual economy' is considered quite different from the individual or private ownership which, under socialism, plays 'an irreplaceable role in expanding production, meeting the people's daily needs and providing employment'.[4] The October document pledges to remove obstacles in the way of collective economy and individual economy in both cities and rural towns in order to facilitate their rapid development. Future policy will encourage 'diverse and flexible forms of cooperative management and economic association among the state, collective and individual sectors of the economy'. For example, some small state-owned enterprise may be leased to individuals or collective bodies on a contract basis.

The document recognises the contradictions between antagonistic international political relations and cooperative and close economic relations among states. It repudiates the past self-isolation and declares 'National seclusion cannot lead to modernisation ... We have taken opening to the outside world to be our long term, basic state policy, a strategic measure for accelerating socialist modernisation. Practice has already yielded marked results. We must continue to pursue flexible policies, reform our foreign trade structure.'[5] Pledges are also made to strive for the success of the special economic zones and in opening up other coastal cities. Foreign funds, technology, and foreign businesses for joint ventures are beneficial complements to China's socialist economy. Domestically, all parts of China should be open 'to do away with blockades' between more and less developed regions, between coastal and interior and the border areas. In short, China pledges to speed up economic rationalism in both organisational management and geographical distribution, with the help of foreign technology and investment.

Reform on such a wide scale clearly calls for a 'new generation of cadres' and 'a contingent of managerial personnel'. The urgent task is to educate and train 'thousands upon thousands' of middle-aged and young managers and technicians. Party reform is linked to recruiting qualified cadres who are free from past factionalism. Completion of the reshuffling of leadership in key enterprises was to be accomplished before the end of 1985. The Central Committee of the Communist Party has called for rapid training of directors, chief engineers and accountants. Education has been given a special task of developing human resources in the next several decades.

Finally, the success of economic structural reform depends on the leadership of the Communist Party. To proceed cautiously, the document states 'make reforms one by one when conditions are ripe, and make experiment when we are not sure of success. We must not try to accomplish the whole task at one stroke'. The party began its own consolidation after 1985. The Four Cardinal Principles of the party are to be strictly emphasised in cadre recruitment task.

Area by area, the document carefully reviewed the economic situation and provided detailed reform guidelines. In total, it has set out an enormous task to be accomplished in the next several years. There is no arrogance expressed, no dogmatism adhered to, and only a minimal socialist ideological reference was employed during policy discussion. The entire document appears most frank, straightforward in problem analysis, and rational in programme suggestion and recommendation. In short, the October document calls for an ambitious undertaking. Whether or not the Communist Party or the country as a whole can fully accomplish what has been called for remains to be seen. Even if only 50 per cent of the task is accomplished in the next several years, it will be a success anyway because of the experimental nature of the reform itself. The document does not impose a timetable for completion. Many future new problems are expected during reform implementation. Many unexpected new circumstances may emerge beyond the leadership's control. The fact that the party in 1984 drew up such a reform document is itself a significant evidence of rational planning and programmatic progress. It will be seen how the private individual enterprises in China are to be linked to the planned command socialist economy as a whole, and how the small collectively owned enterprises will operate in competition with the powerful command economy is of great interest to economists and sinologists. The democratic operation of an enterprise under a single powerful manager, who is to be aided by the Communist Party leader within that enterprise, may or may not be as smooth and ideal as now expected. In short, there are many unanswered and unanswerable questions on the way toward successful reform implementation. Indeed, the document has dramatised Deng's 'Socialism with Chinese Characteristics'. However, such characteristics as now perceived in the reform are not so unique to China itself because they are economic rational devices, progressively conceived and universally understandable. What is quite characteristic is Deng's leadership in the Communist party, which is able to transform itself and to integrate into Chinese socialism many classical features of economic free enterprise. Such a new socialist economy, in my judgement, will be quite acceptable to all Chinese people everywhere. Deng's new socialism will bring the benefits of modernisation to the whole country, and it will be carried out without a Maoist class struggle. Indeed, this reform document is another evidence of Deng's characteristic statesmanship. If these major reform items are successfully implemented, China will have institutionalised its socialist economy which will in itself be a new model of innovative development.

Three implementation reports are to be discussed briefly as follows: one of them is the Premier's Report on Government Work on 27 March 1985, to the sixth National People's Congress.[6] Another document is the Draft Plan for National Economic and Social Development. The third deals with Report on the Execution of the State Budget for 1984 and of the Draft State Budget for 1985. All of these documents were adopted by the same National People's

Congress as official policies for implementation. Together, these documents help explain the state of the economy as viewed and dealt with by the different departments of the executive branch of government. Each document contributes to a better understanding and solution to the economic situation as seen in fiscal year 1985.

The premier declared 1984 the year of 'great achievement' in industrial and agricultural production, in the acceleration of the modernisation drive and in further improvement of the people's living standards. For several years the nation has achieved a new economic situation marked by 'sustained, stable and coordinated economic growth'. In 1984 the total value of both industrial and agricultural growth exceeded 1000 billion yuan. This welcome growth followed an average annual increase rate of 7.9 per cent. The 1984 growth represented a 14.2 per cent increase over 1983. And national income and state revenue both scored an increase of 12 per cent over 1983. In agriculture, another bumper harvest was registered. Grain output was more than 407 million tons in 1984 (a 5.1 per cent over 1983). Cotton output registered 6.08 million tons (a 31.1 per cent increase over the previous year). Rural China continued to diversify its productive innovation toward a growing commodity economy. The average per capita amount of grain and cotton in 1984 rose to 400 kilograms and 6 kilograms respectively, almost double that of the early 1970s in many part of the country. With the exception of few far removed areas, the people have generally 'attained sufficiency in food and clothing'. In the industrial sector, energy production, for example, exceeded its target production in 1984, with the coal output reaching 770 million tons and crude oil over 114 million tons, an increase of 8 per cent for both over 1983. Good progress was registered in 1984 in other industrial areas as well, including chemical, building material, machine building, electronics, textile, metallurgical, and other light industries. By December 1983, 43 out of 65 major projects of the Sixth Five-Year Plan (1981–5) had been completed one year ahead of time. By the end of 1984, more than 42 million urban jobs had been found for city residents between 1979 and 1984. According to a survey of the State Statistical Bureau, the annual per capita income of urban citizens has reached 608 yuan in 1984, and a net per capita income for a peasant was 335 yuan by the end of 1984. Farmers' per capita increase was 14.7 per cent over their city counterparts of 12.5 per cent in the 1984 average.

The main features of Chinese economic development in recent years have included the following: (1) a balanced rational growth between agriculture and industry, and also between light and heavy industries has been achieved; (2) a correct ratio between consumer consumption production and capital investment accumulation has also been obtained. These two main achievements represent a major accomplishment in the readjustment process. Agricultural expansion in recent years has resulted in light industry growing at a faster pace, a healthy 11.2 per cent between 1979 and 1983, with 13.9 per cent for 1984. Due to rapid expansion in light industries, especially in areas of woollen fabrics, washing machines, television sets and refrigerators, heavy industries have also picked up rapidly. Rising consumer demands have stimulated the growth production to meet the popular demand for higher living standards of the people. Statistics indicated that, between 1978 and 1983, average per capita consumption rose from 175 yuan to 288 yuan, and in 1984 to 320 yuan. Thus the average annual growth was 7.3 per cent after making allowance for price changes. This growth rate far exceeded the 2.2 per cent increase during the twenty-six years between 1953 and 1978. These figures in economic achievements, which may suffer from technical inaccuracy, have been the result of the success of the four-fold policy of readjustment, restructure, consolidation and improvement. The economy has broken the 'closed and rigid pattern that had taken shape over a long period'.

Beginning in 1979, the economic policy success in the countryside led the government to experiment in urban enterprise reform on the tax system, enterprise decision making and other reforms concerning the construction industry, the system of commerce, and banking. Because of the reform effort to 'introduce diverse forms of urban economy and method of business operation', the urban economy has begun to experience a vigorous growth unknown for many years. Now, the government is confidently entering a new stage of restructuring the entire economy with an emphasis on urban aspects.

On the other hand, many new problems resulting from the recent reform, in addition to those inherited from the past, will require solution. Aside from the persistent difficulties over, for instance, energy supply, transportation bottlenecks, supply of raw materials and semi-finished materials, 'a conspicuous problem' is the issue of too much currency as a result of 'lax control' over credit and consumption funds in 1984. This was unavoidable because of the increase in consumer goods production, in rapid business turnover, and in higher income for people to spend. The lack of a rational wage and price system has made control of bank credit and floating currency more difficult to regulate and adjust. 1984 was the first year of the implementation of the economic reform decision of 1984. The nation's political situation has been marked by 'increasing stability and unity' in recent years. This has helped the economy to maintain vigour and vitality. The principal guidelines have been: 'Be steadfast, be prudent in fighting the first battle and be sure to win'.[7] The government seems fully aware of its lack of knowledge and experience in opening up a complicated urban economy for reform. In the past few years, the cities aided reforms in rural areas. And larger enterprises helped smaller enterprises. The government will continue to 'invigorate small enterprises' for still greater vitality. But future emphasis will be on large enterprises. The reform focus will emphasise the need for low production costs, less use of raw materials and the increase of the factories' ability to initiate proper changes on their own. In terms of new forms of administration, 'economic responsibility systems' will be introduced to suit each particular enterprise for efficiency and accountability.

The most urgent areas for structural reform in 1985 were the wage and price systems. The old practices in both areas are now out of step with new strategies and economic changes. They were not much in need when the state authoritatively decided wages and prices, and the supply of goods in the market and in rationing. The consumers, who had no say, bought whatever was available or could not buy what they wanted even at a higher price. There was no need for knowledge of price theory and wage mechanisms to regulate the growth, production and distribution in the economy. Today, all that has changed. The economic 'command sector', the 'collective sector' and the 'market sector' of the economy must coordinate and compete in the name of 'socialist commodity economy'. All three sectors do mutually influence each other. But they must also interact for purposes of harmony to meet the overall growth efficiency and the structural modernisation. Today the market conditions of less regulated and less planned rural and individualised sectors of the economy can affect the collective components and the commercial activities. This can very seriously produce painful consequences for the average consumer and wage earner. The negative effect of prices and wages must not be allowed to destroy the basic purpose of raising the living standards of the masses. The central government, however, is not at all experienced in dealing with the price fluctuation of the free marketing economy and with the wage system resulting from enterprise reform between labour and management. Secondly, with the command and collective sectors of the economy in the hands of the government, the less regulated fluctuating 'market price' can easily be victimised if wrong measures are adopted to prevent natural price fluctuation which often affects the entire consuming population of the nation. On the other hand, the new reform strategy itself depends on the healthy growth and vitality of the free marketing mechanism from the countryside to the urban daily commodity exchange. To maximise the worker's production efficiency and rural industrial development, the government must treat prices and wages as two major phases of the same growing problem. Presently, the premier has reported that 'the prices of many commodities reflect neither their value nor the supply and demand relationship. They adversely affect the assessment of the operation and management of an enterprise and its economic performance as well as the development of commodity production and exchange. Reforming the wage and price systems has become the key to further encouraging initiative in all fields'.[8] In short, prices and wages will not only affect every individual consumer but also the entire economic growth. Wage restructuring has aimed at removing the irrational and egalitarian practices in favour of a new distribution differential system to pay each according to his work. Future identification of the work value is to be done by specification of 'work past', 'job specification', 'responsibility' and 'contributions'. In state enterprises, payroll fluctuation will be assessed by the specific economic performance record. Every worker, staff member, and manager will be affected by the overall performance of their enterprise as a whole. Wage and bonus reform is being carried out on a one by one basis. Not all the 300,000 enterprises are equally prepared for uniform reform in wages and prices at the same time. Until the wholly new form is introduced, only partial adjustment on wages and bonuses may be introduced. A period of five years is made available for such reform on wage and price. Presently, overall details on wage reform are being studied and worked out. The first experimental phase of wage reform was instituted in governmental offices in July 1985. All levels of all organisations are currently studying their wage system. The payroll is likely to continue to float on the basis of total production, tax, and profit. More strict control over wage funds and bonuses will have to be institutionalised soon against an irresponsible shift of funds.

Price reform in 1985 was equally difficult if not more so than wage reform. The government adopted a short-range policy for 1985 combining 'relaxed control with readjustment' to raise the prices of some commodities and to lower those of others in order to attain the basic stability of commodity prices across the entire economy. The specific points whose achievement is sought are:[9]

1. In the rural area, the government is adjusting the purchase and marketing prices of grain and cotton and is introducing government purchase of both on a contract basis. Other farm and sideline products will be subject to market fluctuations through gradual relaxation of price control. This will stimulate rural production increases and the price competition of market commodities;

2. Increase of railway freight charges in order to promote the full use and expansion of waterways and highways;

3. Widening of price differences for products of different quality and large price differentials between regions. Expensive or unmarketable products will be eliminated in favour of the production of brand-name and high quality goods in competitive commodity circulation;

4. Prices of raw and semi-finished materials in 1985 remained unchanged, while other finished products by enterprises were subject to market forces. This policy will likely continue.

Eventually a rational price system will emerge in a stabilised economy. It is a laborious process which has been designed to involve 'less risk and greater chance of success'. The government is determined to control the currency circulation through (1) prevention of an increase in consumption funds and the forbidding of all units to use public funds for any unjustifiable purpose (banks are used to control the funds of enterprises as financial supervisor of the latter); (2) introduction of a unified credit and monetary policy to strengthen the regulatory function of the People's Bank of China over major economic activities. The interest rate for bank deposits can be raised to encourage savings over currency circulation (the bank will decide on currency ceilings for its branches in various parts of the nation); (3) over-investment, however, will be subject to a tax penalty in order to protect business and economic expansion through adequate currency circulation in the financial market; (4) a stringent budget cut was imposed for 1985 against administrative expenses, a cut of either 10 or 20 per cent was imposed on administrative budgets of all public institutions on the purchasing of durable goods; (5) encouragement of increase of consumer, marketable, high quality brand-name commodities for expanding market supplies. These measures are presently being implemented in various parts of the nation through cooperation from local government units. The premier's report observed that with one billion people in over 200 million households, the domestic market has shown an enormous capacity. If people rush to buy the same commodities at the same time, no state could cope with the man-made strains on commodity supplies, thereby providing opportunities for lawbreakers and dangers to the state, the consumer and the economy itself. Today, China is trying intelligently to stretch the use of the price system or the wage device to stimulate economic growth and to achieve certain social goals.

The premier's 1985 government report suggested several broad policy making strategies and long term-goals in summary as follows:[10]

1. 'Adhere to the principle of seeking truth from facts and making steady progress and resolutely guard against blindly pursuing a higher rate of development and vying with one another to this end.' He expressed his faith in quadrupling the nation's economic growth value by the end of the century. The nation should see, he said, 'better results rather than too high a growth rate';
2. 'Invigorate the economy and improve management.' The premier asserted that 'we should continue to emancipate our minds and stress opening China to the outside world'. We should, he said, 'have control over major issues and flexibility on minor ones'.
3. 'Take overall interest into consideration and overcome selfish departmentalisation.' He warned all 'localities and departments' not to interfere with the unified policy decisions and plans of the central government and damage the overall interest of the country;
4. 'Continue to follow the principle of gradually improving the people's living standards through increased production, and of building the country through thrift and hard work.' He feels it wrong to seek blindly a higher level of consumption regardless of productive capacity and actual conditions;
5. 'Continue to check all unhealthy practices and remove all obstacles to the current reform.' He listed several malpractices as being extremely harmful to the reform: excessive bonuses and allowances in cash or in kind, profiteering, price raising, power abusing in reselling goods of short supply, giving lavish dinner parties and gifts, and offering and taking bribes.

4.2 ECONOMIC AND SOCIAL DEVELOPMENT THROUGH BUDGET PLANNING AND EXECUTION: PROBLEMS AND SOLUTIONS

On 10 April 1985, the Sixth National People's Congress adopted two major reports from the State Council Members as official policy documents. One of these is called 'The Draft 1985 Plan for National Economic and Social Development' delivered by Song Ping, Minister in charge of the State Planning Commission and State Council. The other document, 'Report on the Execution of the State Budget for 1984 and on the Draft State Budget for 1985' was delivered by Wang Bingqian, Minister of Finance. These two documents provide a large amount of important information on the state of the Chinese economy and on the implementation of development plans. Information quoted in the following pages is taken from these documents.

Song Ping's report deals with a review of 1984 and a draft plan for 1985 in economic and social development, the last two years of the Sixth Five-Year Plan (1981–5). He listed, first of all, the major achievements in 1984 in industry and agriculture as follows: total agricultural output value was 330.3 billion yuan in terms of the 1980 constant prices, a 14.5 per cent increase over 1983. Grain output went up by 19.84 million tons over the 1983 increase of 32.78 million tons, for a total of 407.12 million tons. Cotton totalled to 6.077 million tons, an increase of 1.44 million tons more than in 1983. Other major areas in outputs all surpassed the planned targets. On the other hand, the total value of industrial output came to 707 billion yuan, an increase of 14 per cent over 1983. Coal output came to 772 million tons, a 7 per cent increase over 1983. Crude oil output was 114.53 million tons, representing an increase of 8 per cent. Several rare and high cost commodities, such a refrigerators and washing machines, increased in production by 45 to 200 per cent. Thus, better growth results generally were attained in 1984. The railway, road and water transport, civil aviation and postal and telecommunications departments 'all exceeded their plans by their best use of existing resources'. Secondly, he reported on the work on key construction projects and the technological transformation of enterprises. Work was speeded up generally in these areas in 1984. Investment in capital construction for state-owned enterprises came to 73.5 billion yuan, an increase of 14.1 billion or 23.8 per cent over 1983. Of this an investment increase in energy growth reached 25.1 per cent and in transport and postal services, 34.2 per cent. Capital investment in cultural, educational and public health areas and in scientific research rose by 30 to 50 per cent or more. Investment in equipment replacement and technological transformation was 42.5 billion in 1983, an 18 per cent increase over the previous year. The Anshan Iron and Steel Complex, the country's number one automobile works and other key enterprises are all making 'fairly rapid progress' in technological transformation.

Thirdly, Minister Song said 'the urban and rural market was more thriving than ever'. More consumer goods reached the market in 1984. The total volume of retail sales of commodities was 335.7 billion yuan, a rise of 50.8 billion yuan or 17.8 per cent increase over 1983. A new record on foreign trade expansion and notable progress in the use of foreign funds and technology were set in 1984. Total imports and exports reached 120.1 billion yuan, a 39.7 per cent increase over 1983 or 19.6 per cent 'after allowing for currency exchange and price fluctuations... Grain imports were reduced and cotton exports exceeded imports'. Chinese imports in 1984 registered a considerable increase in the areas of new technology, rolled steel, chemical fertilisers, raw materials of the chemical industry, and timber. More foreign funds were actually used in 1984 in the investment of joint ventures than in the previous year. Progress was made in the areas of science and technology, the training of qualified personnel, culture and public health. Colleges and universities in 1984 enrolled a total of 475,000 students, an increase of 84,000 over the previous year. Adult education at the college level is being developed rapidly. There were 1,292,000 students taking correspondence, television, and evening classes at various universities in 1984. Technical and vocational training was making rapid progress. In 1984, the total number of 'workers and other employees reached 118.24 million'. The document further says:[11] 'The situation in the national economic and social development of our country is better than ever before... There is immense potential in production, construction, circulation and in other fields.'

In surveying the difficult problems in social and economic development ahead, the report listed the following: shortages in electric power supply, in railway transport, shortage of raw and semi-finished materials, failure of manufactured products to keep pace with changes in consumption patterns, acuteness in market supply and demand, high priced low quality consumer goods, a rapid increase in consumption funds, unreasonable raises in wages, and bonus by enterprises and other administrative offices. Many of these problems indirectly or directly contribute to price fluctuation and to excessive currency supply in the market. The target for social and economic development in 1985 consisted of three phases: price reform, wage reform, key construction projects, and the technological transformation of enterprises. More specifically, the task consisted of greater production growth, greater grain output, promotion of animal husbandry and aquatic production. The development plan pledged greater availability and priority in raw material supplies, capital construction, bank loans and foreign exchange to such factories that innovate and produce high quality goods for domestic consumption and for export. Another development emphasis for 1985 was on conservation in consumption of fuel, electricity, raw and semi-finished materials and many other industrial material supplies. All of these suggestions seek, in short, to achieve economic efficiency and social cooperation. The total investment in capital construction in 1985 was set at 80 billion yuan in the draft plan. The preference of spending was given to technological transformation, renovation of plant facilities, and expansion of existing enterprises (54 per cent of 80 billion is assigned for improving the existing enterprises). Forty-four per cent of the land was assigned to capital construction. Thirty-six billion yuan was allocated for technological transformation. The plan seeks to achieve a unified method of state distribution of materials to new developments. Such priority for material distribution, as advocated in the 1985 plan, should follow four criteria:[12] (1) 'Most of the newly added materials earmarked for unified state distribution will be used to meet the increased production projects. As for routine projects, material supply will be kept at the 1984 base figure, or lower in some cases'; (2) 'No additional outlets will be provided to supply materials under unified state distribution at fixed prices. Rather, they will be reduced'; (3) 'Fulfilment of the allocation quotas as fixed in the state plan must be guaranteed. Where the quotas are not fulfilled owing to subjective reasons, the proportion of raw and semi-finished materials and the energy supply allocated by the state will be deducted from the distribution quotas of the following year'; (4) 'Markets will be opened up for public sales of key materials so that products and buyers will come into direct contact through trade centres'.

The 1985 plan for social and economic development also emphasised the service role of urban and rural markets in catering to the improved living standards of the people. For example, retail sales of commodity goods for 1985 was expected to reach 378 billion yuan. The supply of market goods in value and the total purchasing power of the people must be 'basically balanced'. Extra plan attention for 1985 was given to the urgent production of high quality commodities to meet market demand, especially in areas of textile products, household appliances, brand name bicycles and foodstuffs to 'suit people's changing consumption patterns'. Some commodity shortages will be supplemented by imports to meet more urgent consumption demands in accordance with the plan. The plan for 1985 called for vigorous development of tertiary industry, especially in the areas of repair and service trades. The quality of service industries must improve to meet popular needs and safety standards.

Regarding relations with the outside world, the 1985 plan called for a total volume of two way trade at 126.5 billion yuan. Some restructuring in foreign trade must be made to harmonise with the regulations of the State Council to achieve greater trade expansion. Expansion in exports through vigorous campaigns was called for the purpose of bringing in more foreign currencies to pay for China's import needs. The plan emphasised the following areas for fast development: (1) the Four Special Economic Zones; (2) the newly announced opening of fourteen coastal cities; (3) Hainan Island, the Yangtze River delta, the Pearl River delta and Southern Fujian Province.

In the fields of education and intellectual resources, the 1985 development plan called for rapid expansion and utilisation of known scientific and technological achievements in China. Better economic results depend on their rapid transformation into industrial and modern agricultural production. Funds were budgeted for pilot projects, industrial experiments, and, especially for the 'transfer of advanced technologies from the defence industry and scientific research to civilian use'. Emphasis was also made to apply new technology to transform the traditional cottage industries. In 1985, one of the major reforms took place in July in the field of educational administration. Vice premier Li Peng was put in charge of education as the head of the Educational Committee which absorbed the existing Department of Education of the State Council. For example, the 1985 development plan projected an enrolment of 41,000 post-graduates and 522,000 undergraduates in higher education. More students were encouraged to take short-term training at the college level. Faculty improvement and field specialisation were also emphasised. The restructuring of secondary education had begun, vocational schools were being rapidly promoted, and in the economically backward areas, compulsory primary education was strictly enforced.

New emphasis was made in adult education, especially through television and radio courses, part-time colleges, correspondence schools, and the make-up effort in secondary education for those whose school time was wasted during the cultural revolution.

The development plan for 1985, was drawn up after the completion of studies to map out a new planning system. The central new planning system has incorporated the following guidelines to (1) reduce the scope of central government's 'mandate'; (2) to incorporate all the economic levers and the market forces; (3) and to expand the scope of 'guidance planning' with more flexibility and choices available for low level planning agencies. The 1985 development plan emphasised the 'provisional regulations on the improvement of the planning system' which was recently approved by the State Council. Mandatory planning in China will be applied to products or areas which have a 'vital bearing on the national economy and the people's welfare'. Local governments will be charged to balance the planning functions between 'guidance planning' and 'market forces', while the central government will strictly enforce the 'mandatory planning'. Local governments in the future will have to 'decide how to coordinate such plans with those of the enterprises'. The state, for its part, will guide and help their implementation primarily by flexible use of such economic levers as pricing, taxation and credit, and through the allocation of economic funds, foreign exchange, and other major materials and equipments at its disposal. Future 'manufactured products under mandatory planning will be reduced from 135 to over 60; there will be a corresponding decrease in the number of manufactured products covered by the mandatory planning of other departments and the provinces, autonomous regions and municipalities. And the number of varieties of materials earmarked for unified distribution by the State Planning Commission will decrease from 256 to 6'.[13]

The 1985 economic and social development plan took serious note of the party's awareness that the 'more vigorous the economy, the more attention we should pay to macro-economic regulation'. Consequently, the 1985 development plan called for prudent management of the macro-economy through the following measures:[14]

1. Effective exercise of control over credit, loans and currency;
2. Tight grip on funds for consumption;
3. Keeping the scale of investment in fixed assets under control;
4. Strengthening control over foreign exchange; and

5. Enforcing strict financial discipline and the elimination of unhealthy practices.

The report on the 1984 state budget practice was given to the National People's Congress by Finance Minister Wang Bingqian. He prefaced this report with the comment that 'with the sustained, steady and harmonious development of the national economy, and with a considerable increase in state revenues, the 1984 state budget was over fulfilled'.[15] The details of this third document are summarised as follows.

Statistics recorded that the 1984 total revenue was 146.5 billion yuan and total spending at 151.5 billion yuan. There was a deficit of 5 billion. On the revenue side, domestic receipts came to 143 billion yuan, which was more than the budgeted expectation (111.1 per cent of the budgeted figure). Foreign loans were 3.5 billion yuan (only 68.6 per cent of budgeted figure). Other breakdowns are summarised as follows:

1. Tax receipts totalled 93.78 billion yuan (115.8 per cent of budget figure). This increase in revenue was due to faster expansion in industrial and agricultural growth and improved tax administration.
2. Tax receipts from enterprises was 25.98 billion yuan (or 87.1 per cent of the budgeted figure). The shortfall was essentially due to surplus state purchase of grain and cotton and state price subsidies for both in order to promote the income of growers.
3. Depreciation funds of enterprises turned over to the central financial authorities was 2.66 billion yuan (or 115.7 per cent of the budgeted amount).
4. State treasury bonds amounted to 4.15 billion yuan (as expected by the budget authority).
5. Money collected for the construction of key energy and transport projects for 1984 (149.4 per cent above expectation).

On the expenditures of 1984, the following breakdown represents a fair picture of how the government performed in promoting the economic growth through financial allocation:

1. Capital construction of 47.58 billion yuan (or 108.4 per cent of the budgeted figure). Overspending occurred in energy and transport development and in more key construction projects to meet the need of external economic development.
2. Spending in financing technological transformation and in subsidising the manufacture of new brand products totalled 9.82 billion yuan (or 132.6 per cent more than expected). Spending

went much further because additional funds became available during the year for this specific purpose.

3. Expenditure on aid to rural production and fighting natural calamities amounted to 9.43 billion.
4. Culture, education, public health and science amounted to 26.343 billion (112.1 per cent of the budgeted figure). More local contribution became available during the year.
5. National defence accounted for 18.075 billion yuan (or 101.1 per cent).
6. Administrative spending reached 12.077 billion yuan (or 144.1 per cent more than expected). Apart from the need to strengthen public security, judicial work, additional spending was due to failure to control personnel expansion.

On the whole, the execution of the 1984 state budget was satisfactory. It was achieved largely due to the success of economic readjustment and restructuring as well as opening the country up to the outside world. Several major points can be made about the success of budget implementation in 1984. First of all, production expansion and management efficiency helped increase revenue. Government assisted enterprises to increase their profits and in turn, produced more taxes for the state. As statistics indicate, the total 1984 production output increased by 14.2 per cent over 1983. This helped raise a revenue of 143 billion yuan which registered a revenue increase of 21.9 billion yuan (or an 18 per cent increase over 1983). Secondly, in education and capital construction of key projects, government spending increased by 22.3 billion yuan, a 25 per cent increase over that of 1983. More was spent in 1984 in these two areas than was originally budgeted. Thirdly, through budget execution, the government helped the enterprises to reform for their invigoration of production. The new taxation system had completely replaced the profit system by October 1984. From now on, large and medium-size enterprises must pay income tax to the state and small enterprises pay a fixed amount of contracting charge. All profits after tax will remain at the disposal of the enterprises. As a result of this reform, state revenue, enterprise profit, production increase, and competition among enterprises for efficient operation for higher income are all part and parcel of an invigorated economy. Early statistics indicated that, after tax, total profit of the enterprises reached 31.3 billion yuan in 1984, an increase of 3.4 billion over 1983. The new regulations from the State Council in 1984 has further extended the autonomous decision-making power of the industrial enterprises. These include greater enterprise self-control over production, planning, purchase of materials, sales of products, personnel and labour management, use of funds, and handling of assets. The government also obligates itself to financially assisting key enterprises with their depreciation costs of fixed assets and on their special financial need for technological transformation and new experiment on new product manufacturing. Finally, in 1984 the state budget authority provided support to the development of the special economic zones and the opening of coastal cities. In 1984 the state subsidised the infrastructural construction of these cities to create a favourable environment for foreign investment. Special regulations on reduction and remission of income tax and on industrial commercial consolidated tax in the special zones and coastal cities are now in full operation. Preferential treatment is also given, in addition, to Chinese–foreign joint ventures, cooperative enterprises of joint partnership, and other enterprises run exclusively with foreign capital. In 1984, the government succeeded in signing trade agreements with Japan, the United States, Britain and France to prevent tax evasion on the one hand, and to avoid dual taxation on the other. Progress in negotiation with other countries on the same tax issues will further smooth China's trade progress abroad.

Based on the progress made in the 1984 budget execution and with 1985 being the last year of the Sixth Five-Year Plan period, the 1985 state budget took into consideration the urban economic reform as decided in October 1984. As a result, the 1985 budget consideration included the following guidelines:[16]

> Work hard to explore new financial sources and increase revenue on the basis of expanded production and improved economic efficiency; satisfy the need of key construction projects and the economic structural reform, of the continued development of cultural, educational and scientific undertakings of the continued improvement in the people's living standards to the extent of actual capability; and strictly control expenditures and ensure a sustained basic balance between revenue and expenditure through better overall balancing and financial management.

The 1985 total revenue of 153.5 billion yuan and total outgoings of 156.5 billion anticipated a deficit of 3 billion. This budget represents an increase of 7 billion over that of 1984. The essential revenue break-downs were as follows: (1) tax receipts expected to be 162.18 billion yuan; (2) enterprises tax of 4.284 billion; (3) state treasury bonds 6 billion yuan; and (4) construction funds for key energy and transport projects to be 12 billion yuan. Budget expenditure has the following breakdown: (1) capital construction 48.363 billion yuan (an increase of 1.1 per cent over 1984; (2) subsidies to enterprises for technological transformation and the manufacturing of new products, 5.26 billion (a decrease by 46.5 per cent from 1984); (3) allocations for geological prospecting, 2.75 billion (a 5 per cent rise over 1984); (4) aid to rural economy 9.4 (as in 1984); (5) allocation for urban construction and maintenance project and for civil defence 5.45 billion (33.5 per cent increase); (6) expenses for culture, education, science and public health 29.3 billion; (7) national defence account 18.67 billion; (8) administrative account 11.9 billion; (9) repayment of foreign loans and interests 2.8 billion; (10) general reserve fund 1.5 billion; and (11) meat price subsidy 2.2 billion.

The budget office is known to be determined to help maintain an economic stability with minimum budget expansion and little deficit if at all. Secondly, the budget office was conscious of its increased spending relative to price and wage reforms in 1985. Wage reform in government departments and institutions alone required 3 billion yuan as increased expenditure.

When the budget office reported on the execution of the 1985 budget, the budget officer voiced in the new budget message of April, 1985 several urgent guidelines which are summarised as follows:[17]

1. 'Improve enterprise operation and management efficiency and increase economic efficiency.' Presently, China still has some 3000 industrial enterprises running at a loss. Price reduction for overstocked products in state enterprises represent a loss of 4.5 billion yuan

2. 'Do a better job in tax administration and use taxation to regulate economic activities and help ensure state revenue.' Under recent tax law and practice, the success of tax administration depends on the cooperation of 'all state and collective enterprises and urban and rural self-employed businessmen ... to report to the tax authority on their production, business operations, and other incomes and pay taxes as required by law'. Tax evasion, bribery and cheating must be prevented. The other major task is to collect construction funds for key energy and transport projects and to manage the issuing of state treasury bonds to meet the target of state revenue for 1985.

3. 'Continue to reform the financial and tax systems, and consolidate and further its achievements.' There are still enterprises that have not adopted the new methods of taxation. The tax system itself needs improvement. The State Council decided to reform the financial management in 1985 as the take-off year. For example, Beijing expects eventually to have a three-category revenue system with one 'fixed revenue' for the central government, another 'fixed revenue for local government', and a 'shared revenue' for both. Financial relations between central, provincial and local governments on revenue distribution and subsidies remain to be institutionalised.

4. 'Control capital construction investment and consumption funds and trim administrative outlays.' Unauthorised investment beyond the plan for the year was an impermissible priority, for investment should be shifted to projects for technological transformation and their innovation and expansion.

5. 'Strengthen control over macro-economic activities and balance the use of funds.'

6. 'Enforce financial discipline and check all unsound practices.' There are still enterprises and units which have wilfully retained funds owing to the state. Others have made unjustified additions to regular costs. Many have indiscriminately raised wages and bonuses in cash or in kind. Ostentatiousness and extravagance at the expense of public funds in the form of lavish dinner parties and gifts 'must be uncovered and prevented'. China's tax system is very new and has not yet become institutionalised. The skills of taxation experts, auditing personnel and administrators are to be gradually improved. Tax evasion will probably be undiscovered in the years to come. The country is moving toward an expanding free market oriented consumption economy at the local level. Some 30,000 new free enterprises are reported to have been set up recently. The government announced on 16 November 1985, that these privately owned markets would cost $1.3 billion in US dollars for their construction during the next five years.[18] When these future private owners and operators fail to report their taxes honestly, it will be quite difficult to investigate without creating a huge tax administration and tax supervision system capable of operating at the township and village level.

4.3 PROSPECT AND CHALLENGE OF SEVENTH FIVE-YEAR PLAN, 1986–90

On 18 September 1985, ex-Premier Zhao Ziyang reported to the Communist party's national conference on the Seventh Five-Year Plan. He explained only a few major points of the plan relevant to economic and social development. Details and process of implementation were to be worked out later on a year-to-year basis. He revealed that this draft plan was the product of a joint effort of both the State Council and the Party Secretariat working for more than one year. The final version was later submitted to the fourth session of the Sixth National People's Congress in the spring of 1986 for its approval. The draft dealt with three aspects: (1) The goals and guiding principles of economic development during 1986–90; (2) strategy direction and policy measures for economic and social development during 1986–90; and (3) economic structure reform and procedure. He asserted that since 1979 the economy has achieved exactly what was expected. The four-fold policy of readjusting, restructuring, consolidating and improving are to remain during the next plan period on the basis of current accomplishment. The draft plan will continue to institutionalise the economic restructuring decision as passed by the Communist party in October 1984.

Ex-Premier Zhao Ziyang reported that the economy has achieved a continuity in growth, stability and balance particularly among agriculture, light and heavy industries, and between capital accumulation and consumer consumption. Agriculture is growing in all its segments, but light industry has progressed faster. Each year finds the economy better than the previous year. There is an average of 10 per cent growth in the national economy, which will continue into the foreseeable future. This rate of growth, the premier has said, 'is rare among nations'. Along with economic growth is the growth in state revenue. The main tasks during the seventh plan, 1985–90, will include: (1) to create a conducive economic and social environment to continue the economic structural reform; (2) to accelerate key construction, technological and human resource development so as to prepare for the economic and social development in the 1990s; (3) to improve the living standards of the people. The main long-term concern is for, during the first half of the twenty-first century, economic stability and growth. 'Without reform, there will be no future economic lasting stability and growth ... for better conditions to implement reform, we must not just aim at a high rate of economic growth, but maintain a proper rate of growth and continue the improvement of people's living standards'[19]

The seventh plan period, 1986–90, can be divided into two stages. The first two years will be devoted to control over total social needs: preventing excessive economic growth rate, stabilising productive investment from over-expansion and consumption spending from sudden increase, using 1985 as the basis to make minor adjustments. Gradually solving the existing economic problems in two years is far better than trying to solve them all during the last half year of 1985. The next three years, 1988–90, will follow the results of the first two years to properly increase construction investment within safe control over the entire development circumstances. This strategy is 'based on our past economic development experience'.

On the overall economic structure reform, the seventh plan period is the key stage reforming the economic infrastructure. 'We must insist on reform as the first priority to lay the foundation for socialist economy with Chinese characteristics', the premier said. Structural reform of urban economy is a 'complicated social engineering'. To structure a new economic system under public ownership the Chinese must rely on three major aspects: (1) strengthen further the publicly owned enterprises of large and medium-sized operations; such enterprises must become relatively autonomous, self-managing, responsible for their profits and losses as socialist commodity producers and managers; (2) develop further, according to planning, socialist commodity markets and gradually improve the market structure system step by step; (3) slowly reduce the central government's direct control of enterprises by perfecting a system of indirect control. These steps can be accomplished only through economic measures and legal procedures, in addition to necessary administrative methods.

Based on the experience obtained in recent years of generating economic vitality and flexibility, the future emphasis is on micro-economic activities by strengthening the macro-management for indirect control and guidance. This will include many economic levers for adjustment and supervision. This task ahead seems far more difficult; and the government has yet had no experience, as the premier admitted in his speech. Yet, this is the only way ahead to accommodate the current economic reform in progress. With all the economic levers to be utilised, such as economic legislation, supervision, information systems, banking, taxing, quality standardisation, and industrial and commercial management, the central long-term purpose is to 'generate new vitality into the publicly owned enterprises'. Two key important goals of the seventh plan are namely: (1) to greatly improve enterprises' economic efficiency; and (2) to vastly increase exports to gain foreign exchange. His speech went on to cover other political and social aspects relevant to the Seventh Five-Year Plan for 1986–90. The premier went on to report the Draft Recommendation of the Seventh Five-year Plan.[20] A few major points of the draft recommendation to the party national conference of September 1985 are summarised as follows. The conference approved it as the basis for further micro-planning by State Council for submission to the fourth session of the National People's Congress.

The draft recommendation reviewed the economically poor state of 1980 when Deng's new economic strategy began. The review cited an increase of 80 per cent in the standard of living in rural China during the 1980–5 period. It noted the continuing problems and weaknesses of the economy, including weak agriculture, a food and clothing crisis in remote regions of the country, lack of information systems, raw materials supply and human resource development. The draft recommendation listed the following guiding principles to be followed:

1. Reform takes the first priority to accompany construction;
2. Insistence on balance between society's total demand and total supply
3. High production performance and improvement in commodity quality be seriously emphasised;
4. Strengthen socialist cultural-spiritual construction; 1986–90, as the period to fundamentally lay the foundation for 'a new model in socialist economic system with Chinese characteristics';
5. Maintain an annual GNP at about 7 per cent during the plan period to avoid other economic problems;
6. Place emphasis on policy research and policy making as 'an organic structural part of the planning process'.

On development strategy and guiding principles, the draft recommendation provides a suggestion in three major areas: (1) to meet the people's consumption demands and changes in spending; (2) to concentrate on technological transformation, internal reform and expansion of existing enterprises in order to expand production; (3) correctly solve relations among geographic regions in their economic development. Six major guiding principles are suggested in the draft plan:

1. Reliance on policy science to further improve production conditions and to foster stability in agricultural development. Agriculture occupies a strategic place in economic development. Adjustment in rural production structure is critical toward rural specialising, commercialising and modernising to better satisfy social needs. Food production, for example, must not be overlooked.

2. Expansion in consumer goods and rapid development in the national housing industry: consumers will be interested in nutrition, clothing and housing improvement. Housing construction must be commercialised to reduce the government's burden in providing free housing as was practised in the past.

3. Concentration on all needed resources, including energy, transportation, communication and primary raw material supply as the foundation for future development coordination.

4. Rapid expansion of tertiary industry and the correction of the unbalanced relations or proportion between the service industry and the first and second industries as now exist. Tertiary industry is the inevitable outgrowth of the first and second industries in the division of labour. China's third industry has been backward. It is better to convert certain nationally owned commercial firms to collectively owned or individually contracted operations. Small shops should definitely be contracted out to individuals to ensure better operation and profit. The state must invest in the development of third industry. Manpower training for this sector industry is critical for better and more adequate quality services.

5. Great emphasis during 1986–90 on rapid technological transformation of old enterprises, especially in the specific areas of engineering, electronics and defence. Parochialism and selfish protectionism in technological transfer and advance must be eliminated.

6. Proper attention and care to be given to the relations among regions of East coast, middle section and far western section of the country in their mutual relations and developmental cooperation as both long and short term propositions. Each region must fully explore its potential and its horizontal development. Gradually, different regions should be linked around key economic urban centres with different levels and sizes in their networking characteristics. Development must move westward as an inevitable trend so that people in all regions will enjoy the fruits of prosperity. The middle section and western region will naturally gain in investment, management skill, technology and their improvement from the east coastal region. Ethnic national minority interests of the far west

must be emphasised. Old revolutionary bases, border areas and poverty-stricken regions must develop from their backward appearances.

The seventh plan period will single out education as one of the most critical areas for rapid expansion. Progress in any area depends on knowledge, skill and foresight. Educational investment takes long-term, persistent effort. The draft recommendation lists the following major points for scientific and technological expansion:

1. Promote technology for better results and greater efficiency
2. Concentrate on key technologies and their conversion;
3. Make the distinction between 'applied research' and 'basic research'.

Reorganisation of the Science and Social Science Academies is required also. In social science research, emphasis must include research on Marxist theory, other basic theories, and problem research for China's socialist modernisation theory. China must face the world and meet the future in her new educational task. For example, during 1986–90, nine-year compulsory education of the young to wipe out illiteracy must be carried out. Special education for physically and mentally handicapped is also important. In short, during the seventh plan period, some 2,600,000 university and college graduates must be trained, an increase of 70 per cent over the sixth plan period. Post-graduates must number 200,000 – an increase of four times over 1980–5.

Increase in foreign trade is a fundamental national policy. The target increase must aim at 40 to 50 per cent over the period of 1980–5. China must maintain trade balances in her long-term modernisation approach. Economic special zones must play a key role in foreign trade. The living standard is to be increased by 25 per cent over the 1980–5 period. Population control policy will be continued to maintain 12.5 births annually per thousand individuals. In short, the seventh plan period is a period of continuation of what has been started in the 1980–5 period. The next five-year period is expected to complete the new strategic policy of readjustment, restructuring, consolidation and improvement. If successful, the Eighth Five-year plan, 1991–5, will probably begin a new accelerated economic stage. The last decade of the twentieth century will probably see stable growth with a well institutionalised economic infrastructure. However, there can be many negative political and social forces to make such hope less

The review of the three documents above has, perhaps, given the reader a broad picture of economic problems and developments in China. It is, therefore, clear that China since 1980 has been transforming its economy from one of a Maoist socialist model which broke down to one of a Dengist new model which continues to change. The transformation of reform does not have a new economic ideology independent from Marxist and Maoist framework. However, the substance of reform has taken on a very new and different approach to adapt China's economic structure and growth toward capitalist operations. But the Chinese economy will not be capitalistic because of the public ownership and planning in the changing economy. In theory, it can no longer be called socialism because it follows 'from each according to his work or worth' that 'work more gets more, work less gets less'. This competition is found in China now to be the only way to stimulate and revitalize the economy for rapid growth which the country must have in order to avoid the national starvation and poverty of the past thirty years. By 1990, if reform and restructuring has been completed, the Chinese economy will probably be growing much faster and will be far better managed according to Western capitalistic criteria. If successful, the new Chinese model will attract global attention. This will mean one quarter of mankind under one huge bureaucracy has profited from an indigenous innovation to 'combine public ownership and western management' – or 'socialism within capitalism'. If, by 1990, the continuity of reform does not reach the original goal, which is unlikely, more readjustment and new experiment may be required, but there will be no return to the Soviet model or Maoist utopia.

The reform measures have been under severe ideological and political constraints from Deng's political opponents who are half-heartedly in favour of his reform in both approach and result. This is so because of their Marxist–Maoist ideology which has prevented them from seeing progress in the capitalist world. The only offer to justify what has taken place in the economic field is that the reform is practical. And the common masses in China like it and benefit from it. They have no faith in Maoism. Deng offers instead pragmatism. The masses resent Mao and what he did during the cultural revolution, so Deng and his colleagues are politically popular. This is the positive aspect of the political environment. The negative aspects include party factionalism and the doubtful followers who were purged by Mao, rehabilitated by Deng and may not ideologically go all the way with Deng on his economic reform and new orientation. In short, Deng's cat-and-mouse theory is not an elaborate foundation to replace Marxism and Mao Zedong Thought. Some day, when Deng's disagreeable colleagues and vicious opponents have died or been neutralised, a brand new Dengist 'economic theory of Chinese Socialism' may emerge to finally provide his reform with an adequate theoretical or ideological foundation.

Given the political environment, Deng can be perceived in several ways as the leader of a 'new economic revolution' in China. First of all, he is an accommodationist ready to reconcile political differences with his 'friendly opponents' through compromise in policy and the speed of reform. Deng is himself content with a piecemeal reform approach. Experiment must proceed before policy change so as not to antagonise his opponents. He has gradually removed disagreeable friends from positions of power in order to employ the young and committed cadres of his own kind. Secondly, Deng is an experimentationist. As such he gives his reform movement some time to experiment with new approaches and methods. When the experiment is successful and applicable nationwide, he applies it. This has been true with the dismantling of the commune system. It is also true in urban enterprise reform. He allowed hundreds of enterprises to be put on an experimental basis with new management and a shift in decision-making authority, before the wholesale reform policies of October 1984. Whatever was experimentally a failure he rejected; and whatever experimentally succeeded he adopted. He, indeed, fulfilled the slogan: 'practice is the only test of truth'. Deng is, finally, a reformist or a 'peaceful revolutionary'. He seems a classical socialist revolutionary who believes genuinely that socialism is superior to capitalism. However, as a revolutionary, he wanted to explore economic development peacefully. He does not want class struggle and purge in his reform. He is no longer, in this sense, a classical follower of Marxism in its methods of post-revolutionary economic and political practice as existed under Mao and even in Russia today. He now advocates thought emancipation or other liberal approaches from unreasoned dogmas.

Chinese economic development by 1988 has gone a long way in attracting the attention of economists, World Bank experts and Sinologists all over the world. 'Socialism with Chinese Characteristics' was the theme of several important messages from the Chinese representatives at the Chongqing Conference in September 1985 which was attended by many foreign experts on Chinese economic development and other Sinologists who are eager to hear what the

Chinese can say about the reform experiment.

Professor Xue Muqiao said in his welcome speech at the September conference:[21]

I recall now in 1982 many world renowned economists came to China for a similar economic conference. Some of you here today were at the 1982 conference. The result of that conference was helpful to us. At that time some experts had very serious doubts about our reform. The last three years have proved that our economic reform has made a giant step forward and is progressing. The reform has not yet completed. Greater reform will take place. Our reform can only advance and never retreat. Difficulties will accompany reform. Consequently control and care over untapped areas must have our policy control. Our reform determination will not waver.

Professor Xue confidently declared that the rural reform success will continue to move toward more improvement, while determined policy attention now direct at 'more complicated and more difficult urban reform'. If successful, he said, 'China will be a socialist state full of economic vitality on earth. It will, then, produce long-term global consequences'.[22] China has already decentralised most of the small size publicly owned enterprises which are now totally responsible for their own profit or loss after income tax to the government. Only some 6000 largest and medium-sized enterprises are being slowly guided toward self-accountability, self-management over profit or loss to avoid 'Big rice bowl dependence of the state'. These largest and medium-sized enterprises must pay income taxes amounting to 60 per cent of their total financial incomes. In order to maximise efficiency and profit at the micro-enterprise level, the government must revitalise the macro-economic control.

One of China's current more serious problems is wage reform to avoid decades of wage equalisation practice. The fear, however, is that wage adjustment may go over the budgeted expectation to flood the consumer market with large sums of cash. If so, it will affect price stability. If housing construction, for example, progresses too rapidly, it too will create new currency problems. Such examples illustrate a lack of economic infrastructure to handle problems and a great lack of management knowledge in China. Academic research in this area was not possible in the past. Foreign experience on macro-management did not come to China until recently. Presently, Chinese economists are most eager to acquire comparative knowledge on models of macro-management in other Western countries. The State Council continuously searches for new and acceptable measures to correct economic behaviour, especially on policies concerning currency, finance, budget systems, fiscal philosophy. Professor Ma Hung, former president of the National Academy for Social Sciences, pointed out at the 1985 Chongqing Conference the central difficulties in the economic managment.

He said [author's translation]:[23]

> Presently China is in the midst of an enormous historical reform. First of all, China is economically in a rapid transition between a backward agriculture and a modernised new economy. Secondly, Chinese economy is moving from a closed, feudalistic model toward a socialist planned commodity economy. During our Seventh Five-year Plan, 1986–90, or later, a new model of economic system will take shape, a key period in our reform.

Economist Ma listed several areas of reform contradictions:

1. 'In the midst of economic structural change, annually hundreds of thousands of workers want to enter the non-agricultural sector of the economy; this overheats the economy.'
2. 'Our economic reform and transition is from uneven development to balance, from agriculture to industry, from collective ownership to state enterprise, from consumption concern to production expansion, from small to large enterprises, from coastal region to hinterland. Slowly the reform becomes easy to be accepted. It is difficult to meet expected and also unexpected new demands from reform itself ... Investment hunger, consumption hunger, import hunger are tied together to make greater supply demands.'
3. 'Movement from single measure, area-oriented reform to multiple structural existence, thus creating macro control problems.'

One of the contradictions in the investment area, for example, is the structural lack of control by the government over the execution of budgeted investment. This is so because presently about two-thirds of total investment derives from the contribution of publicly owned units. The other one-third is from the contribution of the collective ownership and from individual investment. Only one-third of the two-thirds of the publicly owned units is reliable from budget commitment. The rest of the expected annual investment accounting depends on administrative methods and control to cut other expenses and through the issue of new currency.[24] In short, such practices produce negative impact against economic structural improvement and investment results. The banking and currency sectors require experience to make investment more predictable and successful.

In short, economic structural changes in China since 1979 can be divided into three stages. The first two stages have been governed by the new strategy of readjusting, restructuring, consolidating and improving. The first stage has focused on short-term adjusting and long-term dismantling of inefficient practices of the past thirty years, 'big rice pot' philosophy. The second stage has focused on restructuring and improving during 1983–5. The third stage covers the Seventh Five-year Plan, 1986–90. which will focus on reshaping of a socialist commodity economy that will require greater decentralisation of decision-making powers to the production management level, leaving the central government in charge of macro-management of the economy as a whole. The Seventh plan period may reveal the maturing of the process entailed by the Chinese socialist model with Chinese characteristics.[25] In the final analysis, the government will continue to do the same two things: first, to revitalise the economy at home, and second, to open the country wider to the international community in trade, investment and technological transfer to China.

5 Rural Economic Development

5.1 AGRICULTURAL DEVELOPMENT

Chinese farmers have always loved the land. In an agricultural society land is the only means of livelihood for most of the population. Therefore land ownership, development policy, and the distribution of land by the past imperial government is of grave concern to those who owned land and those who farmed it. From the ancient practice of 'well-field system'[1] of cultivation to other policies of land distribution and ownership, China has gone through many systems of land disposition. Historically, land was concentrated in the hands of the few rich, educated ruling elite of the society. It was a perpetual system of landlord exploitation which began with the Sung dynasty. Over the centuries those who became rich would invest their money in land ownership, while the poor were reduced to the status of tenants. They had to work hard in order to pay the landowner and still have enough to live on. In bad years they relied on the mercy of the benevolent landowner for support to prevent them from starvation. Such a practice had disastrous consequences. Eventually, the system was disrupted by Western imperial powers toward the end of the nineteenth century. Sun Yat-sen's revolution of 1911 proposed a land distribution policy of peaceful reform to give ownership of land to the tillers. He suggested that increased land value should belong to the public through higher tax or government repossession of the land if the owner did not want to pay the high tax. Big landowners and land speculation would be abolished. The communists, on the other hand, adopted a very cruel method of confiscating private land and punishing landowners between 1949–52. The communists first distributed land to the tillers. Shortly thereafter, they took land away from the farmer and put it into the cooperatives or communes. Today, the government owns the land and has the right to dispose of it in ways and methods it chooses.

The communist confiscation of land was accompanied by violence to the owners in the late 1920s and again in the early 1950s. In the late 1950s the party leadership was split over the ownership of land and the emergence of rural communes. The moderate faction headed by Liu Shaoqi was opposed to the radicals led by Mao Zedong himself. Rural

126

production development went through several stages which required different policies of the government as follows:

1. Mutual aid production teams in 1953–4 under private ownership;
2. Early stage of cooperatives in 1955–6 involving more families and private land;
3. Advanced cooperatives in 1957, collective land ownership with private family plots;
4. People's commune in 1958–9, state land ownership, no family plot, public rationing;
5. Modified people's commune in 1963–78, with ownership at the commune level, brigade level and production team level, with private family plots;
6. Production responsibility system since 1979 and gradually eliminating the vestige of the commune system.

These changes reflect the failure of land policy against the wishes of the rural population. More than that, it reflected a lack of knowledge about successful agricultural economic development. Partly the failure was due to blind adoption of the Soviet system of rural experimentation. In short, the Communist Party's failure in agriculture was largely due to Mao's eagerness for a leap forward, his egalitarianism and his radical utopianism or revolutionary romanticism.

China's rural areas remained largely the same before and after the communist victory in 1949. Substantial improvements have occurred only since the 1980s. This has been verified by Professor Fei Xiaotong of Beijing University, who studied Kaixian Gong village in 1936, 1957 and 1980, in addition to publications in 1955 by Professor W. R. Geddes of the University of Sydney, Australia, from his own tour of research to the same village. The two sociologists have given us an accurate insight into changes and progress of Kaixian Gong village in Jaingsu Province.[2] On the other hand, there is quite a contrast in policy results between land reform in Taiwan and those on the mainland. The former was done peacefully with no interruption in rural life. Land reform and commune development, on the other hand, produced enormous painful experiences for the rural population. Both land reforms, however, have succeeded in getting rid of a feudal land system of exploitation. But Taiwan's success in rural economic development laid the solid foundation for its later industrial modernisation and general economic prosperity; on the other hand, on the mainland today, the new leadership under Deng Xiaoping has to undo and correct Mao's mistakes in rural China in order to lay the same foundation for Beijing's success in the four modernisations by the end of this century. Mutual aid teams, cooperatives, collective communes, private plots, etc., have to be done away with entirely or readjusted to bring about an efficient collective or individual ownership of land for increased productivity. The story of rural failure under Mao is illustrative of many theoretical and policy differences between the radical leftists and the pragmatic moderates who were at first led by Liu Shaoqi. Liu, Zhou and Deng in the early 1960s succeeded in correcting Mao's mistakes in the aftermath of the commune fiasco of 1958. But Mao's jealous response was his cultural revolution which entailed dismissing and humiliating all the moderate leaders. There has been, of course, positive progress in rural China since the 1950s. For example, some rural electrification, enormous irrigation projects, road building, primary educational expansion and the improvement in rural law and order were clear evidence of major communist achievements. However, these achievements did not directly benefit the people in their per capita income and in other freedom to improve their own livelihood as is now possible under Deng. In short, Mao's failure in rural economic development and rural industrialisation has delayed the nation's schedule in building a modern industrial and powerful state. Had Mao not deviated from the party's policy line of the Eighth Congress in 1956, the communists could have succeeded far more even than the progress made in Taiwan by the Republic of China. In a real sense, the development experience and the economic progress of Taiwan and mainland China must be evaluated in competitive terms, because both governments were eager to succeed under a revolutionary urgency.

Returning to the review of rural development in the People's Republic of China. What did Fei Xiaotong say after his 1980 visit to Kaixian Gong village? He wrote the foreword to his new book:[3]

> I could feel the changes brought about in the village by the new economic policies immediately. These changes were shown not only in the abstract figures of a threefold increase in average income, from 100 yuan to over 300, but also to the smiling faces and optimistic words of the local people ... Before the Communist Party's Third Plenum in 1978, the village had very little sideline production or industry. But soon after this crucial meeting, at which new and flexible economic policies were adopted, the village's sideline production developed rapidly. And this was followed by the swift growth of its industrial enterprises. These changes altered the

previous economic structure of the village, in which 90 per cent of the population engaged in farming. In 1980 the proportions had changed to such an extent that over 50 per cent of the population were working in sideline production or rural industries. Their achievements encouraged me to think that they were paving the way for the future development of rural China and providing a means of rationalising China's economic structure through rural industrialisation.

Professor Fei's microscopic focus on a small village for more than forty-five years, from 1936 to 1980, provides other scholars and economists a valuable reference of what the Chinese people can do for themselves if given a sustained period of peace, stability, freedom to initiate, and a right policy which encourages them to experiment, even after some thirty years of rural regimentation.[4] His village, Kaixian Gong, is located eighty miles west of Shanghai on the south side of the famous Tai Hu (Lake Tai). The soil here is rich and the growing season lasts more than 300 days a year. The villagers grow rice, wheat, rape seeds and vegetables. Moreover, the silk industry has been more than a sideline occupation for the people. In his first research tour in 1936, he found that the village represented a typical picture of a traditional small village in the southeast part of China (only 1500 people in 1936). Villagers here loved the land as people do elsewhere in China. 'Land is there. You can see it every day. Robbers cannot take it away... the incentive to hold land is directly related to the sense of security... the best thing to give to one's son is land.'[5] When the Communist Party in the middle of the 1950s took land away from those who supported the revolution and expected to hold on to their newly acquired land ownership, it broke its promise of revolution since the 1920s and 1930s. To the farmers Mao made a mockery of the land reform of 1949–52. He pressured rural cadres to convince the peasants to hand over their lands to cooperatives and communes. Mao's personal restlessness and ignorance reinforced by his subjectivism and arrogance, indeed, caused most of the subsequent crises for the nation. In his 1955 preface to the book of *Socialist Upsurge in China's Countryside*, Mao wrote:[6]

The problem facing the whole party and people is no longer that of criticising conservative ideas about the speed of socialist transformation of agriculture. That problem has been solved. Nor is it the problem of transforming the whole of capitalist industry and commerce trade by trade into joint state-private enterprises. That problem too has been solved. The speed of transformation of handicrafts should be discussed during the first half of 1956. ... [the problem] lies in agricultural production; industrial production; handicraft production; the scale and speed of capital construction in industry, communication and transport.

Mao unwisely argued that 'right conservative thinking is still causing trouble in many spheres and prevents our work from keeping pace with the development of the objective situation'. He did not realise his so called 'objective situation' was totally at variance with true reality and the real wishes of the rural masses. In support of Mao's impatience with the slow pace of rural growth, party cadres worked in rural areas trying to convince the peasants of potential benefits of land recollectivisation. The *People's Daily* blindly suggested in an article, 'The Direction for 500 Million Peasants', that:[7] 'As a matter of fact, the direction taken by these three poor peasant households is the direction the five million peasants will take. All peasants now farming individually will eventually take the road resolutely chosen by the three poor peasant households.'

The press in China can cause enormous damage if used by the wrong people. The same mistake, incidentally, happened during Jiang Quing's struggle for power. No peasants in China wanted to give up land, thus causing their own insecurity. Since the late 1920s and with only a few exceptions, newspapers in China have often been used as a tool of oppression by one man, one party, or one class. Freedom of the press has not really existed in China before and after the communist victory in 1949. One of the reform measures in China should be the policy effort to discover the real voice of the people through a free press against the re-emergence of another Mao.

Professor Fei was quick to discover in 1936 the usefulness of traditional practices of mutual aid among peasants and the system of mutual allowance. The interest rates on borrowed money in rural China, on the other hand, made worse 'the hunger of the people everywhere'. He strongly urged that 'a final solution of agrarian problems in China lies not so much in reduction of expenditure of the peasants but in increasing their income. Therefore, industrial recovery (sideline incomes) is essential'.[8] The Nationalist government after 1945 and the Communist government after 1949 both failed to pump income into rural China. On the contrary, some of their policies were to exploit the peasants for rapid urban industrial capital accumulation. Only since Deng's New Policy after 1979 has the government through careful planning purposefully raised rural income to help the peasants in helping themselves. Writing in 1946, Professor Fei even had nice words to say about rural gentry who were both exploiters and benefactors of the peasants within the traditional social structure and institutional limits.[9] However, in his 1957 visit to Kaixian Gong, he found 'the supplementary industries do not match those of twenty-one years ago [1936]'. They had declined by 50 per cent. Rural collectivisation created new enthusiam and slogans for the higher production of rice. But soon afterward, Fei noted, the peasants gave way to 'three meals a day; we'll eat our way to socialism'. In 1981, after less than two years of Deng's new rural economic recovery policy Professor Fei found his villagers in Kaixian Gong had achieved a per capita income of 300 yuan per year as opposed to the then national average of less than 100 yuan. Thus, Kaixian Gong villagers belonged in 1981 to the 300-yuan income brigades.

Professor Fei found that the 1958 establishment of the commune system 'a premature move' and the 1962–6 rural readjustment a 'welcome improvement against the ultra-leftist tendencies'. Finally, it was the post-1978 new policy that 'removed the various negative effects of the leftist phase,' Fei said. On the other hand, agricultural contribution to national gross income after 1949 much increased proportionally. The government, in return, also made a few major investments in rural China. The crisis, however, was the lack of policy continuity and premature transformation of production and management with no regards for peasant wishes.

To mention just a few of the positive improvements in rural China, land reform itself in 1949–52 was a success. Between 1952 and 1976, the government invested an amount of 130 billion yuan in agriculture, 68.4 billion of which was used for rural capital construction in such projects as water conservation to make possible 18.5 per cent of cultivated land to come under irrigation (about 360 million Chinese mu). There were improvements in farming machinery, fertiliser produc-» tion and rural electrification (for example, the tractor-ploughed acreage increased from 2.04 million mu to 523.69 million mu in 1976). Networking in scientific research gained enormous progress through the coordination of the Chinese Academy of Agricultural Sciences. Nearly two dozen of the agricultural colleges were built and some 270 secondary agricultural schools were established. All together, about 250,000 students have graduated from agricultural colleges and half a million more from secondary agricultural institutions.[10] Rural livelihood improved steadily during the early 1950s of

Communist government. Improvement was resumed again after the commune fiasco and natural calamity in the early 1960s. There had been starvation nationwide in scope.

Because of Mao's erroneous population policy and the planned imbalance between agriculture and industry, actual per capita consumption in rural China, in fact, made little or no improvement in thirty years or even declined in remote and less productive regions. For example, the per capita grain consumption of 306 kilograms in 1957 declined to an embarrassing 300 kilograms in 1976. Cotton consumption declined from 2.55 tp 2.2 kilograms, while oil-bearing crops dropped from 6.6 kilograms to 4.35. These sorry records of agriculture failure were acutely affected by 'high targets' for production and by 'arbitrary guidelines'. Forests and grasslands were destroyed in many parts of the country in order to grow foods in their place. Lakes were reclaimed as farmland. Flood and soil erosion resulted from these man-made disasters. During the cultural revolution years, the slogan in agriculture was 'learning from Dachai'. In his report to the National People's Congress in 1964, Zhou Enlai characterised Dachai as 'putting politics and ideological work in command of the spirit of self-reliance and hard struggle'. In reality, agriculture became a tool in the class struggle against 'the masses and the cadres, and wantonly picking out the so-called capitalist roaders'. The communist agricultural policy was simply unintelligent before 1978. Farmers could not see the need to work, although he was present in the fields.[11] Agriculture was but one segment of communist economic failure. The real causes were ideological, wrong planning and corrupt administration in the entire economy before 1978. A general knowledge of the Chinese is necessary to understand and to see how agriculture and the rural people became the victims of bad socialism which did not care to learn about the nation's most needed knowledge on managerial skill, production incentive and the power of 'free marketing'. Most especially, the highly centralised administrative system demonstrated several defects. One of them was to subordinate productive enterprises to bureaucratic organs which themselves were too ideological and inefficient to guide the production units. The second cause of economic stagnation was China's enormous expansion in socialist command planning and its rigidity. And finally the system of 'unified income and expenditure' meant no one needed to work hard in this egalitarian distribution of goods and service. The government over the decades emphasised capital accumulation at the expense of consumption by the people. The result was less production and more poverty which was further accentuated by natural disasters and still lower productivity. China's failure to develop foreign trade was in itself a denial of wealth which could have easily accumulated capital gains through international trade competition in which Taiwan and Japan have done their best and become wealthy. Wrong emphases of planning made 'better progress' in less needed areas and 'less progress' in much needed areas. For example, Table 5.1 shows less production in grain and clothing and more in steel and oil.[12]

Table 5.1 Output of selected commodities, 1980

Category	1980 (in million tons)	Rollover increase over 1949
Grain	318	.8
Raw cotton	2.7	6
Steel	37	230
Coal	620	19
Crude oil	106	880
Chemical fertiliser	12.3	2,050
Eectricity capacity	300,000 million Kwh	70
Cotton cloth	13,000 million metres	7

It is clear that through authoritarian planning the government decided where increases or deductions should be made in allocation of resources. Steel, for example, was excessively produced and stock-piled, while grain production only gained 2.8 times over the 1949 figure. Central command planning did not reflect the wishes of the people, did not allow initiative for the enterprise, and did not incorporate flexible methods and options to execute the plan. Between 1958 and 1960, heavy industry grew by 230 per cent while agriculture declined by 23 per cent. There was in 1960 a shortfall of 6 million tons of grain supply for the urban grain market. The planned capital accumulation rate still reached 39.9 per cent in 1960. It was then adjusted to 10.4 per cent by 1962 because of natural calamities. On the other hand, due to inefficiency and lack of control many enterprises with huge production expenditures or capital losses were forced to stop production or shift to make other products. When the economy was not in accord with the planned objectives in 1960, for example, the central government simply sent back 20 million factory workers to rural areas from which they had been recruited only two years previously. Through drastic readjustment in 1961–63, the economy got back on track for normal growth. It would have been utterly impossible to restore the economy 'without correcting bad planning'. Centralised micro-economic planning can easily go wrong as admitted in a recent publication:[13]

> We failed to observe the law of value and did not adjust the prices of agricultural and industrial products in accordance with changes in the cost of production. We did not strictly adhere to the principle of 'to each according to his work' and did not raise the living standards of the workers and peasants in proportion to improvements in labour productivity. As a result, there was an excessive concentration of revenue in the hands of the state.

Having recovered from the nightmare of her economic failure through overly centralised micro-economic planning, China is now moving toward more macro-economic planning to allow flexibility and incentive in the economic operation and production:[14]

> The state plan should therefore deal with such things as the overall direction of economic development; the rate of growth; the balance between the major economic spheres; the scale and regional distribution of capital construction, investment allocation, major projects and the rate of improvement in living standards. In addition, it must take care of the balance between finance, credit, materials and foreign exchange.

Imbalance in planning until 1978 was, in short, greatly responsible for the suffering endured by the peasants. First of all, the central plan emphasised heavy industry over light industrial development. Secondly, the plan locked up peasants in their own locale as prisoners bondaged to their commune's stagnation. Thirdly, the government took away food and grain through purchasing at fixed low prices and in big quotas. Farmers subsisted on whatever was left. It was, therefore, very difficult to raise living standards by the peasants themselves through production. The more they produced, the more the government took away on a quota basis with fixed low prices. Urban workers and 'white collar' staff members appeared to have gained in per capita income as shown in Table 5.2.[15]

Table 5.2 Growth of annual per capita consumption of peasants and workers, 1952–79 (in current yuan of 1982)

	1952	1957	1979
Peasants	62	79	152
Workers and staff members	148	205	406

5.2 RURAL DEVELOPMENT AND THE RESPONSIBILITY SYSTEM IN FARMING

My first visit to rural China took place in 1979 after exactly thirty years of living abroad. I went through many communes, brigades, production teams and many visitation briefs which were made available usually to Chinese descendents of foreign nationality. What I had seen in 1979 was quite different from what I later saw in my subsequent trips to the same cities and provinces. Rural China was about to undergo rapid changes in 1979. My family and I visited a dozen cities and provinces in my first trip where we had relatives and friends. We acquired a new Japanese expensive camera with long lens for my son to take pictures of memorable sights and events. Everywhere we went we were given briefs by local cadres and school principles. We went to see many schools, health clinics, factories and recreation centres, and hospitals. I was much affected by what I saw after thirty years, and was able to compare what I saw and heard of the plight of rural China with what I left behind before 1949. Some of the things pleased me well, while others saddened me for weeks and months afterwards. We had relatives to visit in Kuangzhou, Shanghai, Beijing, Xian, and Yanan. Therefore, this first trip gave me a general coverage of several regions in China for my own comparison of the differences from region to region. My other trips to Guangxi, Yunan, Hubei, Sichuan and Manchurian provinces gave me still a deeper and wider scope for comparison. I can categorically declare that while in theory egalitarianism and equal share of 'big rice bowl' for all was supposed to be true, the reality of shocking differences in living standards between different regions in China was, and still is, incredibly sharp. A commune member in the suburbs of Shanghai or Guangzhou enjoys a much higher living standard than his counterpart in the suburbs of Xian or Yanan. In China, villagers are destined to accept whatever the locality is able to provide. Comparison on the basis of the so-called egalitarianism is simply deceiving.

Chinese villagers have in general, since 1949, lived a better life free of robbery, theft, feudal landlord exploitation, and starvation from natural calamities and disasters. They have not, however, been fully free from rigid government control and from the stagnated commune system until recently. The better living today consists of electric wells, electric mills, bicycles, and sewing machines which rural people did not universally have until recently. Peasants have always loved the land, and this was their major reason for accepting the communist revolution in the first place. I found in 1979 that villagers were generally resigned to destiny and with a sense of powerlessness to do anything for themselves. They had no incentive to do anything for the country or the government. Villagers did not appear to care for anything, nor understand what they could have read from local newspapers. And more likely they did not agree with whatever the newspaper said. It was a shock for me to have discovered this common negative attitude. They knew nothing could be done to improve their own lives. However, when I listened to the short briefs by commune cadres I heard only glowing pictures and lovely statistics. In 1979 I saw only communes and brigades in operation. The responsibility system had not been implemented yet in areas where I visited. Small cities and towns were dead places as compared with the former commercial life before 1949. In rural China there were only early morning roadside 'free marketing' near population centres. I suspected in 1979 that some of the trading was bartered between goods with little currency as the medium. In 1982, 1984 and 1985, however, all that I had seen a few years ago had changed. Free marketing in rural China has become a nationwide phenomenon. Cash has become the only medium of commercial transactions. It was incredibly exciting to see the new varieties of goods brought to rural markets. Indeed, it has become the centre of rural economic free activities. One can see rural China has come back to life after some thirty years. Peasants love this new freedom, which they lost unexpectedly after rural collectivisation during the middle 1950s. They are eager to improve their living conditions. That is to say that with less government they can make more improvements through self-help.

Better rural land utilisation and economic improvement have resulted from the dismantling of the commune system entirely or through its reform. This change has been the heart of Deng's new rural development. The process of this change differed from region to region. Initiatives came from a variety of sources, either from the peasants themselves, or local cadres, or from guided policy experiment from above. Politically the party and the central government did not at first want to commit any risk which might touch off a bigger political crisis within the party. Many party leaders at all levels were ideologically frozen and stiff. They were incapable of evaluating, through economic rationalism, what was wrong with rural economic production and with the sad plight of rural living standards. Ideological indoctrination had deprived most of the communist leaders of innovative thinking. Political survival became the major concern for most low level policy makers in China. No one can completely undo the effects of Mao's ideological argument even today. It was in such a fearful atmosphere that the dismantling of the commune system took place in various parts of China. Some cadres and peasants were bolder than their counterparts in other regions. On the whole, even though most cadres knew the need for change, they did not have the political courage to advocate it. Nor could they champion the reform, on the other hand, which would inevitably reduce their own authority as bureacratic leaders of the commune economy. Provincial leaders of the party and the government might have wanted central leadership to issue new policy directions. A few leaders, however, were allowed to experiment quietly with the responsibility system. The central government had to weigh the political consequences of any contemplated commune reform. The moderate leaders were waiting for more information about locally initiated experimental results. Only the farmers knew best that the commune land should be privately contracted to them for more production if the government would allow them to keep what is left after the delivery of a fixed quota collection. This would encourage them to work hard in the field.

On the other hand, the commune reform over sideline production was another way of encouraging peasants to produce more if they were allowed to keep a large share of profit after fulfilment of the contracted obligation to the commune. In short, reform at the levels of the production team, the brigade and the commune itself was necessary if production relations between the commune and the production units could be arranged by contracts to profit both sides through increased production. The following pages will describe some interesting accounts to illustrate the need for reform and the resulting increase in production. 'The contracted responsibility system' has its myriad varieties in both urban and rural production. During a two-year period in rural China, 1979–81, agricultural productivity increased by 18 per cent. And farmers' per capita annual income increased by 66 per cent.[16]

In three years (1979 to July 1982) some 70 per cent of the rural production teams had gone into the contract system. The main reasons for this rapid transition was the desire of the peasants to work for themselves, for more private profit, and the improvement of their own living standards. The readjustment of production relationship was essential for greater productivity. The leftists up to 1978 had failed to understand the need for rural production incentives. For decades under the leftists, the peasants had been resigned to depend on only three things: 'Grain need depended on government's resale, livelihood depended on government's welfare, and production depended on government's credit lending.'[17] The following incident led to gradual but steady policy changes. During the planting season of the Fall of 1978, Shan-nan district of Anhui Province suffered an enormous drought, and the peasants themselves suddenly took matters into their own hands. They divided up the commune land into a 'family responsibility farming'. The higher authorities at the local, district and provincial levels did not express either their approval or disapproval. In March of the following year, 1979, the *People's Daily* in Beijing was the first to criticise the event in an article. Local authorities immediately decided to declare the farmers' action illegal as so labelled it in the *People's Daily*. However, the provincial party secretary restrained the local authorities and instructed them to await until after the spring harvest before deciding what to do, In 1979, the spring and the fall harvests were enormously increased in volume. And 80 per cent of the farmers requested to continue the practice while, on the other hand, the local party secretary had already ordered a return to the old commune practice. This party leader did so not because he did not approve of what the farmers had done but he feared for his own accountability to the higher party authority. He might be condemned 'as a capitalist roader' if he remained silent. All his subordinate cadres, however, supported the farmers against his 'perfunctory gesture of disapproval'. The farmers and the village level cadres asked: 'Is increase in grain production a violation of law? Must not test of truth be practiced in rural China? Why is this success in grain production not allowed? Our nation still depends on grain import. It embarrasses every Chinese. Why cannot we allow our own production increase?' Farmers and low level cadres proudly advanced their argument in this manner.

The middle level party leaders in Anhui had the same ideological contradiction in their minds. They, too, asked: 'After twenty years of rural work, we now produce less grain than before but still falsely claim our general policy and direction is correct. This new contradiction was similar to an earlier precedent. When grain production was increased in 1961 and 1961 Mr Mao said the policy was wrong. What kind of theory is this?[18] They further asked: 'What is capitalism? What is socialism? Now everything is confused.' They both loved and feared the new success of family farming responsibility. They loved it because grain production doubled and peasant incentives multiplied. They feared it because of their involvement in it: they might be possibly accused of supporting new capitalists. Therefore, these cadres did not offer their support in the transition. Nor did they dare draw a positive conclusion from it. They thus did not take a clear-cut stand before the peasants; they were simply waiting for instructions from the higher echelons.

What is family farming responsibility? It is not giving away the collective ownership of land, animals and large farming equipment. These all still remain collectively owned. The production team at first acquired greater autonomy in decisions about production, but the team did not gain the ownership of anything. In many cases the production team has become the most important unit. It may give points to the members who in turn, receive goods or cash according to these points. As a result, each family, has more income while still under collective ownership. The state now gains in larger purchase quotas because of production increase. Consequently, the collectivity accumulates more capital profit. Thus, the individual, the family, the collectivity and the state can all benefit. The rural individual farmer can sell his goods on the free market. This practice is of value for everyone. It is a form of socialism; it is not a typical practice of capitalism. This is, then, the first argument in favour of individual and family responsibility farming. However, ideologically leftist cadres consider the new practice a step backward in the socialist movement without realising that it is two steps forward for the modernisation of the country.

In 1980, a number of areas of Kansu province adopted the family responsibility system in response to local popular desires. According to an official investigation report, Kansu province for the thirty years after 1949 did not make much progress at all in agricultural production, especially in the dry drought-prone central part. Top soil was blown away by dry wind. In remote areas and hilly regions of the province, no progress had been made at all. Cultivation still depended on draft animals. For example, in education some 65 per cent of the people between the ages of sixteen and forty-five were in 1980 still illiterate. Thus many local cadres did not have the necessary ability to manage collective production. Bookkeeping in most of the communes was confusing. Some cadres often misused and misappropriated the commune's money, while commune members suffered from starvation. Too many of the cadres themselves often refused to work in the field and became themselves a burden for the peasants to feed and to clothe. Up to 1978, peasants in Kansu province received a per capita annual income of 60 yuan (about $US30 in 1980 exchange rate). Thirty-five per cent of production team members received only 40 yuan.[19] When family responsibility farming came to Kansu, commune members could directly manage their own production to avoid waste and exploitation by privileged cadres who used to live much better at the farmer's expense. Now the peasants love the land they farm and their draft animals they keep for work in the field. Production has risen rapidly as has per capita income. With the increase in production enthusiasm, interpersonal relations have improved between the cadres who now work in the field themselves, and the farmers who now have little to complain about. Most important of all, the policy today is in accord with popular desire and working experience in the field. Responsible farming is in short, the first step in rural modernisation because of (1) dramatic production increases; (2) competition between farmers and rural division of labour; (3) emergence of specialisation in production and new job availability; (4) transition from farming to other specialised non-agricultural occupations; (5) new and greater voluntary cooperation among farmers in the future for their own self-interest; (6) rural expansion in husbandry, auxiliary occupations and sideline industries. And rural commerce will be developed by the initiative of peasants themselves with just a little or no government assistance. Land will not be the only means of rural prosperity. Light industry and specialised commerce will absorb much rural manpower. Land redistribution in the future on a voluntary basis in order to mechanise farming for more efficient production is entirely possible and rational without coercion.

The contractual family responsibility system is a new system of readjustment in rural management of the economy and production. It affects not only 80 per cent of the total Chinese population living in the countryside, but also the other 20 per cent of urban citizens who depend on abundant labour and material supply from the countryside to improve their lives. A complicated sequence of changes will result from the reform and revival of rural production initiatives. This peasant enthusiasm to work for the benefits of all as well as for their own self-interest is the antithesis of Mao Zedong Thought or Marxism. It is rather the retreat of ideology, the withdrawal of the party and the government bureaucracy; it is a demonstration of peasants' self-help with less socialist interference. However, China will remain a socialist state, at least, in the foreseeable future. The planned 'command economy' will continue to dominate. The publicly owned enterprises remain closely under the guidance of the central government. Even growing rural prosperity can be reversed by future adverse political policies designed to stamp out the present rural growth. Therefore, no one should be misled into thinking that the role of government and central policy will be less important. On the contrary, they will be far more important in terms of price and wage systems, credit and banking, government purchasing, central policy on educational expansion to improve the technological level in rural mechanisation and production management application, and especially in respect of the total volume of production of goods and services for both domestic consumption and for export in foreign trade. In short, as rural China industrialises further, more government, but with a different kind of planning and intervention, will be critically needed. A cooperative relationship between the central government and rural industry and agriculture must emerge to help and to guide, but not to control, dominate or stifle. This, in fact, has been the policy of the Nationalist government in Taiwan, which provides credit, fertilisers, export information to farmers' own free associations which in turn make their rational decisions on production, marketing and profit calculations. In the people's Republic of China today, agricultural experts are warning about future problems, such as farmers' short-sighted, conserva- tiveness, and the need for more party leadership and consistent policy to guide the healthy development of the agricultural economy.

The reform and readjustment experience in Kansu province is a telling manifestation of thirty years of agricultural failure, a story of tolerating inequality in living conditions of different parts of the province, not a promotion of egalitarianism as Mao's theory promises. The central government did not have the resources to promote egalitarianism which had remained, in Mao's time, an idealistic future goal only. His government had only an organisational mechanism and a political power to oppress the peasants into submission, the organisational power and its efficiency to herd peasants into political discussion and indoctrination which the peasants only listened to but did not believe. The details and episodes are too numerous to be told here. On the positive side, the dismantling of the commune system and the local government reform must eventually lead to such future developments as to require a new outlook as follows:[20]

1. The leadership must be able to anticipate the long-term impacts or implications of responsibility farming and rural light industrial and commercial development;
2. The distant future of rural economy includes new occupational specialisation and differentiation along with production socialisation. Such trends will require a new united effort and new economic concepts and organisations for greater demand for more efficient management;
3. Greater expansion of agricultural development cannot be separated from rapid supportive development in industry, commerce, transportation and the credit system. Family unit farming may soon lead to expansion in family unit production in commercial goods, service industry, and other greater sideline developments. Thus, the market law of supply and demand, market organisation and rational competition, guided production development, and raw material supply for production, etc., must claim the utmost policy attention of the central government and provincial governments;
4. Too many party cadres and ill-fitting bureaucratic organisations in rural China must be subject to continuous reorganisation. Presently, the communes and brigades, etc., are disappearing, and the re-emergence of new local government units is in good progress. However, achieving maximum administrative efficiency to yield positive assistance to rural productive forces will require much upgrading of the needed knowledge, leadership capacity and self-discipline on the part of future local cadres. Past cadres were resented, feared and tolerated by decent peasants who hated the arrogance, privileges, misuse of power and unfairness of rationing by the local cadres.[21] It is up to the Communist party and government to honestly draw lessons and conclusions as to why (1) the practices of the past thirty years killed peasants' enthusiasm for production; (2) why today many rural problems have disappeared as a result of family responsibility farming; and (3) why the new policy in rural China must become the basic foundation for future urbanisation and urban economic prosperity. On the other hand, the government must not tolerate the development of future gaps between the rich and the poor. Future land recollectivisation must be done purely for economic reasons as opposed to ideological reasons. Many peasants must be allowed to leave farming for other

new occupations, and land must be mechanised to produce new materials and more food to feed the entire population. A free economy has often produced its own disadvantages in other advanced economies against the interest of the rural population. China is clearly heading toward a much freer economy through sweeping reforms.

My own interview with Mr Hu Qili, one of the new rising stars in the Political Bureau, demonstrated that he was very well-informed on the dynamic rural economic development during the recent years since the Third Plenum of the Eleventh Party Congress. He stated during the interview several specific policy emphases.[22]

1. Development in agricultural economy has created many new unpreventable and also welcome conditions. For example, he cited the following: the rise of thousands of new middle and small-sized urban centres everywhere for rural commercial exchange and other supply convenience; a policy need to guide and settle population shift to prevent inflow of people into presently existing crowded cities; peasant initiatives to accumulate capital for transportation and navigation purposes (for example, in the lower Yangtze region); merchants making plans to build indoor retail market in the suburb of Beijing; rural human resources will eventually promote light industrial production for export; the need of avoiding the crises in capitalist states such as crime and poverty; the movement of scientists, technicians and educators into the country-side and to less developed western China; and avoiding compulsory immigration from the crowded coastal plain to western and underdeveloped highland (it has failed once);
2. Before the year 2000 AD, the development of a new dynamic national economy remains one of the three major goals of the government (the other two being preservation of world peace and the return of Taiwan to the fatherland).[23]

In short, rural transformation has genuinely begun in the last six years since 1979. However, the experience of constructive contribution under the old commune system is not totally forgotten by the government. Peasants can still be called upon to do labour for the benefit of the community or the village. The role of the Communist party leadership in this economic transformation will remain a crucial one for a long time to come. The quality of life in rural China will improve by leaps and bounds in coming decades. And finally, the purpose of both the revolutions of 1911 and 1949 are showing dividends in both Taiwan and the mainland for the weaker peasantry.[24]

5.3   CASE INTERVIEW IN RURAL NANHAI COUNTY

P. Y. Chen and W. J. Gao of Guangzhou Foreign Affairs Liaison Office arranged for and accompanied me to Nanhai county, which is an hour's drive from Guangzhou. It is, incidentally, the birth place of Kang Yu-wei whose teaching centre at Xiqiao I also visited. I was brought to spend two days with Zhou and his two assistants. Zhou came to Nanhai from Northern Jiangsu in 1949. He became an instrumental leader of Nanhai county for thirty-five years with many assignments in the economic and financial management areas over the past three decades. He held such offices as deputy secretary, deputy county magistrate and magistrate. His success in Nanhai earned many opportunities for his promotion to higher positions. But poor health forced him to remain in Nanhai whose prosperity has been intimately tied to his life-long dedication. Presently he is much respected and loved by the people of the county. They elected him to become the president of Nanhai County People's Congress, a position requiring fewer daily burdens, on account of his health.

Zhou is a leader of smooth personality with a wonderful memory for statistical records in economic progress and dates of events. He used no notes and asked for no assistance from the two assistants whom I also interviewed separately for their responses to my questions resulting from the first interview. Zhou (hereafter referred to as Chairman Zhou of the County People's Congress of the CPC) was purged during the cultural revolution. His People's Congress Committee meets every two months during which time he is in charge for about four days. The People's Congress hears reports from the party secretary and the county chief, Xianzhang. It also elects several officers, including the police chief and judges of the court. There are several special reasons for my selection of Nanhai county for the interview. First of all, it is well known because it was repeatedly considered a model example of success. One of its unique features is that it has its large number of overseas residents in Hong Kong and the United States. Annually the county has been visited by high government officials from Beijing. When Hu Yaobang became the Communist Party Chairman, replacing Hua Guofeng in November 1979, on the first day in office he declared Nanhai as the model experience for others to imitate. When party secretary Xi Chongshun was governor of Guangdong he came to Nanhai repeatedly to encourage new progress and spirit for reform.

Before my report on the interview with Chairman Zhou, it may be helpful to summarise certain information about Nanhai county from the 'Report on Government Work' delivered by the Magistrate (equivalent of county board chairman of supervisors) to the County People's Congress on 23 March 1985. In this report, the county chief made the following points in a language and manner indicative of standardised political practice:

1. Nanhai has closely followed Beijing's new policy direction 'to continue our reform toward material progress and spiritual construction'. 'We have made in 1984 good records in industry, agriculture, finance, public enterprise, collective entity, and individual progress'. The combined production value of 1984 in industry and agriculture was 1870 million yuan, an increase of 20.4 per cent over 1983. Of the total production, industry was 980 million yuan, an increase of 26.3 per cent over 1983. This was a 100 per cent increase in industrial total value in four years. Agriculture made a 14.5 per cent value increase over 1983. Rural development advances toward production specialisation, commercialisation and modernisation. Commercial production has increased unprecedentedly.

2. In 1984, the countryside of Nanhai county registered a total income of 152 million yuan, a 23 per cent value increase over 1983. The thirty-six county-owned enterprises made a total production value of 560,000,000 yuan, a value increase of 28.5 per cent over 1983.

3. Market prosperity and commercial transactions increased at both county and national level in Nanhai.

4. 'We speedily advanced the development of small cities and towns in Nanhai in 1984.' The living standard of the people made another jump to a per capita annual income of 861 yuan, an increase of 101 yuan over 1983 or 13.2 per cent. Workers and factory staff members received a 8.5 per cent wage increase in addition to an average bonus of 40 yuan for the year. Housing conditions in the countryside also improved in 1984. Newly constructed housing in 1984 provided an additional 760,000 square metres for the rural residents. People's savings have also increased over the previous year by 48.6 per cent. The rural

people have accumulated an average saving in their account of 681 yuan (each $US1 is approximately 2.5 yuan, subject to market fluctuation).

5. Nanhai county, by virtue of close proximity to Hong Kong and Guangzhou, achieved in 1984 an export volume of 320 million yuan, a 27 per cent increase over 1983.

6. Nanhai is also speeding up 'its housing construction for our overseas brethren to return and to live or retire in Nanhai homeland'. The county also returned many formerly confiscated homes owned by overseas citizens. In 1984 overseas Chinese from Nanhai county made a total investment in their homeland of 30 million Hong Kong dollars, which has more than twice doubled the total investment value of 1983.

7. Nanhai county is very conscious of technological improvement in production. The county polytechnic office selected forty new technical areas for skill improvement, twenty-nine of which have achieved good results. In education, the county made systematic investigations of secondary and technical school curricula and teacher training programmes. The county has proudly met the following three educational criteria (1) every school is adequately housed; (2) every class of students has a room; and (3) every student has a desk and a chair. There were thirty-six night classes in adult education in the rural areas of the county.

8. Birth control in the county has succeeded yielding a ratio of 17.41 births per 1000 people. Sixteen thousand citizens underwent surgical operation for birth control in 1984.

9. In industrial structural reform, the county is following national instructions to separate politics from enterprises. On industrial personnel, it has moved from an appointment by a superior hierarchy to an election system by the workers. Simplification of the administrative procedures and control is being carried out. And enterprise decision-making autonomy is being granted. In its wage system, the county is becoming less egalitarian.

10. In agricultural contract, the county's production land is mostly put under a fifteen-year contract to assure stability in our farmers' production long-term planning. The county has also adopted a liberal policy toward credit lending with low interest to encourage light industrial development occupational specialisation in rural areas.

11. Rapid expansion in small towns and city construction in rural areas was carried out to meet central government's expectation.

These small cities are needed to meet political, cultural and economic future development in rural China and to avoid spilling the rural population on to existing major urban centres.

12. In short, this county, like the rest of the nation, has suffered from the following difficulties: (1) difficulties in liberating minds from leftist past indoctrination; (2) inadequate energy, transportation and primary resource supplies for meeting rapid industrial development; (3) the slower speed in rural industrial structure reform, especially with regard to the development of tertiary industry in remote areas; (4) lack of personnel in science and technology in rural and far remote areas; and (5) lack of foreign exchange to buy from abroad the necessary equipments and goods.

The above list represents a continuing emphasis on economic development for the six years since Deng Xiaoping's new reforms. Nanhai is the model example in its implementation of such policy guidelines of the central government. Most other counties in remote or border regions of the country are not equipped to follow closely and efficiently the new reform movement. Nanhai county benefits greatly from its geographic proximity to Guangzhou and its rapid economic development. Unlike other counties, it received a substantial amount of investment from overseas Chinese. The level of education, transportation and capital investment in Nanhai are far advanced compared to most other poor counties in other parts of China, including most of the coastal counties.

Let us return to my personal interview with Chairman Zhou of the County People's Congress. I can only select a few instances to highlight how he personally relates Nanhai's economic development to central government's reform policy, to provincial leadership's enthusiastic encouragement, and to the kind of unusual cooperation among county leaders. It must also be true elsewhere that the rural people simply did not believe at first the sincerity of the new leadership in reforming the economic system as practised under Mao to one of open experiment in new and non-socialist economic policy for material prosperity. Chairman Zhou's interview revealed the following: (1) the peasants and city people for thirty years were very afraid of their government. They did not believe the government was sincere concerning a change in Mao's policy. They were accustomed to being like sitting ducks waiting to be led. They were concerned to avoid unexpected troubles which would hurt them; (2) given time, the political system and party leadership eventually were able to convince all the citizens through open campaigns or restrained methods. The party leadership was quick and eager at all times to initiate new ways to change old practice, to reform and to convince everyone. The central leadership was able to eventually convince the people that this time the party is going to remain committed to changing the rural economy of China; (3) the communist leadership, even after thirty-five years in charge of everything, is still revolutionary and experimental in search of the best way to make China a powerful industrial state. Whether under Mao or Deng, the party's willingness to experiment is frightening and even admirable. It can change from past failure to offer hope for future sucess. Therefore, communists do not fail in the long run. But their price of experiment is too high; (4) communist leaders, like their Kuomintang counterpart, are unable to succeed in their original revolutionary goals. They have awakened to realise China's own needs and her ability in self-rejuvenation and self-discovery; (5) The revolutionary failures of 1911 and 1949 suggest that external challenges can only help China transform in her own way. The leaders know eventually what the people really want even though the people do not have a dependable way of informing the government. The leaders learn eventually to follow the people as the only way for their own political survival. Mao did not follow the people and failed. Now Deng takes account of what the people want, so he should succeed in the end. The people always remain patient, and silent under bad leadership; (6) the Nanhai experience verifies that a thorough and peaceful revolution is going on in all parts of China; (7) the Chinese government bureaucrats never seem to raise questions on what is right or wrong. They only follow political dictatorship. So the whole system moves in one direction from the top to the bottom until it fails totally, when a new start is initiated.

Nanhai county has a population of 842,000. It lost some of its people and land to the city of Guangzhou and other fast developing urban neighbours. It is one of the first counties to become rich and probably the richest among them as a result of Deng's reform. Six hundred and seventy thousand people are considered farmers whose 1984 per capita income was 860 yuan. Total industrial and agricultural growth value income in 1984 was 1870 million yuan. Thus, the average 1984 income for all citizens in the county was over 2200 yuan. The average wage bonus per worker was 480 yuan. It exports through Hong Kong a total value of 500 million yuan. Almost in every respect, Nanhai has made enormous progress. Thus it was designated, at the very start of Deng's reform, the 'model county' for emulation in 1979. Why was this success possible? Chairman Zhou spent days with me explaining it. He was and still is totally involved in the county's progress as he had been since 1949.

In 1949, Nanhai had an income of 100 million yuan. In 1979 the total income was 810 million. As already cited, the 1984 total growth was 1870 million yuan. In the county's own statistical record, income increased by eight times in the thirty years between 1949 and 1979. Why was it possible in the last five years for county income to increase by 1070 million yuan? Chairman Zhou made the following summary. First, enthusiastic execution of the central government's reform policy of 'open the country up to foreign nations and revitalisation of domestic economic development'. Chairman Zhou unqualifiedly declared it the only right policy which is welcome to the people. This was a 'policy to make wealth'. As he said: 'Under the same sky, on the same land and by the same people, the policy has succeeded; but Mao's policy failed. To me the only valid answer is that this is a correct and welcome one, Mao's policy was incorrect and without genuine support.' He said the implementation strategy is also correct in terms of readjustment, restructuring, consolidating and improving. Such a strategy involves no drastic departure or sudden change to benefit or hurt anyone. The new policy requires time to transform the economy, to raise wages and bonuses, to pump money into the countryside and to allow the people to adapt to new aims. The new policy allows some people to prosper sooner than others, but all will get there eventually. There is room for all the people to improve their own personal lot if they live in rural areas and wish to manage some sideline incomes.

Secondly, Chairman Zhou stated his second reason was that of support from the central and provincial governments. As early as November 1979 Beijing leadership declared 'In agriculture, learn from Nanhai'. This declaration made his own leadership stronger and more confident. It gave every cadre in 'the county more excited, more dedicated push and made him eager to work extra hard to set the next target of progress much higher and more ambitiously'. Well-known leaders from Beijing came to Nanhai to 'observe our progress, to encourage our people, to remove our fear of policy reverse to make themselves again the victims of condemnation. This pattern of encouragement was no different from Mao's declarations: 'In agriculture learn from Dachai'. The whole propaganda system and the local leadership then listened and followed. In the 1960s there was just as much enthusiasm to learn from Dachai as in 1979 to learn from

Nanhai. For Nanhai, however, the result was different. The people's standard of living was improved instantly. On the other hand, the provincial leaders did their utmost to support Nanhai's own progress. Many came to Nanhai from Guangzhou. The governor, the first party secretary and many others 'were behind us'.

Thirdly, 'the unity and cooperation among some twelve county leadership units' were responsible locally for making the huge economic progress possible. Chairman Zhou modestly omitted his own leadership capacity in leading the county officers and cadres. The people had to work day and night since 1979 at meetings, in the fields, making plans, taking evaluations, plotting schemes and inventing new methods in order to mobilise the peasants to believe and not to be afraid. To become rich in the past was a violation of egalitarianism which would result in a person's being subjected to criticism of class struggle. No one wanted to commit that sin and to violate Mao's ideology. After thirty years of communist rule people have learned to share poverty in disgust, not healthy competition to become wealthy even though they wish they could. It became the task of the county leadership crew to convince the peasants 'to work harder and to get wealthy'. They must change now without fear.

How to campaign against peasant inertia of inaction or resistance? The county leadership units worked hard to devise methods and strategies to move the people for incentives to work. They held public meetings and invited a few courageous people to report on how they had been able to make more money and save more in their bank account. The leaders went to production teams and brigades to tell the people how to aquire greater income, how to think in terms of becoming rich and 'why there is no limit to the growth of wealth'. They created a variety of occasions in which to celebrate those who had become wealthier. In 1979 the county leadership set the target of per capita income from the average 100 yuan to 400 by the end of 1981. This was a very difficult goal to attain. They worked daily to encourage all teams and brigades to meet their separate group goal. A few devices were employed to overcome the fear of becoming rich: (1) write 'a letter to congratulate' those who have achieved more income; (2) 'use a string of firecrackers to celebrate'; (3) give a free 'ticket to a movie'; (4) provide 'a head of pig for feast'; (5) deliver 'a case of wine'. This was their method of encouraging production through their 'Five Ones' policy. When such a celebration was in progress, pictures were taken. The guests of honour often said: 'If the government accuses us of becoming richer, these photos will be our evidence that you people in county leadership are responsible for what we are accused of'. The celebrations for production increases usually consisted of dancing, local music, a brigade meeting and a lion's dance. After some time of such encouragement, more and more peasants took initiatives to take on sideline jobs or worked more hours in the field. Such celebrations were so often held and so numerous throughout the county that only representatives of the county government were sent out to attend these occasions. By 1981, the county leadership delegated the task of organising victory celebrations to the district unit. Later on, certificates of achievements were used to replace big celebrations. Soon more peasants were deeply convinced of the government's sincerity. They might comment that 'we are not afraid any more. If we are in trouble, you leaders will be in trouble, too'.

To change people's attitude toward wanting higher income was the hardest thing to accomplish. They were simply 'afraid to be better off than their neighbours for fear of class struggle and new tricks of the government'. It took the country a great deal of campaigning to convince the people. Thus in three years, 1979–82, per capita income was raised from 100 yuan to 400 in Nanhai. Other neighbouring counties did not follow Nanhai's example. They thought this was impossible in their areas. The county leadership in Nanhai followed a 'four firsts' strategy to stay ahead of other counties in production and in per capita income. The 'four firsts' consisted of: (1) 'first to learn everything'; (2) 'first to know everything'; (3) 'first to be concerned'; and (4) 'first to get the benefit'. This was the county's leadership predisposition to stay ahead of others in the reform policies of the central government. The separate units of the county government, from the beginning to the present, have remained united, so rural production and sideline industries have made 'Nanhai the first among the richest counties in all of China'. Delegates of many other counties gradually came to Nanhai for inspection to do likewise.

Why was the Nanhai county leadership so confident of its success and not afraid of consequences of failure? Chairman Zhou said that the provincial party leaders and governor assured the county not to be afraid. Every cadre in the county was fully aware of the government's commitment to make the country richer, and to raise the people's standard of living. Secondly, Nanhai county leaders undertook a thorough study of Nanhai's potential for development, and its past record in light industrial production and in commercial activities. After a careful analysis of Nanhai's past, they drew four conclusions. First, the geographic location of Nanhai is a positive factor. It is only hours away in transportation from Hong Kong, Macao and Guangzhou. All year round Nanhai can produce vegetables, fruits, chickens and ducks which can be shipped directly from Nanhai to these places during all four seasons both by land and by water. Secondly, historical experience was vividly available to convince that Nanhai could again develop its light industries and revitalise its commercial activities as it had done thirty years ago. Nanhai still had the human resources to recover its lost commerical activities. Thirdly, the study made a correct assessment of Nanhai's sons and daughters living abroad as overseas loyal residents. They are scattered all over the world, the majority of them residing in Hong Kong, Macao, Singapore, the United States and even in African states. These overseas loyal citizens were eager to re-establish relations with their loved ones in Nanhai. They could make capital investment back in Nanhai and act as trade agents, too. Finally, the county leadership has remained united to work together.

What should Nanhai produce? The answer is basic and simple. It should first of all increase food production for people to eat well. Their feelings of security will increase if they are no longer worried about starvation. Secondly, Nanhai should produce supplementary food supplies and other daily consumer articles for both self-consumption and for export. Thirdly, Nanhai should expand light industrial development; 'Without industry there cannot be wealth'. And finally, the county leadership emphasised their effort and determination to redevelop Nanhai's commercial activities. They believed that 'without commerce life has no vitality and dynamism'. In 1980 all these conclusions of the study were put into practice. The people became quickly convinced that their destiny was in their own hands, and that the new policy of reform was not likely to change.

For example, Nanhai reached out to re-establish links with those overseas Chinese. Many of them left Nanhai more than thirty or forty years ago and still had their close relatives there, but they did not want to return yet. Communication with relatives was cut off totally during the cultural revolution. Deng's open door policy to the outside world was, therefore, particularly beneficial to Nanhai which could now help local citizens re-establish relations with relatives abroad. Over the last several years, many Nanhai officials have visited Hong Kong, Macao, Singapore, the United States, Canada and even parts of the African continent to seek closer contacts with them. Seventy thousand of them were scattered elsewhere besides the 200,000 of them still living in Hong Kong. Others are in Taiwan, Macao and various parts of Southeast Asia and Europe. In total, Nanhai has more than 300,000 former citizens and their descendants living abroad. They have been invited to return to their homeland to retire, to visit relatives, to seek trade opportunities and to invest in local industries.

The result of such visits by Nanhai county officials abroad has paid off handsomely. Many former inhabitants have returned to visit or to invest. Former residents or descendants in Hong Kong have reversed their political allegiance in National Day celebrations after 1980. They have stopped hoisting the Nationalist Government flag on 10 October every year. Nanhai's Chamber of Commerce in Hong Kong has been in active existence since 1910. Members of it have been eager to contact their relatives in Nanhai. When Chairman Zhou himself visited Hong Kong in 1980, they all wanted to see him personally. He was kept busy for weeks meeting with them. Nanhai's total foreign trade with Hong Kong annually accounts for more than 100 million Hong Kong dollars. These overseas Nanhai descendants remit a large portion of their foreign exchange to their relatives. They also donate cash for welfare and education. Some 500,000 local citizens have directly or indirectly been benefited by these new contacts with relatives abroad. Nanhai now has its own foreign tourist industry.

My interview with Chairman Zhou covered other areas which have broad similarities with other parts of China. For example, the dismantling of commune economy, local government reorganisation, education and technological developments, and other local problems of nationwide significance occupied most of the remaining interview time. I asked for his opinion on the development of democracy and the rule of law in China. Chairman Zhou considers this as one of the central parts of the reform under Deng in terms of long-term implications. In conversation he demonstrated his total ignorance of democratic freedoms and rights. He was unaware of local autonomy and practice in democratic decision making, or of the importance of political election with multiple candidates to choose from or of the expression in public affairs or the freedom of the press. However, what he avoided mentioning or did not know about non-communist practice of political democracy was itself most important to me. I suddenly realised with greater depth that no nation can practice any form of democracy which is alien to itself and is not in demand by its citizens, especially its rank and file political and administrative leaders. Chairman Zhou is not just anybody else. He is a gentle, thoughtful, experienced, and dedicated communist who is open-minded and genuinely loved by most of Nanhai's citizens. I believe, that by comparison, most of his counterparts elsewhere in the nation as chairman of county people's congresses would know much less about the varieties of democratic governments in practice. Chairman Zhou has made official visits during the last several years to the United States, West Europe, Africa, Singapore and Hong Kong. In short, this example illustrates that Western scholars or Sinologists have to be careful when they inadvertently attempt to impose on China Western standards of democracy, such as respect for human rights, freedom of religion, civil liberties as guaranteed by the national constitution, or multiple party practice in the election system. Chairman Zhou was proud that China has come out of the chaos of the cultural revolution and that the 'Revolutionary Committees' at the county and provincial levels have finally been replaced by reform-minded officials in recent years. To him, China is now already quite democratic. There was no response from him to my question on the practice of democratic centralism in China and absence of election for central government officials by direct popular methods.

Zhou happily told me that since before 1980 Nanhai county has had an elected people's committee which meets under the direction of the county chief, who was himself theoretically elected by the committee. The minimum voting age in China is eighteen. Members are elected to the county people's congress which, in turn, selects members of its own standing committee to exercise the 'legislative or consent' power when the Congress is not in session. The congress meets generally for a period of five days or seven days annually to hear a variety of reports and to approve the needed actions. Real democracy appears to exist in the method of practice, not as guaranteed by legal or constitutional devices. For example, the county people's congress elected the county administrative chief (county board of supervisors' chairman), police and fire chiefs. Members of the county people's congress are directly selected by districts, towns, the units of local military and security forces, commun ist youth league, women's organisations, worker's unions, and fire departments. Every three years an election is held for members of the county congress. Re-election is possible for another three-year term. The standing committee of the people's congress must meet every two months and also meet anytime on an emergency situation. The members of the standing committee annually make two visits in small groups to every community in the county to hold discussions and other meetings with county voters on matters of their interests.

I asked Chairman Zhou what the voters perceive as democracy in practice. He happily replied that voters want their representatives to 'have power, a sense of duty, an interest in local, county and provincial matters and participation in their solutions ... Representatives must be just and unselfish, resentful of political factionalism, communicative both upward and downward, willing to hold street or village open meetings to tell voters the positions of their government on various issues. If this kind of democracy conveys genuine popular judgements on issues, it is then, a true democracy and a form of 'New England town meeting'. Another major routine practice in Nanhai county is that the chairman of the County People's Congress must invariably request all delegates to survey voters' ideas and opinions in advance of the next session. The voters may directly initiate 'legislative proposals' with their own signatures. People's delegates also enjoy 'a Chinese postal courtesy' to mail letters and information to the voters, in addition to their frequent tours to visit voters.

Nanhai county has 820,000 people. The people's congress has 400 delegates. Only one-third of the delegates are communist cadres. An elected county chief may not even be a communist party member. Approximately 15 per cent of the 400 represent the intellectual class (those with high school education or above). Some 60 per cent of the 400 members, in fact, are not party members in Nanhai. Their youngest delegate was twenty-three years old when elected. The average age of the Standing Committee of the People's Congress is fifty years of age. Roughly 25 per cent of the delegates are women. However, none represent the small democratic political parties which are better organised and proportionally represented at the provincial and national levels of congresses.

I did ask for Chairman Zhou's opinion on the future fate of the eight small political parties in China. First, he considers that from the point of view of historical development, China must have a multi-party system. He likes the communist party strategy of forming a united front among minor parties for cooperation. The small parties made their contributions to the communist victory of 1949. They also provided the 'sovereign basis' in the formation of national government in 1949. It was the Chinese People's Political Consultative Conference (CPPCC) which acted as the sovereign central legislature before the adoption of the 1954 constitution. Besides, the CPPCC has existed side by side with the National People's Congress (NPC) under the 1954 constitution. At the national level, the CPPCC can perform a very significant check on the communist exercise of power. Thus, chairman Zhou welcomes a multi-party system because of his views about the role of the minor parties. Secondly, he thinks that the country must have a core leadership at the national level to lead the people toward the achievement of modernisation. Therefore, the Communist party must exercise greater power as the political leading core. Thirdly, he cited the Party Secretary-General's pledge of 'Heart to heart peaceful co-existence forever' with the minor parties. And finally, Chairman Zhou sharply suggested that the existence of such minor parties in mainland China has an important meaning for the government in Taiwan. The nation must some day be unified as one. The minor parties presently worked hard on that issue: they have friends in Taiwan from the days before 1949.

Our interview shifted to the rule of law and Chinese legal or judicial independence. I respect his experience of leadership in thirty-five years at Nanhai. As a top leader at the county level, he was able to stay closest to the basic rural social hierarchy where 90 or 95 per cent of the people live and die. The other 5 or 10 per cent of the Chinese citizens and leaders remain in 'the ivory tower of big cities'. They have less practical experience or knowledge about the majority of the people who have suffered more and were condemned to poor rural areas and small cities. As a result, his definition of democracy in practice and understanding of rural people and their immediate government is of great importance to me. His definitive responses to my questions on the 'rule of law' and 'judicial independence' are very original and of practical use for my further contemplation. His reasoned answers are summarised as follows:

1. 'The rule of law must be under strong leadership of the communist party'. Judicial independence requires party direction or institution. A judge's work can be independent: but he must be 'under the communist party, not superior to the party'.
2. 'Rights, democracy and ideology are mutually related.' There is 'no need to emphasise democracy', 'no need to stress ideology'. 'Emphasis either way is wrong.' He declared 'talking about democracy without food in the stomach and talking about ideology without food in the stomach are both meaningless'. Economics must have the first priority. After only a few years of the current reform, we have already eliminated the rationing coupons for food and clothing. People who talk like young Wei Jingseng and Wang Xiche, are ahead of their time. It seemed to me that his stand is relative only to economic changes. Chairman Zhou is an economic determinist.
3. Chairman Zhou very sharply emphasised that the good and common people in China 'cherish, first of all, peace and stability'.

They have suffered too much from revolution to revolution, from class struggle to class struggle in the 1950s and again in the 1960s. Finally, they were 'rescued by Deng's peaceful reform to improve their economic conditions'.

Toward the end of our interview, I simply wanted to hear from him 'what will the majority of people want in the next ten or fifteen years?' Chairman Zhou's answer emphasised familiar issues. However, he claimed to speak from the common people's point of view. 'Energy supply, transportation and education are important to the average person in China, today and in the next fifteen years.' 'People do not have energy to cook food in the kitchen.' Coal, wood and electricity are in very short supply for daily use by the people. He cited popular complaints: 'Under the Kuomintang government before 1949 we had fuel but no rice to cook; under the communist government since 1949 we had rice but no fuel to cook.' He explained that, during the cultural revolution, the 'rebel slogan was to open up the mountains to make rice field because rice production was the key policy'. Since Deng, the key policy emphasis is to close the mountains to make forest because reafforestation is indispensable for energy and raw material supply.' On education, he said 92 per cent of Nanhai's primary school-age children are in school today. The county is rushing to build more schools for students of junior high school which is now compulsory. Senior high school education, polytechnic occupational education and university opportunities are extremely limited everywhere, especially in remote and border regions of the country. Nanhai is one of the best places for educational opportunities. A grave crisis, however, has been 'teacher shortage everywhere'. During the cultural revolution, Mao simply closed schools at all levels for many years. Nanhai county is rich. It has been able to build thirty-three new junior high schools. The entrance examinations for senior high school and university are too difficult to pass. No more than a dozen or so lucky candidates out of one hundred are admitted into good universities and colleges. The other top 20 per cent find other post-high school training opportunities for jobs. The rest are wasted annually. Qualified professors are also in short supply everywhere. The people today are fond of comparing educational opportunities before and after 1949. He said, that before 1949 'there were books and schools, but parents did not have the money; now parents have the money but there are no books and no schools'. Nanhai county has only four senior high schools for 33 per cent of the senior school age. One of the crisis solutions has been to request universities at the provincial city, Guangdong, to accept some Nanhai students for whom Nanhai will pay the university the entire expenses of each student. Nanhai has also created its own television university and has hired professors to come to Nanhai county at specific times to meet with students on their questions and other difficulties at the county television centre classrooms, student dormitory and other university facilities. Because of Nanhai's advanced economic prosperity, the county must train its own varied human resource supplies. For example, Nanhai has even one specialised training school for foreign languages. The adult education campaign is a nationwide movement. Nanhai, too, takes care of its adult victims of the cultural revolution period when all levels of schools were closed. Chairman Zhou himself is spending three days per month attending classes offered by professors of Chongshan University in Guangdong.

In conclusion, I must remind the reader that Nanhai's experience is unique, because it is one of the best developed counties in the entire nation. It is wealthy, conveniently located for foreign trade and transportation, and is close to the big city of Guangzhou. Nanhai possesses a good background in education, light industry development, and has better climate for a longer growing season per year. Above all, Nanhai has its own brethren living abroad who are making investments in their home county and are engaged in its foreign trade. The rosy picture in Nanhai must not be applied to other counties in other regions, and even in other counties of Guangdong Province. The most significant discovery in my interview was how the Nanhai county leadership fought to promote reform for a higher standard of living for the people who were themselves still afraid of becoming rich. They feared future class struggle. My second discovery was that all the documents I read, in addition to this interview, demonstrated a high degree of knowledge on the part of the county political leadership concerning current government policies in all major fields of national affairs. My third surprise was that Chairman Zhou himself could so easily adapt to all new policy and political circumstances at the national level. He was very well adjusted, softly spoken, mild mannered, and with a strong sense of pride in his and the county's achievements in the last six years under Deng's leadership. He rejected many offers of merited promotion for health reasons and, I suspect, of his love for Nanhai. Coming from North Jiangsu in 1949, he has become completely identified with Nanhai's recent past and its foreseeable future. And finally, besides the differences in levels of wealth between Nanhai and China's other 2800 counties, Nanhai reflects common national problems and the critical need for capable leadership dedicated to making satisfactory economic progress, if not the miracles that this particular county has achieved in the last six years since Deng's reform began in 1979.

5.4 CONCLUSION

China's economic future and urban prosperity very much depends on how solid rural diversities and development will be, but the prospect is good. The present economy has come a long way through difficulties.[25] In general, the village level economy in various places still retains some collectively centred features. Such weak collectivity in ownership consists of specialised production, individual or household contracts, with or without equal income for participating households as mutually determined by the contractual terms. Often, formal policy adaptation in rural China has lagged way behind changes that have occurred. This phenomenon was confusing in rural China during 1983, when change was still experimental in rural policy.[26] Local government since reorganisation has recently (1983–4) replaced the commune structure. This government reorganisation finally has eradicated all the vestiges of the commune in economic experiment. Production team and brigade as economic accounting units have now been replaced by village committees.[27] New rural production incentive and income diversities are both encouraged and easily adaptable as new experiments. Xian level government (county government in the USA) will slowly become the transmission belt between rural and urban economic relations. If the central government can develop a much improved nationwide transportation system of rail, highway and waterway to link rural regions together, China may be able to avoid the adverse impact of economic urbanisation which has occurred in many non-Western countries. If so, the slum cities of the developing countries may not come into existence in China.[28] Rural enterprise at the town level may become the most promising new experiment in China's free marketing economy. A large portion of government revenue may depend on its development. Rural products do not rely heavily on government's policy for marketing success. The people will gain or lose on their own accountability. Such town-level enterprises depend essentially on local surplus cheap labour, village-level capital accumulation, and the indigenous raw material supply. In some distant future, China may have to introduce economic special zones in the interior hinterland of the far west where underground resources are more available and technological transfer is most needed to catch up in development with the coastal regions. Recent economic policy seems to suggest 'all get rich at the same time rather some now and others later'.[29] It is clear that a middle course socialism in Chinese economic management and its profit distribution is a departure from the Soviet economic model but not an unqualified acceptance of the capitalist profit model. The retention of land ownership for example, means little when the land contract itself now allows fifteen or fifty years in duration. We may be able to witness another policy change in rural land ownership. Land recollectivisation may precede mechanisation in farming as the next rationale for policy change. As rural economic policy continues to be experimental in nature, other problems of economic considerations will add new pressures to the government's rural decision making. One China expert on the rural economy has put it this way:[30] 'There are other major areas of concern which tend to enhance the government's policy dilemma. Water conservation works represent a crucial one ... The lifeline of agriculture is by no means firmly secured.'

The Chinese people in rural areas and the hinterland seem to be the best resources for the nation's economic development. If for no other reason their motivation to work for a profit, their self-discipline and industriousness can be easily counted on to move the nation forward. The real concern may simply be whether or not bad central planning and bureaucratic bungling can be avoided. For example, lately the nation finds itself short of vegetable and meat supply. In early 1988 meat rationing is being instituted in several urban areas. Shortages are caused by lack of government support in meat price. Larger profits are possible by abandoning farming and devoting them to non-farming trade and sideline productions.

6 Urban Economic Reform and the Case of Shenzhen

Chinese revolutionary leaders from 1911 to 1949 of both the Nationalist and the Communist persuasions have indeed wanted to build a modern and powerful industrial state in East Asia. The Japanese modernisation success provided the inspiration and the United States provided the ideal of democracy for Sun Yat-Sen on the one hand; on the other, the Bolshevik victory in Russia in 1917 offered a new revolutionary alternative to Mao Zedong and his idealistic predecessors. Both Sun and Mao not only once cooperated but also agreed to make China strong enough to be treated with equality in the international community. Sun did not know the Western nations were not prepared to aid him and circumstances forced him to accept assistance from Lenin in 1923. Mao Zedong, likewise, failed to realise until 1960 that Stalin was not prepared to help China become a strong partner. A new Sino-Soviet conflict eventually compelled him to be reconciled with the United States in the 1970s. All of these twists of history help illustrate clearly one of the many genuine Chinese expectations, to build China into a strong industrial state capable of self-defence and a higher living standard. The May 4th movement in 1919 further demonstrated how young intellectuals were devoted to the same purpose through democracy and science.

Sun proposed an 'industrialisation plan' which suggested the use of Western capital and technology to convert China into an industrial state. Deng Xiaoping today is doing almost exactly what Sun wrote about some seventy years ago. Only Deng calls it four modernisations – in defence, science and technology, industry, and agriculture. Urban industrial development was also the central emphasis of Mao's revolution in order to speed up progress so as to catch up with Britain and Japan. However, Mao again failed miserably. It has been Deng's task to revise Mao's timetable to achieve the success of modernisation by the end of this century to give the nation a 'Socialist Economy with Chinese Characteristics'. Deng has seen in his lifetime the failures of Sun and Mao who both idealistically insisted in following either the US or the Soviet model. Deng, on the other hand, wants to experiment in China his own way. His strategy of success follows two basic paths: enliven the economy at home and keep the nation open to the outside world.

161

6.1   INTRODUCTION: MAO'S ECONOMIC FAILURE AND DENG'S INNOVATION

When Taiwan and Hong Kong economically prospered, and while Mao's China in 1970s was suffering from economic decline, reform became really a matter of survival of Marxism and the Communist Party in China. Intellectuals and youth were faced with a crisis of confidence in Marxism and the party. Deng in the 1970s had to restore and reform from the basis of a new crisis for the party's survival as he had done in 1961–3. In three years, reform in rural China had succeeded and the experiment for urban economic reform was underway in 1984. Confidence slowly returned. Living conditions were so improved that Deng was ready to launch a greater urban economic reform plan.

The Soviet economic model had to give way. It did not provide work incentives in China: Chinese people work hard only when working for themselves. Mao's policy after the First Five-Year Plan (1952–6) further disrupted the normal inefficiency of the Soviet model. He made his worst mistake in communising land in the late 1950s against the advice of the party and his Defence Minister, Peng Dehuai, who begged him to discontinue the communes. A short-term policy revision soon followed to restore the economy between 1961 and 1963. When Mao became restless again three years later, he launched a new revolution to replace his loyal followers, and to further radicalise the economic and political system during the next decade, 1966–76. He did not trust anyone except Lin Biao, his wife Jiang Qing and a few others. He put up Dachai as the rural production model and Daching as the urban production model. Both models survived only two years under his hand-picked Premier Hua, who had his own 'little leap forward' during 1976–8 which also failed. The nation was eager for a new economic model, and peasants themselves began to dismantle the commune system. Hua soon lost the majority support in the Political Bureau of the Party and by 1978 was on his way out as Mao's successor.

Deng's urban economic reform followed his success in rural reform. He had allowed a larger plot of land to each farmer, encouraged more sideline private production, permitted rural free marketing, improved individual income, and enlivened light industrial growth throughout rural China. Deng made rural economic revitalisation the cornerstone of urban industrial development.[1] After several years of new policy in economic readjustment, restructuring, consolidation and improvement, China seems to have blazed a new trail in socialist development.

Although full of theoretical contradictions within Marxist ideology, what Deng has done is what the Chinese people want as an alternative to Mao's failure in improving the people's living standards.

Deng launched his new urban economic reform because it was the main public sector of the economy. Forty thousand major enterprises under public ownership did not function effectively. The Party's strong interfering hand in factory production, rigid administrative domination, and lack of purpose in enterprise initiative for production in the past thirty years had destroyed the real economic opportunities for growth at a satisfactory pace. Deng's four modernisations would be in serious jeopardy unless the urban economy was enlivened. Maximum efficiency of enterprise production, individual enthusiasm for his work, correct leadership in management, enterprise responsibility for planning in production, in the marketing of goods, and the desire for better income for all were all in need of drastic reform for new economic growth. Under Mao 'politics took command'; under Deng 'economics takes command'. Under Mao the 'red expert' planned the micro-details for economic progress. Under Deng the 'economic expert' is allowed to exercise greater leadership. After several years of unpublicised enterprise reform experiments, the government declared in October 1984, its grand scheme of urban economic reform to be carried out in three years.[2]

Growth and expansion in industrialisation is the key to the transformation of the economy. Western technology and science, capital investment, and management skill are part of China's strategic need. This is why one of Deng's long-term policies is to keep China open to the outside world. Chinese import and export will play a major part in the economy in the decades to come. The Special Economic Zones in the coastal areas will be the middle ground to bind China to the rest of the world. Among the Four Special Economic Zones, Shenzhen is of greatest importance for a variety of factors. First of all, Shenzhen is near Hong Kong which is a part of the free world economy and will be a part of China in 1997. Secondly, together with Zhuhai, Macao, and Hong Kong, Shenzhen will play a major role in the economic and technological development of the great Pearl River Delta scheduled for rapid industrialisation when the oil of the South China Sea is further explored and refined. Schenzhen development represents a Chinese multi-purpose innovative regional experiment which will enjoy the easiest access to the outside world by air and by sea, while at the same time acting as a transmission belt for technology in the development of China's hinterland.

6.2 THIRTY YEARS OF UNSTABLE POLITICAL ECONOMY IN CHINA

In the socialist state, politics and economics are much more combined into an integrated whole. Politics and policy from the political arena dominate the economic development not through the science of economics but through the dogma of Karl Marx, Engels and Lenin. Records show that all communist states are doing poorly in terms of economic growth as compared with non-communist states. Political economy in the communist world has an entirely different emphasis, such as the theory of class exploitation. Thus the operational, organisational and structural aspects of the economy are sacrificed to the ideological pre-eminence. As a result, political rulers remain powerful as decision makers and the citizens are powerless victims without opportunities to take initiatives to maximise their own private income potential. Thus, the Soviet economic model has failed in Russia, East Europe, North Korea and in a few other socialist states as well. In the capitalist countries, greater productivity does bring about a greater enjoyment of material life by all citizens who have a far higher standard of living than citizens in most of the socialist states. Politicians, and policy makers in capitalist states are much less able to dominate production and competition among the common citizens, who are also able to reduce economic inequalities. China has learned about economic wastefulness and the disadvantages of the Soviet model of socialism. It has learned also from its Russian big brother the painful experience of Soviet economic aid cut off in 1960 and the withdrawal of the 1000 technicians, aid materials and project blueprints. In short, as a loyal socialist member in the Soviet orbit, China paid dearly since 1949, especially in its sacrifices during the Korean War years. Chinese leaders found, to their surprise, the Soviet leadership never intended to treat China either as an equal partner or with trust and confidence. This fact led to mutual distrust between the two nations in the late 1950s and was a critical factor in Mao's radical economic policy. Mao was a restless leader, eager for quick results. Moderate and more rational colleagues failed to restrain him from his radical leftist policies because they, too, were shocked by their treatment at the Soviet hands, whether under Stalin or Khrushchev. These reasons were part of the basic background in China's thirty years of instability in both politics and economics. The painful experience resulted in her backwardness, following Taiwan, South Korea, Hong Kong, Malaysia and Singapore in economic development.

Deng had to reform the economic system, but this could not be done without some fundamental reorientation, first of all in the political system and its new relation with economic development. For a better perspective, it is worthwhile summarising the past thirty years of political and economic instability. This sequence of instability and changes can be divided into stages as follows: a period of rehabilitation, 1949–52; efficient growth with popular support, 1953–6; Mao's economic disaster, 1958–61, corrective adjustment, 1961–6; political chaos and economic decline, 1966–76; failure of Hua's 'little leap forward', 1976–8; and Deng's readjustment and reform, 1979—present. During all these years, the emphasis was on urban economic development or reform in order to build rapidly a modern industrial state. The facts in the following pages will best illustrate the past instability and failure as well as significant achievements made in some areas under the communist regime.

In 1949 the communists inherited a bankrupt economy which did not have a large segment of modern industry. According to Beijing's statistics, production of grain (−25 per cent), cotton (48 per cent), and peanuts (−60 per cent), for example, were all way below the production level of 1937 by substantial percentages. China's production of steel, electricity and coal were below one or two percentage points of the world's total in 1949.[3] Upon achieving power, the communist government confiscated all segments of modern industries owned by former government officials and foreigners. All enterprises handed in their revenues to the government for unified control of expenditure. The state became responsible for allocating grain, cotton and all industrial equipment. Such complete control reduced the need for currency and market exchange. By 1952, restoration following war damage was largely completed, and production of steel and pig iron had greatly increased. Economic transformation accelerated during the four years from 1952. The 'state economy' became the leading economic force. It consisted of enterprises taken over from the Nationalist government and new enterprises created after 1949. The 'cooperative economy' was owned by the working people, and the 'individual economy' owned by the people privately still constituted a freer segment of the economy. These three segments co-existed in the early 1950s. By

1955–6, agriculture was transformed into rural cooperatives and farmers' production mutual aid teams.[4]

The worst crisis occurred in late 1950s when Mao's leftist mistakes damaged the economy gravely. He was not satisfied with the speed of transformation into a socialist economy, because it still included the handicraft industry which counted for nearly 8 million full-time craftsmen and women in 1955, and small businesses of traders and street peddlers who supported nearly three million households in 1956. Between 1952–67, strong emphasis on economic growth was placed in heavy industry at the expense of the standard of living of the people. The rural population suffered most while industrial workers were relatively better off. Grave imbalance was imposed on the people because of concentration on capital accumulation and negligence of daily consumption. Therefore, growth achievements were made in spite of management and leftist mistakes (see Table 6.1).[5]

Table 6.1 Rise in the output of major industrial products, 1952–80

	1980 output	*Increase over 1952*
Cotton yarn	2,930,000 tons	4.5 times
Coal	620,000,000 tons	9.5 times
Electricity	300,600,000,000 kwh	41.0 times
Crude oil	105,950,000 tons	241.0 times
Steel	37,120,000 tons	27.0 times
Machinery	127,000,000,000 yuan in value	54.0 times
Metal-cutting tools	134,000 units	9.8 times

A defence industry was built up from nothing. Many new industries were built in China's hinterland which accounted for 36 per cent of the annual industrial output. In agriculture, large-scale irrigation projects were undertaken to make possible 20 million more hectares of land under irrigation. Flood control measures were undertaken to improve water flow in the Yangtze River, Yellow River, Huaihe, and the Pearl River regions. Grain output by 1980 reached approximately 318 million tons which almost doubled the production figure in 1952. In rural China, the means of production were drastically improved as shown in Table 6.2.[6]

Although the nation's population nearly doubled between 1949 and 1982, China is today able to feed and clothe its people. The progress in education and road construction in rural China must be counted as a major achievement to overcome some physical isolation in the

Table 6.2   Means of production improvement in rural China, 1952–80

	1980	Increase over 1952
Tractors of all sizes	745,000	570 times
Pumping equipment	74,645,000 hp	583 times
Farm trucks	135,000	474 times

countryside and illiteracy among rural people. However, progress would have been far more impressive if China had not gone through the phases of economic disasters and political upheavals. The disproportionate allocation of resources between heavy industry on the one hand, and agriculture and light consumer goods on the other, the blindness in following the Soviet economic organisational model and the ignorance in seeking faster industrial growth were all serious policy mistakes. Several times economic readjustments were made to correct the government's own mistakes, especially during 1961–3, 1976–8, and 1979–81 before the current long-term new policy of readjustment, restructuring, consolidation and improvement during the Sixth Five-Year Plan (1981–5). This economic instability was caused by political instability which itself was caused by the blind following of an alien, inapplicable ideology – Marxism and the Soviet model of economic structure. A great deal of time in the last thirty years was wasted in political campaigns and mass mobilisations. A period of ten years was given to futile ideological battle among Communist Party members and factions during the cultural revolution. Everything suffered setbacks and there was much human sacrifice, educational neglect and economic decline.

Hua Guofeng did not have anything new to offer the nation, although he was eager to correct some of the political and economic mistakes of the previous decade. He did not make any changes at all on the ideological front. On the contrary, he depended on Mao's old prestige and political legacy to govern post-Mao China. He deliberately tried to imitate Mao's personal style of appearance to create his own legitimacy for succession. Hua failed to join hands with the Dengist reformers who held very different views regarding Mao's personality cult, leftist ideology and the class struggle. A new round of political instability occurred, therefore, during the policy struggle after Deng's return to power in 1977 until Hua's departure in 1981. Even after Hua's departure, anti-reform conservative senior leaders still remained within the party hierarchy. A retirement system had to be implemented after the party's Twelfth Congress to formally, or legally, separate them from the policy-making function. However, even now they still interfere indirectly in political and economic policies. In short, political compromise and the potential for instability, has always been present since the communist takeover in 1949. Some party leaders, whom Deng has rehabilitated from purge, refuse to relinquish their executive power in the economic sphere. They have been quite reluctant to accept fundamental but peaceful reform in recent years.

The urban economy has been at the core of Deng's reform to enliven the economy at home and to open the country to foreign technology and trade. The early measures of readjustment between 1979 and 1981 can be summarised as follows.

First, a readjustment of the relation between capital accumulation and consumer spending changes has occurred in a number of ways. His policy included the raising of government purchasing prices for grains and other sideline rural products, and the lowering of, or exemption from, taxes for all poor communes. The government paid prices to farmers higher even than the free market prices for grain, cotton and other products to enliven the rural economy. The government buying prices, for example, rose 22.1 per cent in 1979 as compared with the previous year and another 7.1 per cent in 1980. In two years, the government spent 48 billion yuan in higher-price purchasing. Furthermore, farmers are allowed to grow anything they see profitable in order to increase production. On average, a peasant gained 89 yuan in 1979–81. Farmers were encouraged to exercise greater production initiatives. They could do anything they wished after the government's quota purchase has been fulfilled.

With extra income, peasants have begun to build additional housing units, to buy sewing machines, radios, watches, etc. In urban areas, 26 million people found new jobs during 1979–81. Wages and bonuses for industrial workers in 1981 increased by some 25 per cent on the average, from 614 yuan in 1978 to 772 yuan in 1981. Like that of rural areas, more housing construction took place in 1979–81, from 30 million square metres per year previously to 220 million square metres of housing for the three-year period. National income distribution between capital accumulation and consumption is shown for a four year comparison as follows in Table 6.3[7]

In socialist countries, the living standard is controlled by govern-

Table 6.3   Accumulation vs consumption
in national income distribution, 1978–81
(percentages in 1981 prices)

Year	Accumulation	Consumption
1978	36.5	63.5
1979	34.6	65.4
1980	32.4	67.6
1981	30	70

ment allocation. China after 1949 never placed people above heavy industry and capital construction.

Secondly, a new policy of faster growth of agriculture and light industry has increased and enriched the supply of consumption in rural life. This was a reversal of the practice of the previous thirty years. The implementation measures were: (1) ensuring the policy independence of rural communes, production brigades and teams in their production decisions through a system of contractual obligations and for long-term contract duration; (2) diversification of production specialization and sideline production through encouragement for rural free market commercial exchange; (3) subsidies for rural sideline production through price supports. These policies induced more peasant enthusiasm to produce for their own assured greater income, for example, grain production reached an all time high of over 332 million tons in 1979. Even terrible floods and droughts in both north and south China did not prevent grain production from reaching approximately 318 million tons, in 1980, the second highest since 1949. Gross agricultural output value was augmented by an average of 5.5 per cent in 1979–81. The same high rate of growth was true for cotton, oil-bearing crops, forestry, animal husbandry and fishery. Light industry received in the 1979–81 period larger sums of government loans for expansion. For the first time since 1949, light industry grew faster than heavy industry. Thus, market commodity supplies suddenly increased. Annual retail sales rose by several times in 1979, greater than for any single previous years and more than the entire decade of 1960s. The growth rate of heavy industry was purposely reduced through control of resource allocations. A comparison between light and heavy industry is shown in Table 6.4.[8]

During 1979–80, because policy emphasis was on improving the living condition, tax exemptions and financial subsidies reduced government revenues. Due to practical difficulties involved in reducing capital

Table 6.4   Proportion of light and heavy industry in gross national output value, 1978–81 (in percentages)

Year	Light industry	Heavy industry
1978	42.7	57.3
1979	43.1	56.9
1980	46.9	53.1
1981	51.4	48.6

construction and other government administrative costs, a huge deficit occurred for both 1979 and 1980 for a combined total of nearly 30 billion yuan. This deficit in turn caused inflation and price rises, which were controlled effectively in the following year through budget revision.

Thirdly, greater effort was still needed to readjust the economy beyond 1981 which was not originally expected. A new policy was adopted to continue the readjustment in five more years during the Sixth Five-year Plan (1981–5), and beyond. Drastic economic changes, though policy guidelines and specific steps finally did come in October 1984 when massive urban economic reform measures were announced. The reform thrust called for changes in the following specific areas:[9]

1. Creation of a dynamic socialist economy in China;
2. Invigoration policy as the key to restructure the national economy;
3. Creation of a planning system to foster development of a socialist commodity economy;
4. Reform in price system and utilisation of all economic levers for competition in production and management efficiency;
5. Separation of government from enterprise in the latter's internal decision making and operation through 'enterprise autonomy and internal collective decision making';
6. Institutionalisation of responsibility accountability through wage differentials and salary reward;
7. Development of diverse economic forms in both domestic and foreign economic exchanges;
8. Training of 'a new generation of cadres' and a managerial personnel for the new socialist economy; and
9. Strengthening the party leadership 'to ensure the success of reform'.

The Sixth Five-Year Plan has now been completed (1981–5). The Seventh Five-Year Plan was presented to the party conference in

September, 1985. For future rapid growth, emphasis is given to coordinating the three segments of the economy: public command economy, collective economy owned by the groups, and the individual economy. Creation of a price system and a wage system in relation to enterprise reform, capital accumulation, and consumption is being pushed forward. A faster economic growth is cautiously expected during the Seventh plan, 1986–90. But rapid economic production take-off is confidently expected during 1990s, but even then, living standards in China are not expected to rise beyond a per capita annual average income of $US 1000 by the year 2000. It seems that there is no doubt that China's gross industrial and agricultural output value will be quadrupled over its 1980 level. There seems to be an enormous self-confidence on the part of the Chinese leaders in the 'inherent superiority' of the socialist system and the control of its productive potential. The command sector of the economy, fully subject to national planning, is looked upon as the socialist weapon to prevent the rise of 'economic anarchism' which disrupts the 'un-regulated free enterprises' of the West. This is the Chinese rational and theoretical claim. Of course, the truth is that there is today no such 'anarchist economy' in any of the capitalist states of the West, including Japan.

The most difficult part of the reform seems to be the government's ability to create a workable and efficient economic management institution consisting of good banking, credit system, inflation control, wage and price relations, etc. Will China eventually have a market economy under socialist planning? Or will it remain a socialist economy with a less regulated but insignificant rural consumer-oriented 'free market'? Much depends on the political leadership after Deng and his immediate followers. The Chinese leadership is attempting to combine the virtues of both the socialist and the capitalist economic systems. Can they be combined without contradictions in ideological consistency? Such a combination was predicted by Chen Yun at the Eighth Party Congress in 1956. He said:[10]

> As regards planning, the bulk of the industrial and agricultural output of the country will be produced according to plan; but, at the same time, a certain amount of production will be carried on freely, with the changing conditions of the market as its guide and within the scope prescribed by the state plan ... This kind of market under a socialist economy is in no way a capitalist free market, but a unified socialist market. In the unified socialist market, the state market is the mainstay and attached to it is a free market of certain

proportions under the guidance of the state and supplementing the state market.

It remains to be tested in China's future economy whether Chen Yun's theoretical prescription is possible or not in actual practice. In fact, China tried in 1958 to decentralise a number of centrally operated enterprises and place them under local government management. The practice did not seem to have produced positive results. In short, the Chinese economy before 1979 had revealed similar defects of common socialist practices. These defects relate to whether the central government directly manages certain enterprises or puts them under local control while itself remains in command of unified planning. In the case of Chinese past economic failures more specifically, the defects were: over-centralisation, extreme egalitarianism and bureaucratic inefficiency.

In the current economic reform of the managerial system, the government has been very cautious. It began with limited 'enterprise decision-making autonomy' in 1978 in six enterprises in Sichuan province. The number was increased to 106 in 1979. Eighty-four of them were state-owned enterprises, while the other twenty-two were under direct management of the central government. The general stipulations in those experiments were indicative of the existing strength of control by central directives or planning. An enterprise could not market its products in free market, for example, until it had fulfilled the planned quota first.[11] Profit for the enterprise was possible only after other costs, such as depreciation, was first taken care of. The enterprise was allowed to hire only 'the middle-level leaders without permission from their leading bodies'.

In 1979, some 4000 enterprises took part in some phase of autonomous management experiment. In the following year, over 6600 enterprises were in these experiments. They made up only 16 per cent of some 42,000 large enterprises which were under law required to hand in their annual profit to the government. However, these 6600 enterprises accounted for more than 60 per cent of the industrial output value and 70 per cent of expected profits for the government. So the experiment was a quiet but significant undertaking. The result was obviously a success. For example, the eighty-four Sichuan local enterprises increased their annual output value of 14.9 per cent over the previous year, their profits by 33 per cent of which 24.2 per cent was turned over to the government. However, small enterprises, which did not take part in the experiments, made even larger output value of 25 per cent and 120 per cent profits and turned over to the state 100 per cent more profits. Upon further analysis, in 5422 enterprises which participated in the experiments, decision-making decentralisation did not have a significant impact on production.[12]

Another experiment in enterprise production and profit making was tried in 1980 in Shanghai, Sichuan and Guangxi. This time the experiment was on the introduction of income tax to replace profit to be delivered to the government. The enterprise was made solely responsible for either profits or losses. The State Economic Commission asked every province to select an enterprise to experiment in 1980 with the new tax appproach in place of profits. In total, 191 enterprises throughout the country participated in this experiment. Toward the end of the year, the State Council issued 'ten provisional' regulations to promote and protect socialist competition throughout the nation against local barriers. In short, urban economic reform had five years of quiet experiment throughout the country before its official inauguration in October 1984.

Among recent reform experiments has been the government's effort to recreate an individual economy of craftsmanship, for example. As it may be recalled, the government in 1955 compelled all peddlers, small shop owners and craftsmen to join cooperatives. More that 96 per cent of them did, that is except those in far remote areas of the country. In 1962 there were still 2 million individual handicraft people and traders within the cooperatives. By 1978, only 150,000 were left. However, between 1978 and 1980, under a new policy of rehabilitation and expansion, the number grew to 810,000 in 1980. More jobs and competition will probably develop as the individual economy is encouraged by the state. In short, competition and growth are related closely to the expansion of the free market. The reform policy is using the market mechanism as an auxiliary regulator of the economy which is basically controlled by state planners. Today in China consumer goods through market channels, as opposed to those handled by the government, account for 20 per cent of industrial production and 25 per cent of total retail sales. One-third of total rural produce is being purchased by the government. The prospect appears that more a market-oriented economy in China is most likely. Rural population will revolve around this free sector of the economy.

Proper handling of the relations between government planning and market mechanisms will always be crucial to managerial reform. The free market as a supplementary regulator of the socialist economy has alerted experts to call for 'four different forms of management'. They are :[13]

1. 'Production carried out under mandatory state plans'. This applies to key enterprises and major products which are most vital to the people and the economy. Their output value 'accounts for the greater part of the gross national product, although the types of goods are limited in number'.
2. 'Production based on changes in market demands, but limited to the specified categories in the state plan'. This type of production includes a great variety of small commodities which are made by large number of small enterprises and individual producers, but their total output value constitutes only a small part of the national gross product.
3. '... goods produced largely according to state plan but a small part of them are made by enterprises or individuals on their own'. These are goods close to those of the first category.
4. '... goods made according to changes in the market demand, and only a small part of them made under the state plan'. These goods are close to those in the second category.

Such a managerial and production structure is to integrate state guidance with enterprise initiative. This may be what Deng calls 'Socialism with Chinese Characteristics'. It will clearly be different from the rigid Soviet economic model on the one hand, and unlike the market economy of free capitalism on the other. It will be a planned economy with a market stimulator. Whatever the reform result, planning and reforming in China is a difficult task. With a large population, and uneven economic development in a huge country handicapped by lack of transportation and technology, it is, indeed, a difficult, if not impossible, task to attempt to secure the desired outcome of any intelligent planning exercise. However, the wishes of the people, and their desire to improve their own living standards must be considered the best guides to planners; they can no longer be ignored.

In conclusion, political upheavals of the first thirty years under Mao's policy caused economic setbacks. In addition, the lack of market knowledge on economic competition and its proper growth aggravated political and policy debate between Mao – who wanted faster growth, especially in heavy industry, at the expense of raising living standards – and the moderates, who failed to resist Mao's economic policy. The people paid a heavy price for the mistakes of the communist party leadership in the economic area, especially in the

Table 6.5   Composition of national income in 1966
and 1976 (%)

	1966	*1976*
Total national income:	100	100
Industry	38.2	43.3
Agriculture	43.6	41.0
Building	3.7	4.9
Transport	4.2	3.8
Commerce	10.3	7.0
Proportion in net industrial output values:		
Light industry	47.2	40.4
Heavy industry	52.8	59.6

imbalance of economic growth and national income comparison during the cultural revolution (see Table 6.5).[14]

Such an officially imposed imbalance in national income composition naturally created general distress over per capita real income for each citizen. The management of the economy simply violated the natural forces of supply and demand and the experience of growth success of the non-communist countries, and thus created unnecessary economic problems. People can suffer for a while in the interest of their nation; they can not forever make sacrifice after sacrifice for unnecessary revolutionary radicalism and egalitarian utopianism. Deng tried to correct the situation in 1974 – 6. He was soon dismissed by Mao for political reasons in 1976. After Mao's death Premier Hua tried to correct some of Mao's mistakes. But he made other grave mistakes of his own, because he, in fact, did not have a new economic and political orientation different from Mao's erroneous economic approach and political dictatorship. The need for economic adjustment and reform during 1977 and 1978 was inevitably delayed for the outcome of the leadership conflict between Hua and Deng in early 1980s. Thus, it is only fair to conclude that political instability and economic disasters from the 1950s to the 1970s were aggravated by repetitious conflicts between politics and economics caused by contradictions in Mao's own thinking.

From December 1978 to the present, Deng's economic reform emphasised the following: increase in people's living standards, greater rural freedom of production and profit making, increase in light industry over heavy industry, reforms in the price and wage system, and the importation of foreign technology and capital investment. In short, Deng's reform has been to continue to enliven domestic economic development and to bring China into closer contact with the rest of the world. Shenzhen and other economic special zones are the transmission belts in China's economic development through foreign investment, technology, and world trade. China has become an integrative experimenting model of both socialism and capitalism, with practical emphasis on Chinese indigenous characteristics.

6.3 THE CASE OF SHENZHEN AS A CAPITAL-TECHNOLOGY TRANSMISSION BELT IN CHINESE ECONOMIC ENLIVENMENT

In January, 1984, Deng Xiaoping and his entourage came to Shenzhen Special Economic Zone for an inspection, or study tour, in order to assess policy decisions for its future. Some members on this tour have been known to be very critical of this non-socialist experiment. Rumours had it that many anti-Shenzhen senior leaders and generals had come to Shenzhen before and wept on sight. They felt Mao's cause for socialist revolution had been eliminated totally in Shenzhen. Special Economic Zones are 'dangerous signals' against socialist revolution for the rest of the country. If such a sentiment was and still is that strong for some leaders, it is easy to realise how significant was Deng's tour in his later economic policy decision. At the end of his inspection on 26 January Deng wrote a one sentence souvenir statement: 'Shenzhen's development and experience has proved our policy is correct in the creation of such economic special zones.' How relevant his tour was to the 20 October 1984 party decision on urban economic reform will be for researchers to discover. In the short-run, his tour convinced him and other 'doubtful colleagues' to end their dialogue over Shenzhen itself.

Whether Shenzhen signals a conversion from socialism to capitalism will be speculated about later. My interview-study tour of Shenzhen in July 1985, made many things clear to me as far as this particular experiment is concerned. I shall first of all introduce certain relevant information about the experiment. Discussion will take place on laws and regulations concerning foreign capital and technology to be attracted to Shenzhen and their profit-making. There are a number of serious questions I raised in my interviews with many individuals especially those with the vice president of Shenzhen University, Fang Sheng, who is an economist and has travelled abroad, and has answered many similar questions I raised during the interview.

6.4   INTRODUCTION TO THE SHENZHEN EXPERIMENT

In their interest for international economic cooperation and technological exchange to advance socialist modernisation in China, the Standing committee of the National People's Congress, in 1981, formally declared Shenzhen, Chuhai, Shantou and Xiamen as four Special Economic Development Zones. Shenzhen is the largest of the four. It emphasises industrial development, commerce, agriculture and tourism. The Shenzhen Special Economic Zone (SSEZ) is part of Shenzhen Municipality along the sea coast and is closest to Hong Kong. It is 327.5 square kilometres in size and is already one of China's largest import-export centres. Whatever Hong Kong represents as a present and future economic advantage for China, Shenzhen is the direct transit port of such advantage. After 1997, Shenzhen and Hong Kong will easily produce joint prosperity because Shenzhen can bring all the available Chinese resources to assure its future expansion and act as a hinterland for Hong Kong. In the long distant future Hong Kong and Shenzhen may simply become one single commercial-industrial centre for southeastern China. According to its current development blueprint, it will have a population of 400,000 (250,000 as of 1985) by 1990, and 800,000 in the year 2000. Since 1981 Shenzhen has developed faster than expected. It is now the best known foreign investment centre in China. As one rides through Shenzhen, one is easily overwhelmed by the number of high-rise buildings under construction compared with other buldings already in use by commerce, industry and as tourist hotels. There seem to be more buildings under construction than those already in use. Construction workers have come from all parts of China besides those from Guangdong province. They have come through competition to claim their share of the profit in Shenzhen's rapid development. So are the many commercial firms here representing all other twenty-eight provinces and municipalities in China. It looks like an emerging twin-city of Hong Kong or its suburb, only more sparsely occupied in population density. Of its 327.5 square kilometres only 17.4 are under use. Some 350 square kilometres are still in the suburbs as future reserved land for development. Land development in Shenzhen began in 1979 and had cost an amount of $US 824 million by 1983. In the Shekou industrial area of Shenzhen, transportation, electricity supply, water system, postal and telecommunications have been more fully completed (the industrial sector of Shekou is only 1.3 square kilometres). A larger area of 20 square kilometres, in addition to the presently used 17.4 square kilometres, is being rapidly developed as the site of a future industrial-commercial complex. Chinese industrial and construction workers in Shenzhen's development today are the best prepared or trained human resources. The city of Shenzhen (which is adjacent to the Shenzhen economic zone) itself has a working force of 100,000. The other 100,000 selected workers came from other parts of the country. These 200,000 construction people have generally completed their high school education. In addition, they now receive on-the-job training for occupational specialisation provided by various factories themselves. For technologically advanced future development in human resources, the central government in Beijing approved in 1982 the establishment of Shenzhen University which is totally financed by Shenzhen itself, and is providing students with a Western curriculum in content and in depth (of which more will be said later). The university promotes basic research in Shenzhen's future technological development. Another major undertaking is the construction of a nuclear power station to supply a fully expected future industrial-commercial use.

Both the land and the water transportation systems between Shenzhen and the rest of the country, and the world at large, are being improved. The special zone will be fully linked with the national network of railroads and highways. Future harbour development for world trade and for Nanhai oil exploration is also under way. Presently 3000-tonnage ships are navigating between Hong Kong and Shekou. Future harbours are planned to handle 10,000 and 100,000 tonnage of ships for an annual total weight of 20 million tonnage of business. This will be especially useful to oil refining for crude oil from the South China sea. The Shenzhen Navigation Company is presently in charge of water transport with most major cities reachable by water in heavy tonnage.

It has been just four years since the experiments began in 1981. Shenzhen has become an attractive centre to people of many interests: tourists, merchants, industrialists, academic experts, China specialists and economists in particular. They have come to Shenzhen from all over the world to learn about recent Chinese economic development through the example of Shenzhen. For example, for economic investment reasons, many foreign banks from Japan, North America, Europe, Hong Kong and Southeast Asia have recently opened branch offices there.

Presently, there are eleven different legal codes and regulations that govern the economic activities in Shenzhen. Other laws are being proposed to deal with growing complexities. On the whole foreign investors or Chinese from abroad can make greater profits here and enjoy more extra privileges than elsewhere. In enterprise management, foreign investors can operate independently, or enter joint ventures with Chinese enterprises. They can invite in foreign workers, overseas Chinese, or Chinese experts from Hong Kong as technology or management advisers. If Chinese workers are preferred, the Shenzhen Worker's Bureau may take charge of the recruitment. Every enterprise can recruit independently and so select the best workers through specific tests administered to job-seekers. After that both sides can negotiate a wage contract. Violations by Chinese workers of the contract may result in either a warning, mild penalty, wage reduction or dismissal. According to the nature of the enterprise, wages may be determined by day, hour or work-piece accomplished.

Free of import duties, an enterprise may import equipment for production, repair or replacement parts, raw material, transport equipment and other production material. Other daily useful articles may also be duty-free, or as determined by contract except whisky and cigarettes, at half of the lowest such duty charge. Products or semi-products made in Shenzhen are duty free for export purposes. Income tax on enterprise is 15 per cent. However, on investment amounts larger than $US5 million, or involved in the advanced stage of new technology, or investment of long-term duration, there is a tax reduction of between 25 to 50 per cent, or even total tax exemption for from one to three years. Foreign investors' profit may be exempted from profit tax entirely, or else reduced, if such profits are reinvested in Shenzhen for a new period of more that five years.

On investors' land use, the Special Zone Authority can satisfy diverse land uses on a variety of stipulations as follows: industrial use for thirty years, commercial and residential for fifty years, school-medical for fifty years, tourist for thirty years, and agricultural-dairy for twenty years. After the completion of a contracted period, new contractural extensions are possible. Rates of charge on land use vary according to types of usage, area of location and duration of contract per square metre per year. These rates are currently as follows (in Chinese yuan, ($US1=2.7): industrial, ten to thirty years; commercial and residential, thirty to sixty years; tourist, sixty to one hundred years, and agricultural-dairy subject to contract negotiation. Those enterprises having entered contracts on land use prior to 1985 have built into their contracts a reduction of fee in land use by a percentage rate of 30 to 50 because of previous inadequate development in land quality or incompleteness in land development itself. Those enterprises having undeveloped land, or slope, hills, or swamp areas, may receive a fee reduction between one to five years at the initial stage. However, the land usage fee is subject to readjustment every three years to future users. Such fee readjustment each time will not be more than 30 per cent of the existing amount. For investment in the fields of education, cultural affairs, science-technology, medicine-health and other social welfare, fees for land use will be substantially reduced. Any investment in the most advanced technology and in non-profit-making fields will pay no fees for land use.

On the control of foreign exchange, all foreign enterprises must open their accounts with the Bank of China in the special zone or with such other foreign banks as are approved and certified to do business by the Chinese authorities. Foreign investors and businessmen, workers or Chinese from Hong Kong and Macao may remit their properly earned profits after having paid their income taxes. Such remittances must be handled by the Bank of China or such other designated foreign banks in the special zone. Foreign enterprises seeking terminations of their business before normal expiration of the contracted period may transfer their capital to other companies, or remit it abroad after having applied for termination as regulated after they have paid all financial debts.

On sales of products manufactured in the special zone, Chinese law requires that such products be exported unless otherwise entered into the contract in advance. If such manufactured articles are those which China imports, they are permitted to enter the Chinese domestic market on a fixed ratio as determined by domestic demands. On the whole, in any dispute or misunderstanding arising from the contract in a joint venture between the guest investor and the Chinese investor, both sides may negotiate for solution on the basis of equality and mutual benefit. After failing to do so, such disputes may then be submitted to the Chinese arbitration authority for mediation and arbitration. And finally, for the convenience of entry to and exit from Shenzhen Special zone by all foreign investors and those having residence in Shenzhen as merchants or alien residents, the Shenzhen authority provides them with special permits issued by Shenzhen Special Economic Zone

Development Company, or other permits with multiple-entry and multiple-exit privileges upon application by the foreign users.

In short, because of these privileges and protections as granted by the Chinese authority, foreign investment is increasing rapidly. Those making approaches for information or contract negotiation are from various parts of the world, including the United States, Britain, Japan, France, West Germany, Norway, Sweden, Ireland, Australia, the Philippines, Singapore, Hong Kong and Macao. The early contacts came from small companies. Many of them today represent large corporations, from big financial combines, and multinational corporations. Early enterprises were generally interested in assembly work of imported parts by Chinese labourers. Today, joint ventures in investment or independent foreign investment have undertaken diversified production of heavy articles. The amount involved in investment companies producing a single article has varied from a few thousands in Hong Kong dollars to thousands of millions. During the first two and half years ending in June 1983, contracts with guest investors reached 2300 in number and the total amount reached 1200 million in Hong Kong dollars. Many of them have already gained big profits from some 120 kinds of products. US Coca Cola exports from Shenzhen to Hong Kong and Southeast Asia are today responsible for a considerable profit. Joint ventures between China and foreign investors in agriculture (e.g. chicken and pig breeding) is so successful that supply cannot meet demand at the present. In short, investment in Shenzhen seems to have few or no problems attached. Profit-making is inevitable because the Chinese want this experiment to be a success. They will be able to regulate the development for mutual benefits as the Chinese government may see fit from time to time as provided by law.

One of the Chinese companies in Shezhan provides varied services to foreign investors. It is a multi-purpose enterprise itself and the largest in the zone. This firm is the Shenzhen Economic Zone Development Company. It undertakes the task of attracting foreign investments and Chinese enterprises to the zone. Its specific functions include: negotiations for foreign investment, cooperation among domestic enterprises, foreign-Chinese joint ventures in investment or foreign independent enterprise in developing land use, expansion of industry and commerce, building, transportation and tourism, management of real estate, collection of land use fees, and promotion of exports. Even before the end of 1983 this company had helped negotiate and sign some sixty-six major foreign contracts for a total investment of 9200 million Hong Kong dollars. The company itself has been divided into thirty-three specialised branches to pursue their separate division of labour. It will likely sub-divide into more functional specialisations according to future demands, as Mr Chen told me during my interview with him on 14 July 1985. For example, some of its branch companies are doing the following: (1) to manage real-estate services together with guest investors to build 100 or more offices or residential buildings of no less than eighteen stories high and several hundreds of luxurious villas; (2) to develop and manage Wen Jin Du Industrial district and Houhai Bay New District's cultural and residential area and to prepare to create an Asian university in this new district; (3) to improve and develop into a new commercial and tourist city, the old city of Huacheng with Chinese cultural-national characteristics; (4) to develop and manage Futian New Town of thirty square kilometres in size; (5) to develop a cement enterprise through a joint venture with Japanese investors to reach 200,000 tons of annual production in cement; (6) to develop and manage Honey Lake Holiday Resort; (7) to develop a science and technology exchange centre, and (8) such other developments for a total of some thirty-three projects under thirty-three subsidiary companies of Shenzhen Special Economic Zone Development Company.[15] In short, this special zone development company is the official vehicle for both the Guangdong Provincial Government and the Beijing Government for devising, developing and coordinating many services in competition with other non-official companies. The creation of some thirty-three subsidiary companies is clearly for the purpose of avoiding a mushrooming growth of the head company bureaucracy. As subunits, each branch company is competitively responsible for its own separate finance and accountability. Many of the Beijing Government policy guidelines are transmitted directly or indirectly through the head office of this giant semi-independent company. The company itself is producing many advance technology-intensive articles, such as orbital satellite ground television reception equipment and micro-computers. Together with the expansion of South China Sea oil exploration, Shenzhen is becoming one of the future oil refining and distributing centres. Petrochemical industrial development will be another potential area for development. At present, to invest in Shenzhen requires following certain steps in contract negotiation as follows: (1) all prospective foreign investors must contact and discuss with the foreign investment negotiation department or its branch offices in Hong Kong or the Hong Kong office of Shekou Industrial Zone. Prospective foreign investors must submit the application forms and an investment proposal indicating its purpose, list of products, amount of capital, land to be used, methods of investment (independent, joint or cooperative in nature), justification for investment success and a list of needs to be provided by the Chinese side; (2) prospective guest investors will receive a reply on whether the proposal is acceptable. If acceptable, there is an accompanying invitation for further discussion; (3) when agreement on the investment is achieved, the contract will soon be formally signed and delivered to the Shenzhen People's City Government for formal approval before it takes legal effect; (4) when approval is given, both sides then work out a list of articles of equipment to be imported from abroad for submission to the Shenzhen City Government for approval. After that, the investor begins to arrange with the Chinese customs authority for the importation of certain materials (5) before the investment enterprise formally starts, registration with and certificate from the Shenzhen Industrial-Commercial Administrative Commission are required. All the documents of approval, enterprise charter, names of the board of directors and registration certificate copy must be submitted; and finally, (6) such later-stage activities can be performed by the Special Zone Development Company's trade service division on behalf of the foreign investors. The company's trade service division also may act on behalf of the Shenzhen city government on matters of real estate transfer, land development fees, etc.

6.5 CHINA MERCHANTS AND ITS SHEKOU INDUSTRIAL ZONE

At the western end of the Shenzhen special economic zone is a uniquely developed subunit. My visit to the area and interview with its deputy director, Mr Jin-Xing Chen, can be summarised succinctly concerning its specific differences from that of Shenzhen.[16]

The primary initiative for the Shekou Industrial Zone came originally from the China Merchants Steam Navigation Co. Ltd (hereafter CMSN), which was established in 1872. In 1978, more than a hundred years later, it received approval from the Beijing Government to expand and diversify its business development from shipping abroad. As a government-owned corporation headquartered in Hong Kong, it applied for and received in 1979 from the State Council an authority to build the Shekou Industrial Zone (hereafter known as SKIZ). This bold action of both CMSN and the State Council opened up a new chapter in CMSN's history. During the last six busy years, CMSN has brought to SKIZ advanced technology, foreign capital, and management experience from Hong Kong, Macao and foreign states. Shekou is a small industrial port. It has completed its first stage of development. Its total area is 10 square kilometres, of which half is now usable land. SKIZ is administered by CMSN, which has converted a 'desolate beach and barren hills' into a small city-port. As a matter of fact, SKIZ is only one of many subsidiary operations and sub-companies built up in recent years by CMSN which has a total capital amounting to 8 billion Hong Kong dollars. Although it is a government agency under the Ministry of Communication with its board of directors sitting in Beijing, CMSN is operating out of its Hong Kong head office relatively free of any interference from the central government. Its business expertise is far advanced and beyond the government's ability to participate effectively or constructively. In the development of SKIZ, CMSN has been able to bring to Shekou many foreign investors in a variety of fields through its Planning and Development Division. Thus SKIZ's success under CMSN is a source of Chinese pride. This success has brought Deng Xiaoping (1984), Hu Yaobang (1983), Zhao Ziyang (1981) and Yi Jianying (1980) to SKIZ to observe its progress.

In July 1984, the People's Guangdong Provincial Government ratified a plan to establish the Administrative Bureau of Shekou District. Although legally under the Shenzhen People's Government, the Bureau exercises its functions quite autonomously as a local administrative body in charge of SKIZ, Chiwan Bay and Shekou town for a total land area of 14 square kilometres. The Shenzhen People's Government has relinquished a large number of its rights to the Shekou bureau, including those relating to the ratification of investment agreements and contracts, import of materials, application for household registration by aliens and by overseas Chinese, and the right to set up its own public security, tax units and postal services. Under the Administration Committee, SKIZ is governed directly by many subunits as functional service branches. SKIZ also has a Nanhai Oil Service office to act as a liaison organ to provide logistic services for oil exploration in the South China Sea and to 'render consulting service to oil companies and contractors'. Like Shenzhen Special Zone, SKIZ has a large volume of joint ventures and sole foreign investment ventures, or other cooperative enterprises. Forty-five per cent of the joint ventures involve investment of 21 per cent from the

United States, 17 per cent from Thailand, 6 per cent from Japan, 5.4 per cent from West Europe and 4 per cent from Singapore. The categories of investment are as follows:[17] industry 77.5 per cent, real estate and construction 10 per cent, commerce and service 8.2 per cent, tourism 2.2 per cent and communication and transport 1.6 per cent.

SKIZ had a population of 12,000 in 1985 and is projected to reach 100,000 in the year 1990. Its future seems closely related to the development of transport of the Pearl River Delta and South China Sea oil resources. Since 1983, China National Off-shore Oil Corporation has concluded eighteen contracts with foreign oil companies, of which twelve are related to the Shekou basin. The second feature of Shekou is its emphasis on industrial production as opposed to the multiplicity of investments in Shezhen or Chuhai.[18] The third feature about Shekou is the fact that it is developed by a Chinese company without any sharing of authority with other domestic or foreign agencies, unlike the situation in Shezhen. It is quite possible that Shekou will always be more efficient in management and easily adaptable to domestic and international market realities or changes. The economic and managerial resources and experience of CMSN is totally behind the development in Shekou, in competition with other economic zones, which are larger but less efficient.

6.6 SPECIAL ECONOMIC ZONES, EDUCATIONAL REFORM AND THE PROSPECT FOR CAPITALISM

One of the most outstanding features in Shenzhen's development is the newly founded Shenzhen University. It opened on 27 September 1983, when Beijing gave its approval to create experimentally a 'new and comprehensive university'. It is new also in its educational methods, its unique curriculum, and its mission to help develop Shenzhen's future development. Under president Zhang Wei, there are four vice-presidents. I had the privilege to interview Vice-president Fang Sheng who is an economist and has travelled abroad to observe the economic development in several non-socialist states. Incidentally, Vice-president Fang attended National Taiwan University before 1949. When I indicated my former university education in Taiwan, he assumed that I was from his Alma Mater and showed a special intimacy toward me. When I identified myself as not one of his fellow alumni, he quickly stopped talking about how well he was received abroad by graduates of National Taiwan University. He seemed disappointed not to be able to continue a sentimental conversation to express his host friendship to an alumnus from Taiwan. He is a very thoughtful scholar and a profound thinker on the most basic economic issues between socialism and capitalism.

Shenzhen University is situated at Yue Hai Men (Gate of the South China Sea) near the coast of Houhai Bay. It has a 250-acre campus. By the autumn of 1984 the first phase of construction had been completed which consists of a modern classroom building, an experimental factory, several student dormitories and living quarters for the faculty staff. After the completion of the second phase construction, which started at the beginning of 1985, there will be a total of 138,000 square metres of buildings of all kinds in use. To meet the needs of Shenzhen's long-term development, the university offers various practical specialities. Ten academic departments were in operation at the time of my interview: Departments of Chinese Language, Foreign Languages, Economics, Economic Management, Law, Architecture, Electronic Engineering, Applied Mathematics and Physics, Structural and Municipal Engineering and Precision Machinery and Instruments. Other departments are being organised, including Chemistry and Chemical Engineering, Industrial Arts and Crafts, Statistics, Tourism, etc. The university presently is divided into four colleges which are: Arts, Law, Natural Sciences, Engineering and Economic Management. Students are trained with practical knowledge and ability to solve problems under varied conditions. Computer and foreign languages are especially emphasised. All students must spend five years for a bachelor of arts degree. There are only about 1000 full-time students at the present and some 300 cadres attending various special courses. Some 400 adults are studying on a part-time basis. In the last two years, the university offered to 5000 people a variety of short-course training classes. Graduates are likely to work in the coastal provinces of Guangdong, Fujian, Chejiang, Jiangsu, and three metropolitan regions of Beijing, Shanghai and Tianjin because they have been recruited from these areas. Only Shenzhen students are admitted as part-time students for short courses.

Unlike other universities in China, Shenzhen University follows a Western credit system to allow students the latitude to select their courses in non-required areas. They can graduate early or late. Less capable students can thus stay on and study longer for their degrees. They can also change their major or minor fields. Some 40 per cent of students receive scholarships. Student loans are also available for those from poor family backgrounds. All graduates will work in Shenzhen immediately after graduation. The government does not find jobs for them: upon graduation, they must work in Shenzhen and find positions for themselves before transferring to other locations. This is a new experience in China which is designed to avoid the assignment of graduates to places with no regard for individual preferences as the country has done for the last thirty-five years. Another feature of Shenzhen University is its support for students to take part-time jobs while still in school: 'running shops, restaurants, guest houses or small factories, selling books, magazines and newspapers, operating postal agency, cleaning grounds around the campus, working as assistant in the university's administrative departments and research centers.'[19] The emphasis is on the student's self-management, self-discipline, self-dependence and self-support to face the real world. Eventually the university will grow into a research institution to meet Shenzhen's development needs. There are several research institutes already in existence. They include Institutes of Special Zone Economic Study, classical Chinese Literature, Comparative Literature, Structural Engineering, New Energy Sources, Hong Kong and Taiwan Literature, and Bio-chemical Experiments. The university is already moving toward graduate studies, such as Industrial Management and Special Zone Economy. In short, the university is staffed with an imaginative and creative administrative leadership which is training a new generation of young people capable of meeting new economic growth demands in Shenzhen and other special economic zones and major coastal cities. Fourteen such cities were recently declared open to the outside world for investment, trade and other activities.

As an economist, Vice-president Fang Sheng expressed his various concerns regarding Shenzhen's economic future. In the lead article of the inaugural issue of the *Journal of Shenzhen University*, he said essentially that China's Special Zone economic development is to expand state capital under socialist guidance. It is a 'multi-faceted' economy in nature which allows several sectors to co-exist with the 'state sector playing the leading role and state capitalism enjoying priority'.[20] He also predicted in the same article that 'it is beyond doubt that there will be an ever broadening range of economic relation and collaboration between Shenzhen and Hong Kong. Cooperation will ensure the two areas in continuous economic prosperity, mutual promotion and mutual complementing, and work division'.[21]

In my interview with him, he provided a historical interpretation of China's failure to meet foreign economic challenges since the nineteenth century: 'from self-reliance and self-sufficiency, economic isolation, foreign economic imperialism, and finally, to certain historical limiting conditions since 1949, Chinese handling of foreign relations, in general, has been too narrow-minded until 1979'. For a long time under socialism, China 'had little or no knowledge in handling her economic relation with foreign countries', no experience to appreciate advanced foreign technology and foreign economic management skill. Poverty in China was aggravated further by 'leftist ideology' and thus created a new isolationist policy after 1949. The cultural revolution made the situation worse. Vice-president Fang happily asserted that international economic-technological exchange and mutual dependence in recent decades has been a correct historic trend, according to the Marxist point of view. China should join it and promote the trend further. China's recent economic policy since 1979, has been, in fact, a real awakening to this trend. This new lesson is the fundamental reason for China's long-term opening of the nation to the outside world. The special zone is the focus of this intensified opening towards the outside world, with such incentives as tax exemptions, high profit percentage and other favourable concessions in order to bring in foreign technology and management science. Chinese special economic zones are more than an effort to build up a processing industry for exporting goods. The most important point, the Vice-chairman asserted, is to 'open up a window to the outside world – a window of technology, a window of knowledge and a window of management'. The Chinese economic structural experiment in the Special Zone is an experiment to train new people, to extend, if successful, to the rest of the nation this advanced new success. Many new experiments are 'carried out without any prior knowledge'. The main message, from Marxist theoretical point of view, is to override the frozen concept that 'individual economy' is inferior to 'collective economy' and 'collective economy' is inferior to 'an economy owned by the whole nation'. In the special zone all sectors co-exist among enterprises owned by the nation (banks, postal services, etc.), cooperative enterprises, domestic joint ventures, joint Chinese-foreign ventures, enterprises owned wholly by foreigners, and others owned by private individuals. This 'structurally unique' economy is obviously succeeding. All sectors are mutually dependent, mutually influencing and competing, and each is full of vitality. The socialist sector, which includes energy supply, transportation, public utility, and currency management, is controlled by the government. The sector of the joint venture consists of both socialist shares and foreign capitalist shares. So Shenzhen is a 'mixed enterprise' or 'mixed economy'. Many of 'our socialist laws and regulations are applied to capitalist joint ventures. Thus, such Chinese-foreign joint ventures become partially 'a state capitalism'. The wholly foreign-owned enterprises enjoy even more management autonomy in a socialist state. Except taxes and expenses, all the profits belong to the entrepreneurs. However, such wholly foreign-owned autonomous enterprises are being guided, supervised and licensed by a socialist state. In the final analysis, 'without socialistic national capitalism, there cannot be a Special Economic Zone'.

Furthermore, the Vice-president added, the special zonal economic 'management structure' is basically 'a combination of planning adjustment and market adjustment'. The zonal economic structure itself and its management structure are part and parcel of overall national planning. For example, zonal commodity production and marketing and transportation are basically under Chinese national planning. How to properly manage the planning and market adjustment is itself a plan and is a theoretical problem which enlivens the Chinese economy at home. In the past, Chinese Marxist theorists perceived 'socialist planned economy' and 'market adjustment' as mutually exclusive or 'unmixable'. Certain Marxist theorists denied that market adjustment was functionally useful. They thus planted the seeds of China's economic failure in the thirty years before 1978. From 1978, however, the government began to realise the utility of consumer commodity production and the adoption of capitalist management. It learned how to prevent blind economic development while not neglecting the usefulness of market adjustments.

China's special zone economy is an 'advanced commodity economy'. Its growth is closely related to future prosperity in international commodity market. This will soon bring greater understanding so that Chinese policy makers will see the inevitable commodity competition in international markets and China's need to respond to the international market challenge.

Vice-president Fang emphasised especially the need to dispose of one critical question, which is: is the Special Economic Zone a capitalist development? He said that he had been repeatedly asked to respond to this question during his travel in the United States. He kindly gave me a copy of his recently composed essay on this question. We discussed some of the main points during the interview. He emphatically admitted that the special zone development is for the interest of socialist China. It is a method of demonstrating the 'superiority of socialism by learning the best of capitalism'. In the special zone, China invites foreign investors to make a profit, which is a form of exploitation. However, this 'exploitation' is in China's own best interest because it is the means of acquiring foreign technology and a way of providing incentives for foreign investors in order to advance China's four modernisations. In any case it takes place within certain limits, such as income tax and re-investment. In practice, China makes the special zone economy serve the socialist economy in general, not the other way around.[22]

6.7 SPECIAL ZONES BENEFIT BOTH CHINA AND FOREIGN INVESTORS

Many questions can be raised about this new venture which began in 1981. In fact, this scheme to stabilise long-term economic relations between a socialist nation and all or any capitalist investors has never been attempted before by a socialist state. Why does China have to choose this path? Is this a stop-gap approach or a serious experiment on China's part? What will be the political effects if it fails? How well have the experiments been accepted by the leftist elements in the Communist Party? How can one relate this experiment to democratisation in China and the government's goal to quadruple the national income by the year 2000? Special zone experiments conform to Deng's two revolutionary goals: (1) to keep China open to the outside world, and (2) to revitalise the economy. The commitment to these twin goals since 1979 has been so strong and so well accepted that it seems impossible for any future leadership to abandon it without unpredictable consequences. Even if setbacks and corruptions should occur in the special zones, they would not be likely to reverse China's policy to remain open to the outside world. On the other hand, foreign investors have made their long-term investment decisions when they came to invest here. They will not be able to withdraw easily under any adverse changes in Chinese politics. After a closer observation of this economic experiment the special zones can be related to four long-term benefits: (1) foreign investment security and guaranteed profits; (2) assurance in foreign capital retrieval; (3) gateway to technology and capital inflow; and (4) internal need for continuity. These four 'preliminary observations' are based on a long-term assumption that China needs constant inflow of foreign technology and capital. It must allow greater investment competition for both profits and security to foreign investors. If one examines Chinese laws and regulations on the Special zone experiment, it will be found that the above four observations are well-supported. A simple explanation for each is as follows.

Foreign Investment Security and Guaranteed Profit

There are now some twenty-two separate pieces of regulation and legislation from both the National People's Congress and the provincial governments in Guangdong or Fujian. The more important ones are: The Law of the People's Republic of China on Chinese-foreign Joint Venture, Procedures of the People's Republic of China for the Regulation and Administration of Chinese-foreign Joint-venture, Interim Procedures for the Handling of Loans by the Bank of China to Chinese–foreign Joint Venture, the Income Tax Law of the People's Republic of China concerning Chinese-foreign Joint Venture, and Rule for the Implementation of the Individual Income Tax Law of the People's Republic of China. Other regulations may concern foreign exchange control over enterprise or individual income and profit, resident foreigners and foreign company representatives, export-import licensing or foreign enterprise registration. These laws and regulations or procedures are fair, well-intended and so far well-administered. The percentage of tax on profit is low and outflow of profit is quite easy. Joint ventures between Chinese and foreigners 'to organise company enterprises or other economic organisations' are to take place 'in accordance with the principle of equality and mutual benefit and subject to approval by the Chinese Government'.[23] Article 2 of the National People's Congress (hereafter, NPC) in its first piece of legislation in July 1979 on foreign investment declares: 'The Chinese Government protects the investment of joint ventures, the profits due them and their other lawful rights and interests in a joint venture.' There is an agency and investment commission to handle applications for such joint ventures. Foreign investors do not have to contribute more than 25 per cent of total capital to a joint venture, and this investment need not be in cash and can be in the form of 'advanced technology and equipment that actually suits our country's needs'.[24] All enterprises, joint venture or not, must be governed by a board of directors agreed upon among the investors. The chairman of the board must be a Chinese and the rest can all be foreigners. The board 'decides on all major problems' of the venture. The 'net profit' is defined as that portion left after the enterprise has paid its income tax, set aside a reserve fund, a bonus and welfare fund for staff and workers and enterprise expansion fund. This net profit shall be distributed among investors according to their share of the contribution to the capital of the enterprise. The law encourages the importation of 'advance technology' by any joint venture through 'reduction or exemption of income tax for the first two or three profit-making years'. As a second attraction, the law stipulates that 'a foreign joint venturer that reinvests in China his share of the net profit may apply for refund of a part of the income tax already paid'. The Bank of China or its approved foreign banks in the special zone shall have rights as protected by law regarding the financial transactions of all joint ventures. But enterprise insurance shall be provided by Chinese insurance companies, a protected right to earn premiums but also to compensate for any major loss. This itself is evidence of a sincere undertaking and also an expression of self-confidence in providing security to all joint ventures. 'A joint venture is encouraged to market its products outside China', and 'may also be distributed in the Chinese market'. Finally, the same NPC law states the methods of settling disputes between partners of joint ventures by (1) its board of directors, or (2) through mediation or arbitration by a Chinese agency or any other arbitration agency mutually agreed upon among partners to the joint venture.[25]

According to the 'Interim Procedures' of the State Council of 13 March 1981, the Bank of China will handle a variety of loans of joint ventures, including (1) working capital loans on revolving funds for deficits; (2) loans for settlement of accounts when their production fund is tied up in goods; and (3) fixed asset loans when the joint venture needs to expand its business or needs to make more fixed-asset investment. Details on loans convince an observer that the Chinese government is very seriously involved in the success or failure of the special economic zones in which China cannot unilaterally change conditions to exploit foreign investors or joint venturers.

On income tax, the NPC promulgated a law on 10 September 1980. This law is quite similar to the equivalent in the United States. Taxable income is defined as the amount after all 'deductible costs, expenses and losses'. The rate of tax on joint ventures is 30 per cent. There is an additional local income tax of 10 per cent, making the total 40 per cent. When profit itself obtained from investment is remitted abroad, a tax of further 10 per cent is levied on the profit. The law exempts income tax or reduces it by 50 per cent if a joint venture starts with a pledge 'to operate for a period of ten years or more'. In such a case, the enterprise must apply for its tax exemption or its 50 per cent deduction for the first three years. If investment is made in a low profit region, it may gain an additional tax deduction by 15 to 30 per cent for a period of ten years after the first three years of tax exemption.[26] These are enough examples to illustrate how China is eager to have joint ventures with foreign investment partners even if their share is only 25 per cent, with their taxes being reduced or exempted. In short, due to its interest in acquiring advanced technology and in exporting manufactured goods, China has established this unique special economic zone to benefit both sides fairly. Investment security and guaranteed profits are assured both in the existing law and also by contracts.

Assurance in Capital Retrieval

Investment laws clearly spell out the retrieval procedure from China of the original capital, profits made from such investment, and the wages of foreign staff members and workers. All of these incomes can be remitted from China as described by the laws. The best details in each case come technically from the contract itself of each joint venture, which can include any conditions for details during the negotiation. The Chinese tax system is clearly designed to induce foreign investors to reinvest their net profits in more profitable new ventures. For longer periods of investment commitment, more tax benefit is still available. In short, China is prepared to tie down capital forces as long as it can. If such a successful trend continues, foreign capital, equipment, and national gross income will increase with accelerating speed. Domestic employment, internal market development, foreign trade expansion and new technological gains will be such that China will eventually be deeply dependent on international economic networks and trade transactions. On the other hand, without such unique special economic zones and investment tax benefits under law, foreigners will not be so easily attracted to China, and her four modernisations will not be able confidently to count on such foreign participation. Given all these factors and their critical consequences, it is easy to appreciate why China is institutionalising in the direction of a long-term opening up of the country to the outside world. To provide strong confidence to foreign investors, China must allow easy retrieval of capital from the country by any investor.

Gateway to Technology and Capital Inflow

Any developing country has to be fairly successful in economic growth, political stability, positive social trends, good internal transportation and communications, an ample power supply, good human resource supply, and better domestic consumption market, before any foreign investor is attracted to invest fixed capital in the country. For example, Singapore and Malaysia are often considered a safe place for foreign investment, but the Philippines, communist Vietnam and communist North Korea are not. How could China attract many foreign investors soon after the death of Mao and when the country was still in political turmoil until Deng's resumption of leadership? Yet China must have foreign investment to finance her four modernisations. Foreign investment and modernisation are inseparable for China to catch up with the rest of the world. Foreign capital and technology are critically needed to build up adequate transportation, energy supply and educational standards. There has been, until recently, little domestic market consumption to convince foreigners to invest in China. Deng Xiaoping's leadership skilfully thought out such a special economic zone scheme to provide potential foreign investors with a very attractive offer in exchange for advanced technology and cash in foreign exchange, or foreign exchange cash earned by China at the special economic zones. And thirdly, the joint venture itself may manufacture such articles and heavy machines in the special zone for China's expanding domestic market for industrial equipment and consumer goods.

Internal Demand in Favour of Continuity of the Special Economic Zones

Any visitor travelling in China knows it is a nation on the move. The Chinese people in both rural and urban regions demand a higher standard of living. Many communists themselves are embarrassed that China's living standard remains too far behind Hong Kong, Taiwan, South Korea, Malaysia and Singapore. Thirty years of communist misrule has been long enough to learn the lesson that ideological leftist crisis of the communist party, especially under Mao's last ten years, has been responsible for the embarrassing economic consequences. Vice-premier Deng Xiaoping in 1974–5 had proposed his four modernisations even before Mao's death. Since 1977, he has remained eager to again pursue his four modernisations. The people are also eager to support rapid economic development and the raising of living standards. Deng's leadership seems universally praised in China for: (1) his dismantling of the commune system and his policy to allow the peasants to help themselves economically; (2) his emphasis on economic enlivenment to quadruple the national income by the year 2000; (3) his decision to reform the urban economic structure; and (4) the opening of the country to the outside world. The Chinese population expects more material improvement. Emphasis is on the success of light industry to meet popular demands, something which will probably prevent any future successor to Deng from turning the clock backwards. The special economic zones, therefore, as a vehicle to accelerate modernisation, can only be abandoned with adverse consequences for any future regime. There is today a 'new revolution of rising expectation' in China.

This study has avoided a survey of economic difficulties and crises resulting from rapid growth, which would be the subject of another book. Suffice it to say that China today is still unable to manage rapid growth and inflation, wage system and price stability, economic crime and bureaucratic inefficiency. Above all, many experts at home and abroad are seriously concerned about future political stability after Deng's death, and the possible re-emergence of a factional leadership struggle within the Communist Party itself. Economic planning is currently under trial in terms of scope and depth. Competition between the relatively free market sector of the economy and the planned command sector is an on-going threat to the established guidelines of socialist development. Even if all proceeds as expected, it may require a decade or so for the socialist planners to build a coherent and integrated infrastructure of a new and experimenting economic system. This new system is, indeed, a new model of its own, which Deng has called 'Socialism with Chinese Characteristics'. To this author, it looks like a 'half-way mixed economy' between socialism and capitalism.

7 'One Country, Two Systems'

This chapter will not go into detail concerning the development of both Hong Kong and Taiwan since their separation from Imperial China under the Ching Dynasty during the nineteenth century. However, certain aspects of changes and the evolution of their significance will be touched upon to highlight the contemporary problems and conflicts surrounding both. For Hong Kong, for example, much emphasis will be placed on its evolution, the impending crisis of its return to China, the process of Sino-British negotiation since the early 1980s, the joint declaration of 1984, Hong Kong as a challenge to the People's Republic of China (the PRC), and the Hong Kong settlement and its impact on the solution of Taiwan.

The unification of Taiwan with the PRC, on the other hand, is a far more complicated matter, politically and diplomatically. Even the recent history of Taiwan reflects many conflicts of the Cold War in Asia since 1949. The early Japanese and US positions on Taiwan, shortly before their formal diplomatic relations with the PRC in 1972, were not quite free of duplicity or mixed intentions. The growing ability of the Republic of China (hereafter, the ROC), independent and free of the PRC, deprives the Beijing regime of certain effective methods of putting pressure on the island. The United States continues to play a critical role in stabilising the current status quo. To obtain a true picture, one must fully understand the nature of Cold War and superpower diplomacy on both sides of the Taiwan Strait. Thus, this chapter will touch on the major features of Cold War strategy, the PRC's overture for unification and its determination to recover the island, Taiwan's internal transformation into a genuine democracy, and the continuing threat of separation in internal political development.

7.1 THE HONG KONG EXPERIMENT

From a barren village island in 1842 to the 1980s Hong Kong has never been fully separated from China. It is almost entirely populated by the Chinese. Of its 5.5 million population 98 per cent are Chinese, including since 1898 that of the leased New Territories. It has a total of 5075 square kilometres. It is the most urbanised city adjacent to China proper. The majority of people speak both Cantonese and English. Its economy is modern, with some 75 per cent in industrial production and 24 per cent in tertiary service. Without a rural countryside for agriculture and natural resource supplies, Hong Kong depends totally on China as its hinterland for raw materials and as its market. Most of the citizens in Hong Kong have close relatives in Guangdong Province. In 1949 when the Chinese Communist Party took over the mainland, Hong Kong had a small population of less than half a million. Over the last thirty years, refugees from China have aided in its rapid population growth. Security border control has remained tight against the inflow of refugees by both water and by land. Cheap labour supply from refugees has been the major cause of rapid light industrial growth and commercial expansion. It is, however, necessary to prevent illegal entry of new refugees to protect the high standard of living. The economy is heavily dependent on foreign markets, investment, and tourism.

Due to its geographic propinquity and lack of resouces, Hong Kong is inseparable from the PRC. Water, meat, vegetables and food grains are all imported from China. The major reason for Hong Kong's prosperity is primarily attributable to its colonial status under the British. The British authority in Hong Kong, like Burma on China's southwestern border, has maintained a friendly neutrality toward a politically chaotic country over the last several decades. The PRC, for its part, has been too weak to take over Hong Kong militarily. It could not abrogate the treaties of 1842, which formally ceded the Island of Hong Kong to the British. In 1860 the Kowloon peninsula was also ceded to the British after the Anglo-French War of 1860. The New Territories, which is the largest segment of the three, was rented to the British in 1898 for a period of ninety-nine years. Together, these three treaties constituted the basis for the British to make Hong Kong into a dependent colony free of Chinese intervention. However, the PRC government since 1949 has maintained a position of not legally recognising the validity of these treaties which were unilaterally imposed on China by the use of force. The Beijing regime has always made clear that in due course it would take proper measures to recover all Chinese territories taken by force by foreign imperialism during the nineteenth century, including those lost to Tsarist Russia.

What has made Hong Kong prosperity tenable was the anti-Communist sentiment among the millions of refugees from China and other local Chinese who do not wish to lose their free commercial society with its higher standard of living for communist regimentation. The British have seen to it that no cause should be provided for the PRC to interfere in Hong Kong's internal affairs. Residents in Hong Kong, however, have always maintained their Chinese Nationalistic outlook, but have welcomed the British as an artificial necessity to de-politicise the island. On the other hand, the PRC government has been tolerant of Hong Kong for a variety of reasons: the window to earn foreign currency exchanges through exports, accumulation of Cold War intelligence, its inability to earn political support from the Chinese residents, and lack of physical capacity to take over and administer the area without serious adverse consequences. As a result, Hong Kong has been able to exist for the interests of all concerned: it is a threat to no one and as such it has prospered. But the hidden influence of the PRC in Hong Kong has remained viable. Like Macao, Hong Kong's internal peace and stability has been possible only due to the wise policies of all sides for mutual accommodation. The British, however, have no long-term sustaining and bargaining power against the PRC. Beijing can exercise greater initiative over the fate of Hong Kong which will similarly affect Macao. Thus, mutual benefit, protected by the British in maintaining internal peaceful order, has made Hong Kong a unique place. This uniqueness has served the interests of London, Taipei, Beijing and, above all, the resident Chinese people in Hong Kong.

Yet, Hong Kong's existence under the British since the turn of the century has had a revolutionary message for China. It is a signpost of democratic institutions, free press, free association among civilians and free enterprise for higher standards of living. This fact has inspired many Chinese from China to come as refugees. In spite of its own colonial status, Hong Kong even helped Sun Yat-sen to organise his democratic revolution against the Manchus. Western ideas of democracy, human rights and civil liberties have also entered China through Hong Kong. Often in the present century, Chinese political and intellectual leaders have sought asylum in Hong Kong. During the Sino-Japanese War, many Chinese came here to seek their safe haven against the Japanese before the Pearl Harbor incident. Through Hong Kong, the world can learn a great deal about China, whether under the Nationalist or Communist regime. It is, in short, the southern gate to China. For better or for worse, Hong Kong is a challenge to China because of what it is. Hong Kong, in this respect, represents a potential for progressive and democratic influence on events in China.

7.1.1   The Crisis of its Return to China

As hinted already, Hong Kong is a British colony consisting of Hong Kong island itself, Kowloon city, other unoccupied islands, and the leased New Territories for a period of ninety-nine years. Without the New Territories, Hong Kong under the British cannot survive. Nor can Hong Kong enjoy internal peace and prosperity without cooperation from the government of China. For example, the Chinese government can cut off the water supply or trade relations. Secondly, all Chinese governments, the Nationalist before 1949 and the Communist since then have vowed to recover all their lost territories at a proper future time. Chiang Kaishek seriously discussed Hong Kong's return to China at the Cairo Conference in 1943 with Winston Churchill and Franklin D. Roosevelt. Politically speaking, the PRC government could have stirred up difficulties for Hong Kong at any time since 1949. The reason she did not do so was because she has always felt that the time for such return was premature. Given all the other advantages that Hong Kong provides and the domestic unrest that China itself has had, the PRC government did not want to interfere with the lease until 1982. It was the Hong Kong Governor who first brought up the issue with Deng Xiaoping in March 1979 during his visit to Beijing.[1] Six months later Premier Hua Guofeng hinted at Chinese concern for Hong Kong's prosperity and external investment and trade. This was the first indication from China about the future of Hong Kong. During Premier Hua's official visit to London, he again assured the British not to worry about foreign investment in Hong Kong. Deng Xiaoping himself assured British Foreign Minister Carrington that 'if any change in Hong Kong's future status should occur, the interests of foreign investors will not be adversely affected', when the latter visited in April 1981. Half a year later, additional indirect references were made public when Beijing declared its nine generous conditions for peaceful unification with Taiwan. Observers concluded that all these conditions were applicable to Hong Kong and Macao with the exception of Chinese troop presence to be negotiated. As declared by the Chairman of the National People's Congress, Yi Jianying, the nine conditions for the Taiwan 'Special Administrative Region' consisted of non-interference in local affairs, no changes in the social and economic system as it now exists, no change in lifestyle, no interference in local economic and cultural relations with foreign countries, private property, homes, land, business enterprise and the right to inheritance. By January 1982,

Beijing was eager to discuss the future of Hong Kong. For example, Premier Zhao Ziyang announced on 6 January 1982, that China would respect Hong Kong's status as a free port and a well recognised centre for international commerce in spite of China's future sovereignty over the colony. He urged others not to draw any damaging conclusions that might affect Hong Kong's economic prosperity while Sino-British negotiation were still underway. Three months later, Deng reaffirmed the applicability to Hong Kong of the conditions for Taiwan's unification in his meeting with British former Prime Minister Edward Heath on 6 April 1982. Heath later revealed the possibility of a 'government by Hong Kong residents themselves' as a special administrative region (hereafter, SAR). This approach was to be arranged through the PRC constitution. Everything in Hong Kong should remain unchanged, including local passports for travel abroad. Up to April 1982, the 5.5 million residents had not had any formal or informal contacts with the Beijing government regarding their own views about the future transfer of sovereignty. The Chinese stand appeared firm and consistent.

Repeatedly, reaffirmation of future conditions was made to Hong Kong officials and citizens as they came to Beijing. For example, Deng in April received President L. S. Huang of Hong Kong University and twelve other notable local residents from Hong Kong and Macao on their views of the future. Article 31 of PRC's 1982 draft constitution provided the way to introduce the establishment of SAR for both Taiwan and Hong Kong. On the British side, officially guarded optimism was detectable by the middle of 1982 when the late Sir Edward Youde, Governor of Hong Kong, described at London Airport the future transfer of sovereignty as a 'routine matter'.[2] Members of the British Parliament began to recognise the government's responsibility to negotiate an acceptable agreement for the people of Hong Kong. Everything remained secret regarding other obstacles to be resolved through negotiation. On 22 September 1982, British Prime Minister Margaret Thatcher arrived in Beijing. At the welcome banquet, Premier Zhao Ziyang voiced the need to discuss long-term future mutual interests between Britain and China after the transfer of Hong Kong. He eagerly cited China's much quoted five principles of peaceful coexistence as a basis for friendship among states. The next day Zhao expressed to Hong Kong correspondents China's determination to regain sovereignty and to guarantee prosperity in Hong Kong. In the critical meeting between Prime Minister Thatcher and Deng Xiaoping, they each stated their separate stands and principles concerning the coming diplomatic negotiation. Principally, Thatcher insisted on the validity of the three existing treaties. Namely, the treaty of 1842 which legally ceded Hong Kong Island itself to Britain. The treaty of 1860 further ceded the tip of Kowloon peninsula away. Britain has full sovereignty over both according to treaty stipulations. The third treaty governs the lease of the New Territories since 1898. If the validity of the three treaties had been acceptable to Beijing, the subsequent diplomatic negotiation would have called for different stands by both. The Chinese would not, as expected, accept Thatcher's argument on the grounds that those three treaties were unilaterally imposed on China during the days of Western 'gunboat diplomacy' and military invasion. China never had any reason to exercise free volition to cede or lease her territories away. It is, therefore necessary and legal for a 'stronger China' to regain lost sovereignty over its former lands and to correct the wrongful legacy of past foreign imperialism in China. This has been, in fact, a consistent stand of the PRC over all border disputes, whether concerning Burma, India, Pakistan, or the Soviet Union. However, this time the political and diplomatic implications required delicacy and sensitivity on the part of the regime, to achieve, at least, three major results in the outcome of Hong Kong transfer; (1) no adverse effect on the economic prosperity of Hong Kong despite a rejection of the agreements; (2) the settlement model to be applicable to Macao and the Republic of China (hereafter ROC); and (3) the cultivation of British good will and cooperation during the transitionary stage before 1997 and its assistance afterwards in mutual commercial and other 'long-term interests'. Therefore, the Chinese government had to exercise prudence in bargaining and pattern-setting during the negotiation. It would not want to embarrass the British about their 'moral responsibility' to the Hong Kong people who themselves were not allowed by the Beijing government to participate directly in the negotiation. Had they been allowed to participate, greater bargaining power would have been available to the British side. On the other hand, patriotic Chinese and university students of Hong Kong openly objected to Margaret Thatcher's insistence on the legal validity of the three treaties. The students considered these treaties 'as evidences of insults to China' if accepted. China has always marked such agreements as 'unequal treaties'.

A sense of crisis seemed to emerge over the validity of the three treaties. A feeling of impotence emerged on the part of many local Chinese residents over their own future. This became another source of crisis, a crisis of uncertainty in future trade and commerce, or future potential social and political instability. Watchful anxiety affected the Hong Kong stock market for a while and caused the decline in real estate transactions. For the people of Hong Kong, little could be known about the extent and content of self-government after 1997. This concern reached the level of crisis when industrialists and businessmen contemplated the outflow of their wealth and capital to other parts of the world. Local leaders wanted to become the third party in the Sino-British negotiation or part of the British delegation. It took a while for the PRC government to convince and calm the population in Hong Kong through many local delegations that came to Beijing to ascertain what the government had in store for their future. To quell the anxiety, Governor Youde appealed to the people on 28 April 1983 to understand the difficulties in the negotiation process and the time required for it. But the people seemed to have little faith in empty promises about their future prosperity and self-government. The second stage of Sino-British negotiations did not begin, until after Margaret Thatcher's visit in 13 July 1983. This time, Governor Youde declared that he would represent the people of Hong Kong within the British delegation. His claim to represent the people was not acceptable to Beijing either.

### 7.1.2	Analysis of Popular Anxiety and the Joint Declaration

Residents of Hong Kong remained powerless to influence the Sino-British negotiation which was already deadlocked by July 1983. They depended totally on the British to fulfil their 'moral responsibility to the people'. However, the British had little bargaining power once they gave in on the treaty validity. For the Beijing government, the entire matter was to wait for 1997 for the regaining of sovereignty over Northern Kowloon and the New Territories. The British would have legally no case against this: Hong Kong Island and the tip of Kowloon cannot exist without the New Territories. But the Chinese cannot govern Hong Kong by themselves. They expect the British to stay on in a new advisory capacity after 1997. The entire future stability and prosperity after 1997 depends on mutual good will and cooperation, and Beijing knew this well. The PRC thus remained diplomatically confident and consistent on its negotiation stand. Furthermore, China also thought beyond the reversion after 1997 in offering 'new favoured' opportunity to Britain, including better conditions for investment and trade opportunity in China, besides helping the residents in self-government as a special administrative region of China. Following some debate in Parliament and public airing of the whole matter, it was not after all difficult for Britain to return for the second round at the diplomatic table. Both Britain and China have shown their art at diplomacy in both tactics and strategy, since the treaty validity issue was abandoned.

What was at stake still was the interests of Hong Kong residents. To this, China had verbally pledged repeatedly 'to take care of the people's interests'. The real frustration was the division among the residents whose interests cannot be well ascertained without a detailed analysis of the population structure. Due to this frustration and fear, their efforts to be heard by London and Beijing were pronounced during the interval after Prime Minister Thatcher's first visit to China in 1982. What did the local residents do and say that was important?

Generally, most residents believed the Chinese sovereignty over Hong Kong could not be challenged. Anxiety was focused on how the residents should be allowed to administer their own affairs, with or without British assistance after reversion. They were concerned about what specific changes would possibly be made to protect Hong Kong as a free port and the third largest financial centre in the world. They could not visualise yet how to insulate Hong Kong from the communist system of government, its economy and way of life, to protect their higher living standard of 4000 American dollars per capita *vis-à-vis* a poor one of fifteen times less. The residents perceived their future in a variety of possible arrangements: 'As trust under British Administration', 'under a rental arrangement with Britain', 'joint Sino-British Administration', and 'full self-government under the PRC Constitution', or 'limited local autonomy'. The daily press itself was, of course, divided among leftist, rightest, and neutral or liberal stands. Each orientation advanced its own perceptions and interpretations of the events. The residents were divided, as rich, poor or in the middle who reacted differently to changing of events. Their lack of faith in the PRC promises beyond 1997 was the one fundamental cause for anxiety, even though the Beijing government remained cautious, firm and consistent on Hong Kong after 1997. To summarise the major concerns of the residents, the pro-Beijing *Mirrow Monthly* in its October issue 1982 published a ten-point list of recommendations for the PRC government:

1. There is a need for clear and firm stipulation through the PRC constitution on a set of special administrative laws which should

prohibit any change within several decades after 1997. This would remove the fear for the local residents of future administrative discretion which may cause uncertainties;

2. To protect Hong Kong's capitalist economy and its free port status, the Communist Party should declare publicly that party organs will not participate in the SAR administration and no municipal communist secretariat will be established in Hong Kong;

3. The Communist Party should declare that its 'four cardinal principles' (Marxism–Maoism, the socialist path, Communist Party leadership, and democratic dictatorship) are not applicable to Hong Kong;

4. Hong Kong's own modernised educational system, professional people and their social status and high personal income must not be downgraded in order to keep such modernity replenished for good performance;

5. Local customs and practices must be respected;

6. Residents of Hong Kong should continue to enjoy rights to travel abroad, to emigrate and study abroad. The PRC government should negotiate with other governments to maintain free port privileges for Hong Kong;

7. The Beijing government should declare a general policy toward residents from Taiwan about their rights, press and publication freedoms, and other enterprises so long as they do not carry out 'two China' activities, or violate Hong Kong's laws and public security, or use Hong Kong to carry out underground counter-revolutionary activities. They should come and go freely and carry out their activities openly;

8. The British system of laws should remain in practice after 1997 and recognition and protection of all legal contracts and obligations and interests made legally before 1997 should be maintained;

9. Hong Kong's foreign exchange should remain uncontrolled; favourable balance of payments should be kept in Hong Kong and not be reported to Beijing. Hong Kong should have no obligation to purchase PRC bonds and treasury certificates. This policy concerns the protection of local prosperity. (Britain only requires Hong Kong to reimburse it for the expenditure incurred from defence protection); and

10. Unless in a war emergency, Chinese military forces should not be dispatched to Hong Kong. With prior consent of the PRC government, Hong Kong should be able to welcome friendly visits

by foreign warships.

Mirrow Monthly emphatically declared that if the PRC can practice these ten policies, the 'crisis of confidence' would be likely to disappear for the people.

If this ten-point recommendation can, in fact, be put into practice after 1997, Deng Xiaoping's doctrine of 'one country, two systems' will truly be revolutionary. It seems that the Joint Declaration of 1984 can accommodate all these points except the dispatch of Chinese troops.

When the British government gave up the sovereignty argument, the second round of negotiation quickly convened in Beijing in July 1983. Negotiation moved forward smoothly. The Joint Declaration was consummated on 26 September 1984. It is a good document and well received everywhere, including Western Europe, Japan and the United States. The government of the Republic of China on Taiwan denounced the Declaration as invalid and not binding. The Declaration consists of PRC requirements; it felt the 'so-called appropriate future time had come' for China not to reject its own territory. The deadline for transfer from the British to the PRC is 1 July 1997. All of British Hong Kong, with a total area of 404 square miles, will be returned. China could not just take back the New Territories without also taking over the Hong Kong Island and lower Kowloon, nor could domestic politics in China allow this logical inconsistency. On the other hand, the British government could not administer Hong Kong under Chinese sovereignty without full control of the New Territories. Thus, the PRC government accepted favourable opportunities for future British trade and investment in China and a special guest role to assist Hong Kong after 1997. China has secured long-term cooperation for, perhaps, the entire fifty years which the Joint Declaration has granted to Hong Kong as a special administrative region of China.

The major stipulations of the Declaration appear to be satisfactory to the residents of Hong Kong, many of whom had established in 1983–4 a high degree of mutual understanding with the Beijing government. Many Hong Kong delegations, personal visits to the PRC and official statements by the Chinese government were made in 1983 and 1984 before the real negotiation began in July 1983. The Chinese government meanwhile bought properties and opened business firms in Hong Kong. It acted to stimulate and restore activities of the local stock market. The Shenzhen Special Economic Zone, across the border from Hong Kong, received large investments from Hong Kong businessmen. Gradually but steadily, the Hong Kong residents understood better the Chinese intent to succeed in the practice of 'one country, two systems'. It also intends eagerly to apply the Hong Kong model to Taiwan for the unification of the country.

The major stipulations of the Declaration include many well-devised means and procedures to assure prosperity in the post-1997 period which will last for fifty years. The Hong Kong Special Administrative Region is being enacted into law through Article 31 of the PRC constitution of 1982 which empowers the National People's Congress to create such regions and to exercise shared supervision with the State Council. The major points are as follows:[3]

1. Hong Kong will implement a new system of government to be based on the people's choice as allowed under Article 31 of the PRC Constitution. Foreign affairs and defence powers are, however, to be exercised by the central government in Beijing;
2. Internal autonomy shall include executive, legislature and judicial power. Final adjudication power is vested in an independent judicial body without interference from the central government;
3. The present economic and social system, which includes free speech, free movement, free association, freedom of religion, and right to strike, will remain unchanged and to be protected by law. Private property rights will be protected;
4. The economic structure and trade system shall remain unchanged for fifty years;
5. The chief executive after 1997 will be appointed by the central government after elections or constitution locally. The future government will be run by the local people;
6. In addition to displaying the PRC national flag and national emblem, Hong Kong may also display a regional flag and emblem;
7. The government of Hong Kong may join 'relevant international organisations' and enter into international treaties. It can also establish trade missions and economic agencies in foreign countries. In each case, the name 'Hong Kong, China' must be used when it enters into agreement with other states, regions and relevant international organisations; and
8. Chinese defence forces stationed in Hong Kong 'shall not interfere in the internal affairs in Hong Kong' and the expenses of such forces shall be borne by the central government of China.

Clearly, residents of Hong Kong should feel adequately assured of self-government with a minimum of routine central government participation, namely, the appointment of a chief executive through consultation or as a result of local election. Foreign affairs and defence are the two major areas in which the PRC central government will exercise independent decision making. A local flag and emblem are concessions to enable Hong Kong to retain and create international economic relations as an independent identity. All things considered, the real test is only, indeed, the PRC's good faith to enact a genuine basic law to create the Hong Kong Special Administrative Region based on the stipulations set down in the Joint Declaration. Direct representation of Hong Kong in the NPC through some forty delegates will help achieve communications between the central legislature and Hong Kong. The legislature of Hong Kong itself shall make local laws in accordance with the basic law for Hong Kong as enacted by the National People's Congress or its Standing Committee which may also interpret local enactments in accordance with the basic law itself. Thus, during the fifty years after 1997, the special administrative region of Hong Kong shall be self-governing under the central legislature only.[4]

According to Article 89 of the PRC Constitution, however, the State Council (central executive) has the power to alter inappropriate decisions and orders issued by local organs of state administration at different levels. Whether this clause is applicable to Hong Kong after 1997 is debatable because Hong Kong is not 'a state administration' at a local level in the usual sense. It is governed by the special basic law for Hong Kong. Professor Hungdah Chiu thinks that the State Council can alter enactments in Hong Kong.[5] On the other hand, it is easy to agree with Professor Chiu's analysis if the PRC central government does not act in good faith. It is difficult to believe that the PRC can afford to act in bad faith if it wants to earn the confidence of the people in Hong Kong. The real difficulties are those not foreseeable at the present time. These might include, for example, factional conflicts and struggles within the Chinese Communist Party, political instability inside China, or an economic crisis and failure in China's four modernisations. Any one of these could easily interrupt the PRC's ability to implement the Joint Declaration of 1984. In short, the real guarantee for the 'high degree of autonomy' for Hong Kong must come from an examination of long-term interests of China *vis-à-vis* the interests of an autonomous Hong Kong which will be part of China and cannot be totally insulated from the common interests of both. Any unforeseen future circumstances will affect the success or failure of relations between Hong Kong and China after 1997. The sincerity of China's professed aim to make Hong Kong 'A Show Model' cannot be doubted. From the PRC point of view, any failure to win the confidence of resident citizens in Hong Kong will have a disastrous result for her attempt to unite with Taiwan.

7.1.3 Hong Kong as a Challenge to the PRC

It has been four and a half years since the consummation of the Joint Declaration. Hong Kong proves to be a challenge to the British to implement and interpret the Declaration up to 1997 to prepare for the reversion. To discharge Britain's self-imposed moral obligation to the residents of five and a half million is not easy. They are divided among themselves in interests and in expectations. The next nine years of British effort is to be made under watchful scrutiny of the PRC agencies and personnel already in Hong Kong. So far all things seem to remain rosy for all concerned. Hong Kong has an open and free press and freedom of speech to guide the development and to facilitate the exchange of ideas. The local residents are likely to support the British authority to accomplish as much as it can before 1997, while all will look beyond 1997 with reservations.

The PRC has begun to work on the drafting of the basic law and on the organisation of the advisory group to voice their opinions and recommendations from the local residents. For the next four years this task itself will not be easy. The residents, as groups of divergent or conflicting interests, may have difficulties cooperating easily. Each group or class wants to have a basic law that can best guarantee its future interests. All will look for assurance and safe devices to protect future autonomy. The PRC government, on the other hand, is not willing to see too many changes occur before and after 1997. However, Beijing wants to expand its influence among the population now in order to be able to steer future development to its own liking. Thus, the challenge of the implementation of the Declaration will increase in its momentum as 1997 approaches.

A different challenge of implementation will come after the reversion in 1997. This is when self-government begins. The Beijing government will exercise supervision over the execution of the Declaration and the basic law. There will be no 'buffer authority' when the British administration disappears to prevent direct conflicts, should any arise between the local autonomous regime and the PRC authority. Hong Kong has been a very different society in itself. Its social, cultural, economic and political realities manifest essentially the characteristics of a free and open democratic system. It has a very highly educated population who all are business oriented and have incentives for self-achievement. Their organisational knowledge and management skills have enabled the people to build up Hong Kong as the third largest financial centre of the world. Hong Kong must remain sensitive to international commercial reality, otherwise it cannot succeed in world trade. It does big business with the rest of the world without interference from big government bureaucracy. Can Hong Kong after 1997 remain free from heavy-handed supervision or intervention from the PRC agencies locally or from the National People's Congress or the State Council in Beijing? Given the planned nature of the socialist economy and the powerful bureaucracy of the PRC, it is difficult to imagine how the central government can remain aloof or self-restrained in the exercise of its supervision. Whether the central government will fully authorise its local authority in Hong Kong to wisely and flexibly exercise self-restraints on behalf of the central government remains to be seen. Hong Kong must not be subject to new constraints and heavy-handedness from the North if it is to compete successfully internationally. Hong Kong will be the first experiment of 'one country, two systems', in a socialist state. It expects, under the Joint Declaration, to remain unchanged.

The positive challenge of Hong Kong to the PRC, on the other hand, is whether or not the central government will be willing and able to take every advantage that Hong Kong provides. For example, Hong Kong's story of economic miracle under the British should be accepted as a positive reference in China's four modernisations. This reference may help the PRC in re-orienting its political and economic structure reform. Can China make all the necessary resources available to Hong Kong after 1997 to make the latter an even greater miracle? China can encourage Hong Kong to expand its commercial and economic relations with the rest of the world. On the other hand, the Hong Kong experiment of economic success can be introduced into the non-socialist sector of the economic, the rural and tertiary sector, for example. There are several special economic zones in China in which Hong Kong after 1997 can be a challenge for success. If the PRC fails to meet Hong Kong's needs and expectations, it will be viewed directly as a failure of Deng Xiaoping's 'One Country, Two Systems'. It is difficult to imagine that this can be allowed to happen if peaceful unification with Taiwan remains high on the PRC agenda.

What has taken place in implementing the Joint Declaration so far? The British side has done well, and the people like what has been done. They expect more to be accomplished before 1997. A few examples can be cited either as accomplishments or as forecasts of future accomplishments:

1. The British government has taken its part quite seriously in its new annual undertaking. The government agrees 'to produce an annual report on Hong Kong for presentation to Parliament between now and 1997'.[6] Community leaders in Hong Kong 'reacted favourably to the move of keeping the UK up to date on Hong Kong';
2. The British government has worked to provide new passport privileges to residents of Hong Kong as British Nationals (overseas) without requiring the carrier to produce an identity card. Discussions on the matter with the Chinese authorities have been under way since 1985;
3. To continue trade expansion since the Joint Declaration, financial cooperation between the Bank of China in Hong Kong and local banking committee has become close. Hong Kong's membership in the General Agreement on Tariffs and Trade (GATT) after 1997 is getting support for its continuation from many trade partners;
4. Since January 1985, the new British political adviser has been building contacts to implement the Sino-British Agreement on the future of Hong Kong. His role involves contacts and cooperation with the Shenzhen Special Economic Zone, the Guangzhou provincial authority and the Chinese Xinhua News Agency in Hong Kong. The late Governor Sir Edward Youde said: 'not much hard work will have to be done in implementing the Sino-British Agreement on the future of Hong Kong; preparatory work has already begun'[7] For example, in the field of legal reform, some 300 multilateral treaties and agreements and 160 bilateral agreements that apply to Hong Kong have been gathered together for review by the Hong Kong Attorney General's office in order to clarify Hong Kong's rights or obligations under such existing agreements. The study result will be turned over to the future Joint Liaison Group which has the task of reviewing and deciding which and how each agreement can best serve Hong Kong's interests after 1997;
5. A significant step was taken to hold elections for the Legislative Council on 26 September 1985 in furthering the development of representative government. The elected twenty-four seats for the first time has joined the twenty-two nominated members and ten

officials in the Legislative Council. Twelve of the elected seats were allotted to district board members and the other twelve to professional groups, including lawyers, teachers, bankers, and social workers. There was an almost 100 per cent voter turn-out among district board members and more than 57 per cent of the registered voters cast their votes in the functionary constituency. Local leaders considered the election a satisfactory start toward future political development;

6. London is aware of the risk involved in deviating from the terms laid down under the Joint Declaration. Peter Williams, Hong Kong Secretary, said in London on 30 September 1985 that 'the first thing that must be ensured is Britain's effectively administering Hong Kong up to 1997. Any deviation from the term will frighten away investment as well as the professional and skilled groups on whom Hong Kong's success depends.'[8] He predicted that 'the early nineties will almost certainly see a new period of uncertainty and we shall have to have well thought out and firm plans for the changes which will then need to be introduced'. The fear in Hong Kong that China might interfere in local affairs during the early transition period has proved to be unsubstantiated. The British introduction of constitutional government, although unjustifiably long ignored, will likely pick up its pace in the coming years;

7. One of the major developments in 1986 was the benefit for the 3.25 million residents of Hong Kong who will continue to hold British Nationality (overseas) passports (BN(O)). These 3.25 million people are Hong Kong British Dependent Territory Citizens (BDTC). The White Paper on the Draft Hong Kong (British Nationality) Order 1986 was released in both London and Hong Kong on 18 October 1985. The new designation of BN(O) passports for Hong Kong residents was for life only. Children born in the first half of 1997 may apply for BN(O) up to 31 December 1997. No one born in Hong Kong after 30 June 1997 is to be eligible to apply for such a passport status. The British government will seek recognition by other governments of this change. This BN(O) status is a significant step with long-term implications. The views of Hong Kong residents were to be voiced on it. The US Consulate in HK has already announced the US's recognition of the proposed BN(O) passport when it comes into use in 1987. Even Her Majesty the Queen in her speech to the new opening Parliament reaffirmed her government's commitment to 'continue to discharge their obligations to the people of Hong Kong; and will

propose provision to implement the nationality arrangements arising from the Sino-British Joint Declaration'.[9]

In implementation on the Chinese side, Beijing has seemed most concerned about residents' popular reaction to the drafting of the Basic Law, which will be Hong Kong's Constitution after 1997. Selection of membership of the Basic Law Drafting Committee was a major effort in 1985. Various social, economic and intellectual groups must be directly represented on the Drafting Committee in proportion to their respective influences among the population. Secondly, the formation of membership on the Joint Liaison Group (JLG) is another major task. It must be, like the Drafting Committee, fairly representative of the British, local and Chinese views. In April 1986, the Drafting Committee had its second plenary session in Beijing. All the members from Hong Kong were in attendance. As reported, the agenda of the session included: (1) discussion and adoption of the outline of the Basic Law; (2) discussion and adoption of the working regulations for the Basic Law Drafting Committee; and (3) classification of special issues and organisation of special working groups of the Basic Law Drafting Committee. It is hoped that an early draft of the Basic Law will be completed in 1988. By 1990 the final version should be ready. The five working groups were expected to present their reports to the next plenary session of the committee. Greater emphasis was given to the future relations between the PRC Central authorities and the Special Administrative Region, the rights and obligations of Hong Kong residents, and the SAR's 'political system, economy, education, science, technology, culture and other matters'.[10]

Ji Pengfei still seems to remain fully in charge on Beijing's behalf over the work and the pace of progress of the Basic Law Drafting Committee. He has been, of course, the director of the Office for Hong Kong and Macao Affairs of the State Council and is concurrently chairman of the Basic Law Drafting Committee. Ji made a trip to Hong Kong in December 1985 and voiced his views and positions during his stay at a news conference concerning the Basic Law. Ji's views were all welcome to the people of Hong Kong. For example, he said at the news conference that he 'has been much better informed after discussions with Governor Youde and many Chinese leaders of many ranks and groups; that Hong Kong is a modern city, free port, international financial-commercial centre ... and that to keep Hong Kong prosperous, stabilising is in accord with the interest of all parties involved. This has been the view and policy of the PRC government consistently since the start.'[11] He acknowledged that, since the Sino-British Agreement, working relations between London and Beijing have been much closer. He expressed gratitude for the views and opinions of the Hong Kong members on the Basic Law and Joint Liaison Committees during his trip to Hong Kong. Over the role to be played by the National People's Congress and its Standing Committee on the future interpretation of the Basic Law, which is of grave concern to the people of Hong Kong, Ji promised that this matter should not be confused with the local implementation process by the autonomous administration authority which can be dealt with carefully when the Basic Law is written. He fully recognised the need for certain flexibility and for changes which may be inevitable under new circumstances in the years to come. Hong Kong always reflects changes in the outside world. China must go along with such future changes beyond its control if Hong Kong is to remain prosperous and protected.[12] In short, it seems that Hong Kong's distant future will ultimately be affected by those who will succeed Deng Xiaoping and Ji Pengfei. Prosperity in China and in Hong Kong will depend on the Communist leadership after 1997 and beyond. On the other hand, the death of Sir Edward Youde in December 1986, for example, was an important loss of one whose devotion and understanding is no longer available during the final decade of transition work.[13] His contribution as Governor of Hong Kong and as delegate of the negotiation team was properly acknowledged at his memorial services.

The following list provides a summary of the problems, progress, and future concerns as expressed by local leaders in Hong Kong and the responses from Beijing and provides also a good agenda for the Basic Law Drafting Committee:[14]

1. Members from Hong Kong on the Basic Law Drafting Committee are most concerned about Hong Kong's future 'degree of autonomy'. They have different views regarding the outline of the Basic Law; for example, that suitable stipulations of the PRC constitution be listed in the Basic Law so to distinguish the PRC constitution from the spirit of 'One Country, Two Systems'. They would prefer a more specific listing of Hong Kong's powers in addition to the 'administrative, legislative and judicial powers' as already mentioned in the Joint Declaration, and are displeased with the wording of the outline of the Basic Law which said 'under the leadership of the Central Government.' They preferred the wording 'authorised by the National People's Congress' only. They

object to the use of Marxist-Leninist jargon in the Basic Law, and refuse to be held responsible to any unit of government except to the National People's Congress;

2. Dissatisfaction of Hong Kong's members of the Basic Law Drafting Committee with what Xu Jiatun had said publicly about his knowledge of the outline of the Basic Law before the Hong Kong members had read the document. As director of New China News Agency in Hong Kong Xu seems to have over-played his hand;

3. Their fear about China's four cardinal principles (communist party leadership, Marxism–Leninism–Maoism, a socialist path and democratic dictatorship) which made it necessary for Deng Xiaoping to assure them that China would not force on Hong Kong these principles;

4. Their 'ardent hope' to retain Hong Kong's legal and political system in order to be 'an independent political entity' to make Deng's 'One County, Two Systems' a trustworthy and credible proposal;

5. The PRC is itself critically concerned about the British intent and implementation of democratic political reform which Britain had failed to provide in the past. The elections of 1982 and 1984 for the partial membership of the Legislative Council and the eighteen district boards have truly worried the PRC. It is clear that Britain and the residents of Hong Kong want political democratisation as quickly and as throughly as possible during the transition period. It is equally clear that the Chinese want to preserve the political status quo with no changes at all. The PRC side has, however, achieved a strong influence and support among the powerful industrial-commercial elite class through local membership in the Basic Law Drafting Committee (consisting of fifty-nine members, of which twenty-three are from Hong Kong and thirty-six from the Chinese side) and the Basic Law Consultative Committee of 180 members (all of them from Hong Kong) who will represent all ranks of the society and will have strong advisory voices in the Basic Law drafting. Thus conflicts or differences over what kind of political system will emerge in both form and substance may come up unavoidably, although both the British and the PRC want nothing less than prosperity and stability. However, the people of Hong Kong, according to a recent survey, seem to still 'have a very low degree of trust for the PRC government'.[15] In the survey, 66.3 per cent did not believe the PRC would let the 'Hong Kong people rule

Hong Kong'. In another survey, 74 per cent of the respondents believed that the current British system, albeit imperfect, is the best under the existing circumstances. Thus, China's constructive responses to the concerns of the local population in the coming years will remain critically important to longterm prosperity and stability in conjunction with necessary reforms under the British before 1997.

On the other hand, since the start of the reversion negotiations in 1982, the PRC has been flexible and consistent. It can be expected to respond more constructively to the continually changing circumstances. The promised 'high degree of autonomy' can not be taken inflexibly or unilaterally. Beyond 1997, the PRC may exercise general supervision in both political and economic development.[16] This can take place for a variety of well-known and unknown future reasons, Meanwhile, steady progress has been made towards the transition, especially during the third session of the Basic Law Drafting Committee in November 1986. The five working groups have given their reports on relations between the central government and the Hong Kong Special Administrative Region and other matters. The basic rights of the Hong Kong residents include the following:[17]

Hong Kong residents will enjoy freedom of movement in and out of the country and freedom to emigrate to other countries and regions, as well as freedom of speech, information, the press, association, forming and participating in trade unions, together with freedom to strike and hold meetings and demonstrations within the framework of law. They will also be free to decide how many children they have, and their freedom of marriage will be protected by law.

In short, Hong Kong is a challenge to the PRC, politically, economically and in the field of democratic civil liberties. This is China's first experiment in giving meaning and purpose to Deng's 'One Country, Two Systems'. Dynamic developments are likely to occur before and shortly after the reversion in 1997. Can Hong Kong succeed? Some do not believe so.[18]

7.2 THE TAIWAN TANGLE

Ever since the outbreak of the Korean War in 1950, Taiwan's legal status and political position have emerged to complicate the Cold War conflict in Asia and in the United Nations. Much of the conflict has resulted from changes in the United States toward the two governments of China. The position of the United States toward Taiwan has affected the policies and diplomatic dynamics of many Asian states, including Japan. Other than commercial and cultural relations with the Republic of China (hereafter ROC), most nations in recent years have terminated their formal diplomatic recognition of the ROC. There are currently twenty-two states with embassies in Taiwan. However, the United States alone is more deeply involved in Taiwan's security and defence even without formal diplomatic relations. Given its regional defence leadership in the superpower contest and in her direct relations with the PRC, policy options for the United States are very limited at the present time. It may be helpful to highlight the recent developments over the status evolution of Taiwan before the discussions of the PRC overtures of peaceful unification, Taiwan's internal politico-economic transformation and the challenge of its independence movement.

7.2.1   The Evolution of Taiwan's Status

The population of Taiwan is of Chinese descent, except for a small number of original 'mountain people'. Taiwan was ceded to Japan in 1895. At the Cairo Conference in 1943, it was solemnly decided among Chiang Kai-shek, Franklin D. Roosevelt and Winston Churchill that Taiwan must be returned to China upon the Japanese defeat. In 1945, the Chinese government took over Taiwan after the Japanese surrender. The local Chinese population in 1945 overwhelmingly welcomed the return to the motherland. Two years later, the unfortunate incident of 28 February touched off an uprising between Chinese of Taiwan birth and those arriving from the Chinese mainland after 1945. This incident seriously damaged the relations between the two groups. In 1949 Chiang's central government retreated to Taiwan while the victorious communist regime was preparing to invade the island in 1950. Suddenly, the Korean War broke out while the US diplomatic delegation was still in the Nationalist Government Capital of Nanking on the mainland.

Surprisingly and suddenly, President Harry S. Truman decided to send the US Seventh Fleet to the Taiwan Strait to protect Taiwan. Within one month, General Douglas MacArthur flew to Taiwan to meet with President Chiang to talk about Taiwan's defence against Communist invasion. Within weeks the US Military Advisory Group under General Chase came to re-arm and train the Nationalist troops. In 1954, a mutual defence treaty was signed between Washington and Taiwan. The United States began thus to insist diplomatically in the United Nations that the ROC was the only legal government of all China. The PRC, for the next 20 years could not receive a two-thirds majority of votes in the United Nations to be admitted to that body. The frozen attitude of the UN towards the PRC had worsened the relations for all Asian states. Suddenly again the United States under President Richard M. Nixon decided on secret talks with Beijing to change the US policy. Still the Taiwan tangle remained one of the most difficult issues in the US policy and in international politics. Much of this has remained from the superpower conflicts.

What is at the heart of the Taiwan tangle? How complicated has the crisis been in both domestic and international dimensions? Because of lack of space, only a few aspects will be discussed below.

When President Truman decided to defend Taiwan in 1950, he also unjustifiably raised a question over Taiwan's sovereignty or legal status. One of his arguments was that Taiwan's position had not been clearly defined at the Cairo Conference. It was decided only that Japan would relinquish Taiwan without specifically suggesting which Chinese government should take over from Japan. Taiwan's position remained to be decided internationally. This line of argument was repudiated immediately by both Taipei and Beijing. Suggestions were then aired in the United Nations as to whether a UN supervised plebiscite should be held in Taiwan to determine whether the majority of the people would wish to become part of China. This foolish suggestion was again immediately dismissed by Taiwan and Communist China. War in Korea between the US forces and those of the PRC was fought and a real possibility of another war emerged in 1958 when the communists launched their heaviest attack on the island of Quemoy which was China's own territory but under the control of the Nationalist troops. To avoid such danger of war with the Chinese communist regime, a 'two China theory' came into existence. If acceptable to both Taipei and Beijing, US relations with both of them would have been quickly transformed. This proposal was unacceptable to either one. The Nationalist government insisted on its legality, as elected in 1948 by the people on the mainland, to govern the entire country once it could achieve a victory on the mainland. The communist government, on the other hand, vowed to complete its war of liberation against Taiwan. Neither government can be blamed by the Chinese citizens for their common claim that 'Taiwan is a part of

China'. In any case, the United States could not untie the Taiwan tangle, legally, politically or militarily. The majority of nations continued in the 1960s to retain diplomatic relations with the Nationalist Government and supported the US position for nearly twenty years. The Cold War certainly was a major cause for nations taking sides. The United States, as the leader of the free world, commanded this position of prestige to retain the support from other nations. However, the 'two China approach' in the early 1960s remained condemned by both the ROC and the PRC.

The PRC's conflict with the Soviet Union and its military inability to confront the United States was one of the major reasons for Beijing's giving up the search for a military solution in Taiwan's liberation problem. China's mad plunge into cultural revolution and power struggle deprived the PRC of the ability to reclaim Taiwan. On the other hand, the ROC became gradually far more powerful after having the armed forces well-equipped and trained by the United States. However, the US would not allow the launching of offensive action along the China coast. Thus, Washington effectively froze the Taiwan Strait against any military action by either side in the 1960s. The Nationalists' hope of returning to the mainland militarily or of negotiating a settlement was thus totally frustrated. The government under President Chiang Kai-shek was not intended to be retained in Taiwan forever. However, he had no choice, given his defence alliance with the United States. Beijing, on the other hand, was kept out of the United Nations and the diplomatic community. Its concentration on its own domestic cultural revolution further isolated it from the outside world, which was watching US defeat and retreat from Vietnam. In essence, both Chinas were powerless to make their own decision about the unification. The superpower contest in Asia did not leave room for any nation to manoeuvre. Thus, two Chinas have existed in practice, but not in mutual recognition and have been at war since 1947. However, the matter of highest order is to find Taipei and Beijing in perfect agreement in their undivided claim and devotion to the unification of Taiwan to form 'One Single China'. No international conspiracy can shake that determination to unite Chinese territories and citizens some day under one single government.

When President Nixon wisely and correctly reviewed US policies toward the PRC, Vietnam, and the Soviet Union, the Taiwan tangle again became a painful reality. For example, the United States could not simply cast away a loyal ally of two decades. Japan and South Korea and the defence of Western Pacific Ocean required Taiwan to remain on the anti-communist frontline in early 1970s. Nixon had to devise a method of defreezing the Cold War in the Taiwan Strait if he was to achieve any improvement at all with the PRC in their mutual relations. First came the Secret Mission of Henry A. Kissinger in 1971. Then came Nixon's own 'Journey to Peace' in February 1972. In his joint communiqué with Premier Zhou Enlai, President Nixon shifted the US position toward Taiwan by declaring that 'there is but one China' and 'Taiwan is a part of China'. Washington, however, preferred a future unification by peaceful means. It clearly indicated that such unification is 'for the Chinese to decide'. Even today there has been no evidence of Washington's intention to be 'a peace broker' between Beijing and Taiwan.

All China experts have long realised the impact on Taiwan by the first Nixon trip to China in 1972. Taiwan became the embarrassed victim and deserted ally for the US to bargain away in order to achieve formal diplomatic relations with the PRC. But China's conditions for normalisation of mutual relations were quite harsh. They included: termination of formal diplomatic relations with Taiwan, abrogation of the mutual defence treaty of 1954, withdrawal of the Seventh Fleet and US forces from Taiwan and the Taiwan Strait, and expulsion of the ROC from the United Nations. The United States could not accomplish all these in a very short time without serious consequences for its leadership in the Pacific alliances. Thus, formal diplomatic recognition was not established until 1 January 1979 during the Carter Administration. All four conditions were eventually met. Taiwan suddenly became isolated in formal diplomacy and left out of the United Nations, the harsh position the PRC used to be under between 1950 and 1972.

However, US interests in the ROC were so overwhelming and genuine that Washington was compelled by the Congress and public opinion to legislate a Taiwan Relations Act in 1979 to protect Taiwan against external military threat and to maintain a uniquely 'unofficial' official diplomacy with the island. The PRC government considers this Taiwan Relations Act by the Congress an interference in China's domestic affairs. In essence, the Taiwan Relations Act is similar to the 1954 defence treaty except it does not require the presence of US forces in the area. Further, the PRC considers American arms sales and support of the ROC an effective obstacle against the prospect of peaceful negotiation for national unification. More will be said about this later. It is, however, sufficient to conclude that the evolution of legal, political and military status of Taiwan has been closely associated with the policy changes of the United States toward the PRC. And the ROC has been either a beneficiary or a victim of the changes. Stability and peace in the Taiwan region, and economic prosperity in Taiwan are, however, the two most positive and direct benefits of US policy. This very success has further complications for Taiwan, the PRC, and the prospect of Deng Xiaoping's 'One Country, Two Systems' as a formula for peaceful unification. The 'ball game' of the future, however, will see the PRC and the ROC to rise above selfish partisanship or not in their negotiation.

7.2.2   The PRC Overtures for Unification

Despite severing formal diplomatic relations, the United States remains the staunchest supporter of the ROC. The PRC cannot do anything about it despite strong objections. Given the need to concentrate all its resources on the success of the four modernisations and the need of growing diplomatic and defence relations with the United States, Beijing will continue to develop greater contact with Washington for mutual benefit. Having met with many diplomatic setbacks and political challenges on the home front, the ROC, on the other hand, has remained strong in economic growth and in political stability. All three capitals, Beijing, Taipei and Washington, seem to understand each other well. In this general state of improved relations, the PRC since 1981 has launched a persistent campaign to unify the country. Admittedly, there are several major reasons for the PRC's eagerness for unification. For example, the aging of President Chiang Ching-Kuo and his general weakening in health, the separatist movement against the Kuomintang in favour of Taiwan's independence, and prevention of the island from seeking contact with the Soviet Union are a few of the serious concerns to the PRC. Therefore, in late 1981, the PRC announced a nine-point unification plan which proposed to start bi-lateral negotiation immediately between Beijing and Taipei.

The nine points are summarised as follows:[19]

1. In order to quickly terminate the national split, the Communist Party and the Nationalist Party should begin negotiation in equal partnership through their representatives;
2. Chinese on both sides of the Taiwan Strait are desirous of mail service, mutual visits among relatives, and trade. Beijing recommends that such activities should commence, including academic,

cultural and sports exchanges;

3. After unification, Taiwan can enjoy 'a high degree of autonomy' as a special administrative region. It can also retain its armed forces. Beijing will not interfere in local affairs;

4. Taiwan's current social, economic and cultural system will remain unchanged. Its way of life, foreign relations, ownership of private and personal property and their inheritance and foreign investment will not be changed;

5. People in authority and representative personages of various circles in Taiwan can take up posts of leadership in national political bodies and participate in running the state;

6. If Taiwan's finance is in difficulty, the national government may subsidise it;

7. For those in Taiwan who wish to come to the mainland to reside permanently, the government can help and assure freedom to come and go without discrimination;

8. The PRC welcomes those in industry and commerce to come for investment and business. Their legal rights including entitlement to profits are guaranteed; and

9. All citizens are responsible for promoting national unification. The PRC welcomes all ranks of people to use all channels and methods to make suggestions on national affairs.

This announcement has been preceded by many other simple public overtures to the people of Taiwan for their efforts to help achieve national unity through peaceful means.[20] The PRC's terms for peace and unification are reasonable and responsively perceived to meet Taiwan's situation. However, Taiwan's responses to these proposals have been completely negative. Taiwan for its part, has different criteria for peaceful unification. For one thing, the Nationalist government's responses to the PRC's overtures are based on its past experience of negotiations with the Communist Party. The ROC has little faith in Communist promises which they violated each time at their own convenience. Taipei fears such deception again. In short, the ROC government often cites the following reasons against the Communists.[21]

1. The communist government's promise to the Tibetans in 1950 was violated in 1959. It finally became necessary for the Dalai Lama to escape to India. The social and religious system was destroyed and the PRC troops moved in to occupy and reform;

2. Past experience with the Communists convinced the ROC leaders

that agreements with them were never kept. Both during the war against Japan and in the 1949 examples of negotiation they found the Communists did not keep their promises – the promise to fight Japan turned out to be a devotion to expanding the Red Army rather than meeting the enemy on the battlefield, and the reasonable peace offer in 1949 turned out to be a demand for unconditional surrender and insistence on punishing the ROC 'war criminals';

3. The PRC's pressure to isolate and destroy ROC internationally has been increased in recent years while talking deceptively about agreement for unification. For example, it tried to prevent the ROC from purchasing arms abroad and establishing commercial relations in friendly countries;

4. The ROC is in a process of political integration in party leadership to include local Taiwan representatives in central government. Democracy in Taiwan must be met with the introduction of genuine democracy on the Communist side. The 'four cardinal principles: (especially proletarian democratic dictatorship under communist leadership) cannot be accepted as a suitable political and economic system for China. Sun Yat-sen's doctrine is the only basis for the unification of China in the future;

5. The lack of political stability in the PRC makes any negotiation and agreement undependable as a solution. Intra-party factional conflicts form a serious cause of political instability. The PRC has not yet succeeded in an institutionalised transfer of leadership through elections;

6. The nine-point peaceful unification proposal would be, in practice, a degradation of the ROC to a provincial level position, not a guarantee of equal footing during the period of the 'Special Administrative Region'. This is really a surrender call. At the same time, the ROC leadership can not fail to note that Beijing has not relinquished the use of force on Taiwan. Once the ROC has accepted the peace proposal, she could not remain independent in foreign trade and in purchase of arms abroad because the laws of the National People's Congress will be applied in Taiwan according to Article 31 of the 1982 Constitution. Even without any direct contact on future unification, the PRC has already strongly opposed the ROC's purchase of arms from the United States. In essence, the ROC does not trust the communist offer for unification. Much can be at stake once the offer is entertained as a basis for negotiation.

On the other hand, the ROC in Taiwan has a series of counter-suggestions. They see the ripe time for the start in negotiation will be determined by the PRC's effort to meet their own suggestions or preconditions. They can all come under the heading of unification through Sun Yat-sen's 'Three Principles of the People', namely, principles of nationalism, democracy and the livelihood of the people. This very doctrine of the revolution of 1911 was once the basis for acceptance of the Communists into the Nationalist Party in the 1920s and again the basis of the second agreement between the Nationalists and the Communists during the 1930s in the war against Japan. Mao Zedong himself personally advocated support and implementation of the 'Three Principles of the People' by all political parties in China at the CCP's Expanded Sixth Central Committee Meeting in October 1938.[22] The ROC leaders, in short, expect more changes to occur in mainland China to narrow the major differences between the ROC and PRC. Former Premier Sun Yun-Suan once declared in Taiwan in a speech:[23] 'If the political, economic, social and cultural gaps between the Chinese mainland and free China continue to narrow, the conditions for peaceful reunification can gradually mature. The obstacles to reunification will be reduced naturally with the passage of time.'

There was no direct response from the PRC to Premier Sun's speech. Nor has there been any official modification of the Communist Party stand on the 'four cardinal principles' in subsequent years. The recent nationwide student demonstrations in the PRC prove the need for more political and institutional reform under Deng Xiaoping. Even Deputy Premier Wan Li of the PRC said publicly in 30 August 1986 that the success of economic reform depends on greater political democracy. Until internal adverse pressure continues to mount, the ROC is likely to continue to adhere to its well-established policy toward reunification, namely, 'no contact, no compromise, and no negotiation'. Unless a new basis for contact or negotiation is found by the PRC, or the nine-point proposal is revised, reunification talks in the immediate future are not likely. For Taiwan, the ROC leadership is determined to preserve the right to maintain their independent international relations, autonomy, and the right to acquire defensive arms anywhere in the world. The ROC has reached a high level of industrial and economic development. It is now undergoing a democratic peaceful transformation into a two-party democracy. A new mass-based political party has emerged in late 1986 and has tested its high popular support in a general election in December 1986 in Taiwan. This new party's demand for greater democracy is both a challenge to the Nationalist Party on the island and to the Communist Party on the mainland. The younger generation in the PRC, given better education and greater opportunities in the outside world, will continue to demand an open society with genuine elective democracy and popular participation. The same remains true on the other side of the Taiwan Strait. Thus, the real gap between the ROC and PRC is the gap in political, social and economic development. Once this gap is narrowed, similarities between the two societies will appear and reunification will come sooner, provided no foreign intervention and no indigenous independence movement in Taiwan intervenes.

What are the main reasons for the PRC's promoting unification? What arguments has the PRC advanced to defend the nine-point peaceful proposal? How does the PRC view the Taiwan Relations Act of the United States? The following is an attempt to answer briefly these questions. A major 'documentary paper' presented by Li Shenzhi to an Atlantic Organisation Seminar has a complete review of the PRC stand on the Taiwan Tangle.[24] It properly asserted that 'Taiwan is China's problem ... which has emerged because of the American involvement'. It went on to emphasise the PRC's preference for peaceful unification for several reasons: (1) to avoid human sacrifice in a civil war; (2) the PRC needs a peaceful environment to develop its four modernisations; (3) peace and stability in East Asia is important to China since its opening up to the rest of the world, especially in the commercial field; (4) China expects to continue to transfer science and technology from the United States, Japan and West Europe. Any war in the Taiwan Strait will interrupt China's close relations with those states; (5) China is determined to improve her once-clouded relations with countries in Southeast Asia. War in the Taiwan Strait may adversely affect the improvement of these relations; and (6) military action will interrupt Taiwan's economic development.

Li's speech stresses the PRC's formula of 'One Country, Two Systems' and its unique reasons for application in Taiwan. True or not, the article asserts: (1) the greatest majority of Chinese in Taiwan identify themselves with China, despite a few elements who hope for an 'independent Taiwan' as influenced by the once popular discussion in the USA of a 'One China, One Taiwan'; and (2) presently, a large majority of people in Taiwan have many doubts concerning reunification; but this is understandable because of some ninety years of physical separation since its cession to Japan in 1895. 'Certain Americans fail to understand the inseparable feelings among the Chinese people. Foreigners thus conclude that the people in Taiwan do not want unification when the problem is merely concerning the conditions under which unification should be consummated.' Movement between fear and confidence among Chinese in Hong Kong can similarly occur in Taiwan. The main difference is that Taiwan is governed by our Chinese people, not the British. Li believed that the PRC has been very generous to Taiwan which will be permitted to keep its armed forces. The article stresses, however, that the PRC has never declared 'not to use non-peaceful means to unify Taiwan', hinting at a veiled threat.

Li's article blames the ROC government's attempt 'to have two Chinas under the slogan of one China' and its claim to represent all of China. The author criticises the ROC government for the expansion in semi-official relations with many nations to bring into practice two Chinas in substance in the national community. The United States is singled out for its double-edged approach toward China's internal problem concerning Taiwan. Li labelled the US policy as 'keep her feet in two boats' or 'two track policy'. On the one hand. Washington officially recognises the PRC as the 'only legal China and Taiwan is part of it' according to the Shanghai communiqué. On the other hand, the US government repeatedly declares 'the protection of Taiwan's security' as its own obligation. The United States has legislated a domestic Taiwan Relations Act to justify its sale of arms to Taiwan. This policy creates and perpetuates several dangerous consequences:[25] (1) it may induce the PRC's eventual unfortunate use of non-peaceful means to achieve unification; (2) it fosters negative conditions to delay the ROC's readiness to begin negotiation for unification; (3) it indirectly aids those separatists in favour of Taiwan's independence movement against the desire of one billion Chinese people for national unity; and finally (4) the Taiwan Relations Act is a direct interference in China's internal affairs. The Nationalist government itself may, in the end, be the victim of US policy which also tends to encourage the long-term emergence of anti-government forces under the disguise of democratisation. Li's paper especially attacks 'the US leaders and government spokesmen for their statements that the solution to Taiwan's future must respect the wishes of the residents in Taiwan'.[26] Li's paper further attacks the development during a US Senate hearing in 1984 when a certain senator asked an official of the State Department what the government might do in case of a PRC military attack against Taiwan's declaration of independence. The direct answer was 'the US would take the necessary action under the Taiwan Relations Act'. Li recognises that the majority of the leaders of the Taiwanese independence movement are concentrated in the United States. Indeed, a substantial number of them have US citizenship. Conservative and liberal factions in the US Congress and among certain interest groups either advocate support to the Nationalist government to adopt a two-China approach or give 'sympathy or encouragement to Taiwan's self-determination'. Both factions are interfering with or obstructing China's effort of reunification. Politically, the US is defending its interests in the Taiwan region. According to international law, however, the author asserts, the USA is in violation in China's domestic affairs by 'keeping the Taiwan issue frozen'.

What is the future prospect of unification in the next ten years? Rightly or wrongly, Li's article attempts to spell out three possible developments: (1) maintain the status quo; (2) peaceful solution; and (3) non-peaceful solution. He goes on to describe each of the three possibilities. He emphasises determinedly that the PRC would never tolerate a 'foreign-supported independence movement to take over Taiwan or foreign powers to take advantage in Taiwan's internal crises'. A high government official in my interview in 1985 declared that China would take non-peaceful means against Taiwan if (1) it declares independence; and (2) if the Soviet Union is involved.[27] Li's article asserts confidence that the PRC–ROC negotiation is not hopeless: 'Under the frozen ice surface there is often a warm current'. Taiwan's present position is 'Totally dependent on the United States'. The United States must, according to Li, choose among four alternatives: (1) continue the present policy; (2) retreat and let the Chinese people decide their own destiny; (3) adopt a positive stand in favour of negotiation; or (4) allow the crisis to emerge to trap it again in China's internal dispute. In the final analysis, the above alternatives will either be in favour of reunification or of separatism. He concludes the article by saying 'the United States has placed a time-bomb in Sino-American relations ... If you participants in this seminar can collectively assist the government to turn off the time-bomb, the interests of the United States and that of the world will be positively served'.[28]

The Taiwan Relations Act came under many attacks in the PRC. The major reasons are the same as presented in Li's paper cited above. However, more detailed debates have focused on US policy contradictions toward the PRC. For example, Washington is equally committed to honour the Communiqué on the Establishment of Diplomatic Relations of 1978 and to implement the Taiwan Relations Act. A US government spokesman when commenting at Congressional hearings or for the public record often hastily added that 'we don't see the two are contradictory'.[29] A communiqué is 'A solemn agreement' between governments. The Taiwan Relations Act is a piece of Congressional legislation having no international standing. The US government must learn to see the differences and choose since it cannot implement both. The United States has 'de-recognised the Nationalist government and recognised the PRC government as the sole legal government of China ... the US has made acknowledgement of one China and Taiwan as part of China'.[30] How can Washington pretend to be blind to confuse others? The Taiwan Relations Act also contradicts, according to arguments from the PRC, the obligations undertaken by the United States in its joint communiqués with China in the following ways: (1) 'the security clauses of the Taiwan Relations Act flagrantly interfere with China's internal affairs and encroach upon China's sovereignty'; (2) many provisions in 'Section 4 of the Taiwan Relations Act regard Taiwan as a country' and also openly declares 'the continuation in force of all treaties and other international agreements concluded by the United States and Taiwan and being in force on 31 December 1978'. This is absurd because Taiwan is merely a province of China. The PRC was disturbed by this kind of agreement during the Senate Hearings on Taiwan in the Spring of 1979 when questions and answers took place between Senators Hayakawa and Glenn and H. J. Hansell of the Department of State.[31] In short, this PRC position on Taiwan is a legal one. A superpower, on the other hand, can always act more politically in its national interest than legally to meet the international rule of law.

So far our discussion has provided a simple summary of the PRC overture for peaceful unification, the ROC response in a counter-argument of its own, and, finally, a PRC attack on the United States over the latter's interference in 'China's internal affairs' in the Taiwan region. What about a more objective analysis among some well-known social scientists of Chinese descent who are observing the development from North America? Although these academic scholars may not be totally unbiased, they each possess a much greater understanding and judgement than other Chinese people on both sides of the Taiwan Strait. It adds constructive insight to bring in their general outlook on the problem of re-unification. My summary below will be, of course, an over-simplification because of the limits of space.

On the whole, Chinese social scientists in the United States do not at all dispute 'the inevitable and eventual re-unification' of the PRC and the ROC. They, too, subscribe to the 'single China approach' which is politically and legally not disputed among Taipei, Beijing and Washington. With the exception of political refugees and refugee intellectuals from Taiwan, no Chinese scholars in North America have advocated or subscribed to the positions of 'Two Chinas', 'One China, One Taiwan', or 'the Republic of Taiwan' through a declaration of independence. Nearly all of them seem in favour of the proposition of of 'One China, but not now'. Re-unification will come when conditions of political, social, economic and cultural developments in both the PRC and the ROC are relatively similar. Thus, re-unification is seen as only a matter of time. This position, on the one hand, directly condemns those who advocate the independence of Taiwan. On the other hand, it requires both the PRC and the ROC to honestly and consistently seek what ought to be the proper conditions to be developed in social, political, cultural and economic fields in order to move the two systems closer together. A premature attempt at unification will not succeed peacefully. The nine-point overture for negotiation will downgrade the ROC and diminish its needed identity as it now exists in the international community for trade, cultural and political purposes. If accepted, the nine-point overture would subject the ROC in domestic affairs to the supervision and legislation of the PRC's National People's Congress, the highest organ of state, according to Article 31 of the 1982 Constitution. Thus, the ROC's rejection is predictable. It simply will not sign its death certificate to give up what it must preserve. Taiwan is economically strong and can purchase defensive arms abroad, especially from the United States under the Taiwan Relations Act. Taiwan can also manufacture a great many of its defensive weapons. Therefore, militarily it is capable of defending itself far more easily against an expensive attack which will require a much larger assembly of arms and men to cross the Taiwan Strait. In addition, there is a predictable popular unity of all 18 million citizens of the island in fiercely defending their homeland and property. Given the above factors, Chinese scholars in the US are able to formulate a general position on the unification issue as follows:[32]

1. Based on its previous experiences in negotiation with the Chinese Communist Party (CCP) that resulted in the CCP becoming stronger, the Kuomintang Party (KMT) is psychologically resistant to another negotiation. If the CCP expects to unify the country via negotiation, it must demonstrate sincerity and avoid the past duplicity of seeking to absorb Taiwan and destroy the

KMT. Unless the CCP is able to remove the KMT's fear of insincerity, the KMT will not negotiate to sign what it sees as its death certificate;

2. Thirty years of economic growth has enabled the people in Taiwan to enjoy an annual per capita income of $US2500 (as of 1982) *Vis-à-vis* those in the PRC of $US300. Popular elections have been in practice for decades as compared to none held on mainland China. Moreover, the political system in the PRC has not been institutionalised. Cultural development has also been different. Under such circumstances, pre-conditions to peaceful unification do not at all exist yet. Both sides must strive to attain them first;

3. Despite the highest common goal of both the PRC and the ROC in favour of unification at the end, lack of the above pre-conditions will make superficial unification less sustainable. If that should happen, large-scale bloodshed may be too costly for the nation to bear and foreign powers may thus interfere. Therefore, both the PRC and the ROC should be devoted to preparing for the pre-conditions or common grounds before the start of negotiation;

4. The present peace overture from the PRC appears reasonable and high-sounding, but behind the reasonableness is the pre-condition which requires the ROC to abandon its independent sovereignty. Once Taiwan lost its sovereign independence, and if the CCP should change the terms of agreement, it would not have the power to rectify the mistakes. Thus, the current peace overture should remain unacceptable to the ROC; and finally

5. Because of the past unpleasant negotiation experience, and because of the divergent developments in the PRC and in the ROC, successful unification requires a 'confidence building period'. During this period both should live in peaceful co-existence and peaceful competition on equal footing across the strait. They should not interfere in each other's international relations, especially not to meddle in each other's right of self-defence (such as purchase of arms abroad). On the PRC side, greater effort should be devoted to political and economic modernisation to shorten the gap between them. The ROC, on the other hand, must pledge not to engage in Taiwan's independence movement. And within the limits of self-defence and security capabilities, Taiwan should establish commercial, cultural, academic and sports exchange with the PRC to increase

mutual understanding. After such a period of transition, both may feel confident and comfortable in peaceful negotiations for re-unification.[33]

7.2.3 Democratisation and the Independence Movement in Taiwan

Taiwan has been under one-party domination since 1945, especially after the ROC government's removal from Nanking to Taipei in 1949. The existence of martial law in Taiwan since 1950 has denied most of the basic civil rights and genuine political participation to the citizens who would otherwise have enjoyed such liberties under the 1947 Constitution. The military garrison command in Taiwan has been fully empowered by the martial law to arrest and punish. It made itself most hated by those who cherish political and civil rights. No mass-based political party, except the KMT, could be organised. Elections at the local and county level were controlled and heavily regulated, although honestly executed and performed in an orderly manner. Municipal and provincial legislative elections were also instituted two decades ago. Political stability and regimentation were considered necessary for general social stability and for rapid economic development. Given the economic growth miracle through land distribution and the introduction of agricultural science, and the enormous educational expansion, Taiwan's lag in political democracy, as a price to pay, has been well worth it as compared with much poorer performance elsewhere in Asia.

What remains difficult to deal with is the growth of demand for political participation and for the rights to form political parties among native born Taiwanese. They have grown up under the Nationalist Party and are well-educated too. They are in the majority of the population who are sons and daughters of the native land. Without removal of martial law, however, they cannot do much short of committing civil disobedience. Thus, in the last half decade, political forces in organised groups outside of the Nationalist Party (Kuomintang or KMT) have grown in strength. They found ways to participate in election politics without a political party of their own. The government was careful to accommodate their needs at election time.[34] In recent years, more elections have been held to select a larger number of representatives to strengthen and expand the Taiwanese voice in the central government – members of the Legislative Yuan, the National Assembly and the Control Yuan. Demand for political participation has also been intensified as a result of other political developments and incidents. For example, native Taiwanese citizens are afraid of the possibility of reunification without their participation in the negotiation or with no regard for popular dissent. Secondly, many elements that have long been inclined toward Taiwan's independence may also camouflage their true colour through demands for political participation. Former citizens of Taiwan now living abroad and political refugees are equally eager to join the native opposition against the Nationalist rule. Thus, the political movement in favour of democratisation of the system has not been as simple as it appears. For example, the political opposition insists on 'Taiwan's future to be determined only by the 18 million people themselves'. There is strong suggestion here for separation from the future prospect of re-unification with the mainland.

Political democratisation through a popular election system has been institutionalised since the 1950s. Campaigns and elections in Taiwan have become, in recent years, major events in the life of citizens throughout the island. The Nationalist Party has devoted a great deal of energy to guide and compete at election time. On the whole the government can count on roughly 70 per cent of the popular vote. Indvidual non-government candidates collect about 30 per cent. Campaign irregularities and money involvement seem to be gradually devaluing the purpose of democracy. With the emergence of a strong middle class as a result of economic growth, demand for participation has gone hand in hand with the demand for social stability in recent years. The policy strategy of the government has been 'seeking progress through stability'. The late President Chiang Ching-Kuo in 1986 overruled, however, all the opposition from within the ruling Nationalist Party to allow the formation of the new Democratic Progressive Party (DPP). This was a new milestone toward democracy of two-party politics, something which has never been possible since the revolution of 1911.

Since March 1986, following a party conference, the government began a series of reforms encouraging political pluralism. Discussion took place over the removal of the martial law. It become legal for the political opposition to organise local chapters of 'political policy forum' and other election-related groups. Suddenly in late August 1986, representatives of groups of political opposition declared in Taipei the formation of the DPP despite its illegality while martial law was still in force. The government tolerated it. DPP thus formally became the opposition party to contest in the 6 December 1986, election. Even more encouraging for the DPP, it won twelve seats in the legislature and eleven in the National Assembly. This was a surprise victory for the DPP, but not a defeat for the KMT government which will continue to enjoy an absolute majority in the legislature. The important progress is that a new dialogue will be advanced at all times in the legislature by the opposition which is likely to grow and to integrate into a better and well-organised institutional party, although it presently suffers temporarily from factional conflicts and from lack of institutional stability.

In retrospect, one must give credit to the government party for its readiness to accommodate political demands through reform. However, the government has set three limits for the opposition party: (1) it must uphold the 1947 national constitution; (2) it must oppose communism; and (3) it must oppose the Taiwan independence movement. Presently, a new National Security Law has replaced martial law. Another proposal is being debated in the legislature for passage to allow citizens the constitutional rights to organise associations among themselves. Since the removal of the martial law, the regular judicial system have come into full play. The garrison command on the island can not freely make arrests and imprisonments any more. There is, already a fresh existence of a much greater press freedom. All these were carried out in 1987. Taiwan in 1988 enters a new age of democracy as a show case for constitutional liberty.[35]

Whether or not the DPP will live up to popular expectations remains to be seen. Its internal leadership itself is yet to be clear. Whether or not the DPP supporters among the voters are willingly and loyally to support the existing constitutional system is a serious matter of political test. Ideally, it is hoped that the DPP will rise as a genuine national party in platform and in activities. Unfortunately, it has to fight itself from within to streamline the party philosophy in a choice between being national in scope to share leadership and support with the Nationalist Party, or remain parochial and working only for the interest of Taiwan's eighteen million people.

All things considered, democratisation is a continuing process in Taiwan. Social, economic and cultural developments in the last thirty years require modernisation in political leadership and in institutional reform. Taiwan is now doing so and is ahead of many countries in East Asia in this respect except Japan. One author has concluded as follows:[36]

> Given the stable, step-by-step manner in which nation building in Taiwan has been achieved by the ruling party, there is every reason to believe that the legal and political reforms of 1986 were motivated

by a rational and sincere belief by the leadership that the Chinese people in Taiwan are ready for more democracy. While the reforms being made may fall short of the goal set by the ROC's hardest critics both at home and abroad, they still are a monumental step forward in political modernisation.

The sudden death of President Chiang Ching-Kuo in January 1988 may already offset the pace of democratisation. On the other hand, the Taiwan Independence Movement is a very vexing problem that may destroy some of the genuine effort toward democratisation in Taiwan. There is, of course, a long history to the independence movement. Many of the early leaders went to Hong Kong and Japan to fight the KMT government from abroad. Before the 1970s many of them died abroad. The new and younger leaders since 1970 have concentrated in the USA. They are articulate and energetic. Some have even conducted urban guerrilla warfare.[37]

More seriously, since 1964, there was a declaration for independence which read:[38]

A powerful movement is rapidly developing inside Formosa. It is a self-preservation movement of the island's twelve million people who are willing neither to be ruled by the communists nor to be destroyed by the Chinese Nationalist regime. Riding high on the universal currents of awakening peoples, we dedicate ourselves to the overthrow of the Government of Chiang Kai-shek and to the establishment of a free, democratic, and prosperous society ... that there are one China and one Formosa is an iron fact. In Europe or in America, in Africa or in Asia, whether or not one has already accorded diplomatic recognition to the Chinese Communist Government, the entire world accepts the fact of one China and one Formosa.

If the declaration were written today, the author would be laughed at, because the real world that most countries have accepted is that there is but one China and Taiwan is part of China. In the early decades many native students who went abroad for study did not return. Some of them eventually became anti-government and joined such groups. As one student said: 'As long as the KMT rules the island, I prefer to live in a democratic country'.[39] A large number of them lived in Japan which was eager to see Taiwan become independent so as to avoid the communist takeover. Japan was worried about its own defence if the Communists were to move closer to Okinawa. There was a large community of Taiwanese in Japan (some 25,000 of them) by the 1960s, although many had come to Japan before 1945. They were, however, split by factionalism. Wen Y. Liao, a well-known leader of them, once said; 'Factionalism? Everyone has a different explanation and they are all partly right'.[40] Those in the United States organised themselves as United Formosans in America for Independence (UFAI) who had their own publications. Others were scattered in Canada and Western Europe. While in Europe, they, too, created their own organisation, Union for Formosa's independence in Europe (UFIE). Their headquarters was in Paris in the middle 1960s. Eventually, after most countries recognised communist China in the 1970s, these anti-government Taiwanese gradually moved to the United States. Factionalism among them seems to be growing worse.

Another type of younger and better educated Taiwanese emerged in the forefront in the late 1970s calling themselves members of 'revolutionary national liberation movement'. They attempted to adopt the Marxist–Maoist strategy in their Taiwan Independence Movement (TIM) to terrorise and destroy so as to interrupt normal urban life. Both in Taiwan and abroad, they spread false propaganda to embarrass the Chiang regime which, they asserted, 'had pillaged the land and the people' and was unable to make economic progress. By the late 1970s these 'radical revolutionary' groups increasingly relied on terrorist actions to accomplish Taiwan Independence through an 'urban guerrilla' strategy. Altogether some twenty-six incidents of violence were committed between 1970 and 1983 as documented by A. James Gregor.[41] The most widely reported violence was the attempted assassination of Vice-premier Chiang Ching-Kuo in New York City on 24 April 1970 by two members of TIM (Chiang Tsu-tsai and Huang Wen-hsuing). They tried to bomb power installations (January 1976), to assassinate Governor Hsieh Tung-ming (October 1976), and to destroy dams, bus, and newspaper buildings between 1980 and 1983 in Taiwan. In foreign countries, they killed ROC government diplomats (Paris, 1983), burned the KMT news department (New York 1979), damaged China Airline Office (Chicago 1980) or planned arson. However, such violence did not stir the people and did not achieve their political purpose. The violent movement itself collapsed. As the KMT government under late President Chiang Ching-Kuo has steadily moved forward to achieve economic miracles, he became more and more popular among the native people throughout the island. Per capita income and GNP rose and political violence declined. The independence movement lost its appeal for the Taiwanese people both on the island and abroad. Rather it was the struggle to open up the political system for pluralism in participatory democracy that has become more attractive in the 1980s. The Chung-li and Kao-hsuing incidents demonstrated clearly that polarisation and politicisation within the political system was transforming the system itself. Only occasionally a sporadic voice is heard about Taiwan's right to become independent. Any serious separatist movement would invite the PRC intervention instantly.

In summary, the Taiwan Independence Movement can be divided into several stages: (1) stage one (1947–64) was a period of strong factionalism and peaceful struggle from abroad; (2) stage two (1964–83) was the period of regrouping, federating in the midst of violence, frustration and defeat; and finally (3) stage three (1983–) has become an open struggle from within the system through election contests, open street demonstrations and the formation of political parties. Perhaps the younger generation has become more sophisticated, articulate, knowledgeable and mature. Social changes, economic growth and the emergence of a strong middle class seem to be the major factors in discouraging any form of violent attempt to destroy the existing political system. Rather, these very factors directly compel the Nationalist Government to initiate new reforms to meet popular demands. Such reform has already been underway since 1986. The prospect for those people living largely abroad and constituting the backbone of the independence movement looks bleak indeed. The DPP seems to have taken over the underground movement from within the island. But a new form of tension of political development will remain strong over many difficult issues ahead, as a result of President Chiang Ching-Kuo's death in 1988. President T.H. Li is both a Taiwanese and the acting Chairman of the KMT.

7.2.4 Conclusion

Hong Kong and Taiwan are too different to be treated in the same manner. It is much easier to obtain a joint declaration from the British. Hong Kong is much within the PRC's reach politically and commercially. There is an inevitable continuity of mutual dependence between Hong Kong and the PRC. None as such exists between the PRC and the ROC as yet. There is a third superpower, the United States, acting on both sides of the Taiwan Strait to exercise a balancing influence as it sees fit. This triangular relation will not change until the PRC is ready or is powerful enough to risk a diplomatic showdown with Washington. Secondly, Taiwan's independent-minded population exerts only strong but negative influence on the ROC government in the latter's attitude toward reunification. Thirdly, the open agreement of 'one

China', which includes Beijing, Taipei, Washington, Tokyo, and most of the other less involved capitals of the world is itself a stabilising force for the immediate future. The evaluation of a dialogue on preconditions before negotiation between Taipei and Beijing will continue. Should there be any sudden or unexpected change of attitude, it will probably come from Taipei. And finally, the process of political reform and the challenge of the new Democratic Progressive Party may yield new understanding and causes for changes on development in the ROC.

All things considered, for Taipei it is worth noting again the proposition made by Professors Hungdah Chiu, James C. Hsiung and Kau Ying-mau that exchange of mail, sports, academicians and other cultural contacts should be seriously attempted between the PRC and the ROC. In my own judgement, given enough time to allow confidence to be built up, both will be able to reflect from their present positions on negotiation. A realisation for 'one China' might come much sooner if political reforms on the mainland move forward faster than expected as a result of the recent nationwide student demonstrations for democracy and civil rights. It is my firm view that the success of Deng Xiaoping's grand politico-economic reform will inevitably move the PRC closer to the Taiwan experience in both political and economic progress. Public insistence on the 'four cardinal principles' will eventually be less and less necessary and meaningful. The interest in the PRC in studying Sun Yat-sen's doctrine of the revolution of 1911 may even influence Deng Xiaoping's definition of 'socialism with Chinese characteristics'. If the ROC succeeds in its experiment with an open and pluralistic democracy in the next decade in Taiwan, she can truly be a catalyst for both democratic and economic success on the mainland.[42] Increase of indirect trade, Taiwan businessmen's desire to seek investment inside the PRC, and the millions of homesick citizens visiting the mainland since late 1987 will jointly have an impact on relations on both sides of the Taiwan Strait.

8 Conclusion: Revolution, Continuity and Synthesis

8.1 NEW CHINA OF THREE TRADITIONS

The preceding chapters have introduced the rise of Deng Xiaoping to supreme leadership through many stages and struggles. Readers are now better able to appreciate the various kinds of problems Deng has had to confront since 1977. China under Deng began to fight all the odds in an uphill battle. Some of the policy goals and methods needed to accomplish his reform he could freely and openly spell out. Other sensitive issues he did not feel free to announce. By 1977, he was a mature and well-seasoned politician after having been humiliated and removed from office several times. He had then few or none of his former close colleagues on hand in 1977 to team up and fight. The leadership authority was still in the hands of Premier Hua Guofeng and his Maoist supporters. Deng remained in the leadership minority for two years among colleagues in the party's political bureau which is the highest real decision making body in China. He has to be very tactful despite his devotion to reform China in a more comprehensive way as he expected at long last.

I have outlined in preceding chapters some of the critical aspects relative to his grand reform. For example, the dynamic nature and demand of the reform, the crisis of his own ideological void, and the need to rehabilitate many of his former comrades with Premier Hua's approval. His search for a new method to begin rural agricultural reform and to experiment with urban production and enterprise management reform were at the heart of his thinking. He wanted to find ways to take steps to convince a closed nation to open its doors to foreign countries for broad contacts in a hope to acquire science, technology, industrial management skill and capital investment. What sacrifices must be made to convince sceptical foreign leaders in the West who for more than thirty years had been locked out of China as enemies? How could a new definition and content be given to his society of Socialist Legality, Socialist Democracy, Socialism with Chinese Characteristics and his promise of Collective Leadership? A host of such problems did not have solutions. He had a strong sense of new direction to move toward. As a practical realist, he seemed confident in what he could achieve and what priority had to be followed to provoke the least resistance and to maximise support from within the policy-making machinery and the population at large. His lifetime experience now became his best inner guiding voice for action or silence. He needed the 'Four Cardinal Principles' to assure his opponents – the socialist path, the Communist Party leadership, Marxism–Leninism–Maoism, and democratic dictatorship. On the other hand, he insisted on 'practice as the sole test for truth' as a justification to free his hand for experiment with his 'black-and-white cat' theory.

As the confident grand reformer sitting on top of a gigantic bureaucracy, Deng had by late 1978, finally found a new team of leaders to set his reform in motion. They did the work, and he guided their pace for reform and the critical thinking for the next right move: from the countryside to urban centre, from the party to the government, and from the undoing of the Maoist cultural revolution to his four modernisations. Detailed policy planning, policy implementation and programme supervision and evaluation were the tasks assigned to others. Deng shared his leadership and decision-making power with chief supporters. As a former bureaucratic chief administrator, Deng knew the importance of respecting the organisational division of responsibility and role assignment. Thus, he could keep himself free from less important decision-making. He had to see far ahead to discover solutions for new problems. For example, on the reversion of Hong Kong and the re-unification with Taiwan, he offered a long-term solution: 'One Country, Two Systems'. To attract foreign technology and investment, he adopted the practice of the special economic zone as a non-socialist sector of economic experiment. These issues required careful judgement in an effort to keep all conflicting political factions and ideological forces in balance.

To depict Deng's role in the PRC we are forced to view him and his responsibility in historical perspective in order to judge whether or not he can meet history's approval. The same applied to Chiang Ching-Kuo in the ROC. There are three major political cultures or ideologies which have interacted with each other since the turn of the century. These three political traditions have never ceased to compete with one another as China struggled to modernise itself to meet the standard in global revolutionary development. They are the indigenous cultural tradition, the new democratic tradition of the revolution of 1911, and the Marxist Sovietised revolution of 1949. The indigenous Confucian political tradition is the most prominent and well-integrated institutional system with which China has been totally and proudly identified for more than 2000 years. The entire treasury of Chinese civilisation is the substance of this tradition. But without change in some parts of this indigenous tradition, China could not bring itself into the modern world. It was inappropriate to resist the challenge of foreign science, industry, liberty, equality, and political democracy. If there was no way to peacefully change the old or traditional China, a revolution to overthrow the old political system was the only approach to revitalise China in order to resist foreign imperialist encroachment which began in the 1890s. So there must be revolution for a new China.

But how to bring about a new China? What new ideology has been introduced into China in the last ninety years has resulted in an excruciating, bitter experience in modern Chinese history. What kind of a future did the revolution of 1911 accomplish for the people? Why did that revolution abort? Certainly many Chinese in general can emphatically agree that the meaning of liberty, equality, popular democracy, and constitutional system of government that they have learned before 1949 are attributable to the revolution of 1911.

Why was there a need for a Marxist revolution in China shortly after the October victory in 1917 in Russia? Unfortunately, lack of space does not permit a lengthy discussion here. However, a simple overview on each of all three traditions is necessary in order to appreciate that all revolutions create changes. Continuity of parts of the indigenous tradition always remains visible. What is changed and what remains visible must be synthesised for the new order to integrate after a major revolution. This is now the task of Deng Xiaoping, to understand correctly historical continuity. Every major revolution, including the American and the French revolutions of 1776 and 1789, has its own ideological tenets to justify the revolt and to bring about a new way of life. What should be Deng's new ideological tenets after having seen the failure of Sovietised Marxism in China and the bankruptcy of radical leftist Maoism in the aftermath of the cultural revolution? The new measuring formula that 'practice is the sole test of truth' is itself not an ideological truth but a working tool in policy-making choice. It is not an ideological system in itself that can be used to debate and defeat Marxism, or to repudiate the doctrine of the revolution of 1911. To meet this ideological vacuum or void, one must carefully identify, first of all, the three major ideological, or political traditions. All three have had their supporters and antagonists in twentieth-century China. As a value system in political culture, what do the one billion Chinese like or dislike after having lived under all three – the indigenous Confucian tradition up to 1911, the tradition of the Revolution of 1911, and the Marxist tradition since 1949? I shall focus below on an over-simplified summary of the political culture of each of the three.

8.2 The Indigenous Cultural Tradition

As a belief system, Chinese indigenous political culture has two diametrically antagonistic aspects. Both were equally applied to justify (1) the exercise of absolute authority by an emperor who received the 'mandate from Heaven'[1] to rule, or (2) the right of tyrannicide to justify the next revolution. The first was applied at the moment when an emperor was crowned to begin a new dynasty hereditarily from emperor to emperor in the same imperial household. The second was to support the popular right to revolt and kill a bad emperor, if the people found physical evidence of his immoral or unethical behaviour. Revolt was justified at the moment when Heaven had withdrawn the mandate from an unacceptable ruler of the people. The real test of a divine statesmanship was easily measured by such clear evidences of good harvest, tranquil climate, perfect peace and prosperity through-out the imperial realm. An emperor deserted by heaven was always surrounded by the opposite evidences, such as earthquakes, other natural disasters, imperial household corruption and sex scandals or poor harvests. In short, the emperor must behave morally and fairly to deserve loyalty from all officials under him and from the people at large. The government became corrupt when the imperial household and the emperor were corrupt. For example, Mao Zedong would have been considered a tyrant, a bad ruler who created chaos and caused poor harvests during the time of his rural commune and the 'Great Leap Forward' in 1958–60. Thus, he should have been killed or chased off the throne of power according to the practice of imperial political culture. On the other hand, Deng Xiaoping would be viewed as having the 'mandate from Heaven' to govern because his government has brought good harvest, prosperity and domestic tranquility. And thus the people should offer him loyalty and support. There was and still is such a popular belief to justify whether or not a regime can enjoy peace which says 'those who win the hearts of the people will succeed in good government; and those who lose the hearts of the people will be thrown out'. This quotation has been one of the most popularly cited 'common watchwords' among the Chinese masses. Its very significance can be equated with the Western belief in 'the sovereignty of the people'. More than 2000 years ago Mencius made the following famous proverb: 'Heaven sees what the people see; and Heaven hears what the people hear'. This was his theory in support of popular sovereignty against bad rulers. He wrote again that 'the people are most valuable (or come first); the bureaucrats come second; while the ruler is least valuable'. Rulers come and go; they can be replaced. So can the officials of government. But the people's interests are the basis for government. In short, in traditional China, there was a well-known fixed standard of good conduct for rulers and officials to follow. The people were the judges and were free to draw their own conclusions about their rulers. According to Mencius, the people can decide on the application of tyrannicide or not. Unfortunately, this political-cultural articulation of theory was not institutionalised as a systematic machinery for 'checks and balances' as in the American Constitution or through a well-built election system to turn out of office bad rulers and the emperor himself.

The other aspect of traditional Chinese political culture automatically compelled the people to accept any new emperor on his positive assertion of having received a 'Heavenly Mandate'. This theory worked every time for more than 2000 years when a new emperor had defeated all other contenders or pretenders to the throne. His military, or political power was so overwhelming or unmatchable by any one else that his claim to a 'new mandate from Heaven' became undeniable. Thus, the bureaucrats and the people of the realm had no choice but to pledge their loyalty and allegiance to him. It resembles Adolf Hitler's ascension to dictatorship when every resistance had been eliminated. This practice, as a tradition or a 'constitutional principle' in traditional China, was completely institutionalised to allow the ambitious victor to legitimately establish his new dynasty. This practice can be compared with the modern British 'unwritten constitution' which is 'written in the hearts' of the British people. This 'unwritten Chinese Constitution' was written in custom and practice for 2000 years. Thus the 'dynastic cycle' repeated itself dozens of times in Chinese political history.

If this practice seemed perfect, why was there the cause for the revolution of 1911? Of course, it was not acceptable any more when China was forced to open up to the Western Nations and Japan. The old imperial system failed to protect its system's functional integrity. Besides, foreign political ideologies of liberalism, theory of rights of man and civil liberties, individualism and equality, and, above all, the doctrines of three-way separation of power and constitutional government slowly but steadily found their way to imperial China. So the Chinese societal integrity and political system became bankrupt before the turn of the century. When constitutional reform under Kang Yu-wei and Liang Chi'-chiao failed in 1898,[2] the only way out to rescue the nation was through Sun Yat-sen's revolution to establish a democratic system of government.

What were other aspects of the political culture in the Confucian system of society? Are any of the traditional values still strongly adhered to by the average Chinese people? How much of the traditional heritage was adopted in the behavioural pattern of many leaders of the Nationalist party and the Communist Party? Any responses to these questions cannot be adequate without knowing the nature of the Confucian society – its structure in human relations, class stratification or mobility and the philosophy of life. To begin with, the Confucian philosophy rests on the belief that every person must play his or her role in a structured relationship of authority to maintain a balance and harmony. Any good government must enforce the well-prescribed code of ethics that is required of each person. For example, filial piety and the extended family of complex human relationships were expected to demonstrate the cardinal virtues in human nature. A gentleman of the society earns his title through learning and his demonstration of classical virtues. He occupies a socially elevated position of prestige. He is entitled thus to enter government service through passing various imperial examinations. Such a scholar-gentry came into existence in the Han Dynasty. The learned men, as bureaucrats or aristocrats, governed continuously while emperors and dynasties came and went. Confucian precepts of etiquette and rituals were sources of law that was enforceable by the state authority. The traditional political system in China was derived from the Confucian concepts of a hierarchical authority structure. Since the Han dynasty, Confucian teaching became the official ideology of the imperial state at the expense of others, including legalism, Taoism and Yin-yang theory. Or rather, other ancient schools of learning were gradually incorporated into 'official Confucian religion of state' under the 'Son of Heaven' as emperor. His authority was unlimited. The people had little to say against the emperor, contrary to modern constitutional heads of state.

The Confucian social-hierarchical code of ethical conduct was fully implemented through education and social organisations to such an extent that individuals, families, villages, towns, counties, as self-sustaining units, governed themselves with almost no support or interference from higher levels of government. In practice, government was an un-necessary evil of corruption and abuse of authority. There was a 'natural way of democracy in self-government' at the lower levels of the society.[3] In the legal and juridical sense, the entire state power was employed to enforce the Confucian way of life. This was inevitable because the scholar-officials were themselves 'little Confucians' by education and conviction. Such a way of cultural life has survived in many parts of China, especially among villagers in rural China and among traditional scholars such as Mao Zedong whose concept of 'democratic centralism' arrogated all the 'last words' of authority to himself. He and many twentieth-century Chinese leaders have demonstrated in their behaviour, consciously and unconsciously, the same legacy of traditional political culture.

Given the emphasis on humanism, the moralisation of politics, the training or indoctrination of people in following various codes of conduct and the monopoly of political power by scholar bureaucrats, traditional political culture remained antagonistic toward democratic values and political rights and equality under any modern constitution. This was the main difficulty for China in modernising through peaceful reform in 1898. It was more difficult to accept a republican form of government with officials elected after the revolution of 1911 which overthrew the 3000 year old system of imperial government. Since then many Chinese leaders have asked whether or not the country should go for 'total Westernisation'. Or whether or not the traditional political foundation should largely be retained and China should adopt only Western science and technology. After the May 4th movement in 1919, some young Chinese intellectuals became convinced that China should avoid Western bourgeois revolution under Sun Yat-sen and go directly to ally with the Soviet Union for Marxist revolution in China. Thus three political traditions soon met in the 1920s to generate confusion, contradiction, and frustration for the feeble and young republic which was still under the domination of regional warlords. Even today we see conflicts being generated by mutual exclusiveness of the three traditions: indigenous culture, Western democracy, and communist proletarian dictatorship.[4] The country naturally cannot totally shake off its past political thought and behaviour in such a short time. Many of the past political ideas are an integral part of the Chinese civilisation in general. Mao Zedong tried to uproot the traditional culture through his 'Great Political-Cultural Revolution' of 1966–76, but he failed completely in his attempt. To many contemporary Chinese people, Mao stands a condemned tyrant who was worse than the First Emperor or the Chin Dynasty, in his radical uprooting of indigenous tradition in favour of an outlandish, inapplicable and bankrupt application of Marxist political ideology.

It is now up to Deng Xiaoping to reverse Mao's ignorance and his leftist radicalism. The revival of Confucian learning in China in recent years is a good sign of constructive attitude toward the nation's cultural past. Restoration of Confucian temples and documentation of his life through movie pictures represent a proper shift in cultural development. Deng's 'Socialism with Chinese Characteristics' will in time demonstrate what characteristics will be discovered and preserved. Compared with the 'bourgeois revolution' of 1911 and the policy on cultural development, Taiwan's attitude toward indigenous cultural tradition is much more in harmony with the goals of life in the past. Individualism and personal rights of the bourgeois revolution of 1911 are in deep conflict with the proletarian revolution of 1949. They both must in time find proper reconciliation if the two parts of China are to be unified peacefully. In short, Deng should be seriously concerned about China's Confucian cultural tradition and its way of life. Every nation values its heritage. Chinese civilisation and cultural values are deeply respected everywhere in the world outside of the PRC. Foreign scholars, for example, admire the Chinese family system and concept of friendship. Chinese arts, poetry, and ancient classics seem more valued elsewhere than in China. Recent tourism in China should encourage many Chinese to realise that their cultural heritage and traditional philosophy of life have attracted millions of foreigners. Any revolutionary excess and the blind condemnation of the past tend to misjudge the past cultural achievement. Creativity in arts and literature should be insulated from any revolutionary condemnation for its immediate political purposes, such as the wholesale condemnation of the past during Mao's cultural revolution of 1966–76.

Future Chinese leaders must realise the need for cultural pluralism. There must be some cultural independence from political persecution for the sake of preserving the culture itself. The Chinese people will continue to love their past culture and will protect the cultural values as part of their real life. Politics must not be in command of everything. Modernisation itself will inevitably lead to cultural pluralism. Deng's reform policies in politics and economics will still come into conflict with indigenous tradition, unless the leadership realises the need for cultural independence.

8.3   THE LEGACY OF THE REVOLUTION OF 1911

Sun Yat-sen was the first Westernised Chinese leader who devoted his entire life to change imperial China through political revolution, or the overthrow of the Manchu dynasty. In its place, a republic of China was to be established to achieve modernity for the nation. This task included, among other things, the following:

1. Development of a national self-consciousness to resist foreign aggression and to abolish the 'unequal treaties'. This policy would bring China to a level to be treated with equality among nations under international law;
2. To create a democratic political system to allow the citizens, for the first time in history, to elect their leaders in government at all levels. This would have made government responsible to the average citizens. Failing in their Constitutional duties, the elected officials could be recalled from offices;
3. To introduce a peaceful system of land reform to divide land equally among the tillers. This would have stopped rural exploitation by landlords. His revolution proposed a mechanism to regulate industrial capital to prevent the evils of Western unregulated capitalism which had occurred in the nineteenth century;
4. To attract international investment and technology to help develop Chinese industries. This would have kept China open to the outside world and also would have enable China to contribute to international peace and security.

In short Sun Yat-sen's doctrines of nationalism, democracy and the livelihood of the people were three tools to achieve modernisation for China. But, for a variety of reasons beyond his control, his revolution failed. Sun himself listed some reasons as follows: (1) Foreign imperialists intervened on behalf of their existing special privileges and interest in China as guaranteed by the 'unequal treaties' which they had imposed on China unilaterally; (2) many foreign states supported Yuan Shih-Kai, the traitor of the revolution, and other regional warlords who succeeded Yuan upon his death in 1916; and most important of all, (3) his followers as revolutionary leaders failed to understand the task of the revolution and to reconstruct a new nation of democracy, industrial development and national unity through new nationalism. Thus, his followers were divided aimlessly, factionalised over minor disagreements, and disappointed with the consequences of the removal of the imperial dynasty. The country plunged into lawlessness, and this allowed Yuan Shih-Kai's followers to continue to exploit the people and to feed foreign powers' ambition for their own protection. Thus Sun was disappointed himself and started the second revolution against Yuan and later his remnants.

Sun himself did not become, like General George Washington, actual ruler of the country. The warlords and their governments, after 1911, were formally recognised by foreign countries. But the purposes of his revolution to make China strong, independent and prosperous in the community of nations were eventually accepted by the entire nation, including the Chinese Communists who joined the Nationalist party in 1923 in order to defeat the warlords and to unify the country. In essence, Sun's hope for Western democracy, liberty and equality, was indisputable. The Chinese intellectuals agreed, especially during and after the May 4th Movement of 1919, that China needed democracy and science. However, some young students after 1917 became interested in the study of Marxism. They eventually secretly organised the Chinese Communist Party in July 1921, in Shanghai. Although Sun died in 1925, his revolutionary followers soon unified the country militarily in 1928, with some effort of the Communists. Soon Sun's 'Three Principles of the People' became 'the bible' for national reconstruction. China under the Nationalists went through a decade of rapid development in many fields, especially in education, transportation, rural assistance, and abolition of most of the 'humiliating unequal treaties'. However, after Chiang's purge of the Communists in the Nationalist Party in 1927, the country remained in a new state of civil war. The Japanese agression in China broke out in 1931 in the Manchuria Incident which provoked China into military armament in anticipation of a large-scale Japanese aggression, which occurred in July 1937. China was at war again with Japan until 1945. Civil war was renewed in 1947.

From 1927 to 1949, the Nationalist Party was in control of China. Indeed, they were confronted with many insurmountable problems, such as the Japanese aggression before and after 1937 and the civil war with the Communists whose aims for the nation were never well understood except their struggle to oust the Nationalists from power. Propaganda from both the Nationalists and the Communists appeared confusing to the masses. Victory for the Communists after 1947 was inevitable in view of the post-war run-away currency inflation, popular antagonism toward the renewal of civil war, greed and corruption of the Nationalist officials, and their loss of popular support. Therefore, by 1949, its armed forces collapsed in indiscipline and surrendered one after another. Sun's doctrine never had a chance for implementaion.

How does one evaluate the democratic revolution of 1911 in view of the total chaos in twentieth-century China? The Nationalists came and went in only twenty-two years on mainland China, but its renewal and rejuvenation in Taiwan has lasted thirty-nine years. This success must be taken seriously; it cannot be irrelevant to the development in the PRC. On the other hand, Mao Zedong's Marxist revolution of 1949 also came and went in twenty-seven years. Deng Xiaoping initiated a new era of peaceful reform. This, too, must be taken seriously in an analysis of future development. Both the Nationalists and the Communists have each created a tradition of its own.

Sun's doctrine of revolution, unlike Marxism, has never been seriously criticised by any Chinese intellectual. Even some eighty years ago, he was able to propose precisely what China then needed and still needs today. His doctrine emerged from three sources: (1) China's traditional culture and institution; (2) modern Western democratic theory; and (3) his own innovation and integration of relevant theories and concepts applicable to China. For example, he praised highly the traditional Chinese civil service system to place government in the hands of educated scholars. He also preserved the Chinese traditional institutional system of censorship. Thus he was able to propose a 'Five-Power Theory' of government.[5] Western concepts of judicial independence and separation of power between the executive and the legislative were adopted to introduce a genuine form of democracy in China. He did not blindly condemn Chinese culture but opposed, for example, such practices as superstitions and the intolerable inequality between man and woman. He advocated the need for strong nationalism as a means of national survival only, but not as a tool of aggression against others. Sun was opposed to the global cosmopolitanism of the strong nations which would lead to national self-destruction of the weak nations. He advocated a global practice of national self-determination against foreign colonialism. To Sun, the recovery of 'national spirit' was the only way to achieve internal unity against external aggression. Chinese 'national spirit and heritage' consists of 'loyalty to state, filial devotion to parents, kindness and love to fellow citizens, justice and harmony in human relations and peace to the world'.[6] Traditional morality and ancient Chinese learning must be fully and eagerly revived. He advocated the revival of Chinese political philosophy as incorporated in the ancient 'Great Learning'. Contrary to Marxism, Sun's concept of nationalism for unity and salvation was easy to understand and to appreciate by all Chinese. Even Mao Zedong supported him on this.

On the theory of democracy, Sun read J. Rousseau, J. S. Mill and John Locke. He was opposed to autocracy, despotism or the justification for the existence of any form of privileged classes. His greatest contribution, however, was in his clear analysis of the differences between his Principle of the People's Livelihood (Min Sheng) and Marxism. On 3 August 1924, when Sun delivered his first lecture on this subject, he said that Karl Marx had been wrong in advocating materialistic determination of human history and human behaviour. Sun considered Marx merely an economic 'pathologist of social disease', not a 'physiologist for its cure'. His own theory of livelihood of the people is the real cure of rampant capitalism. While Marx had foolishly advocated class warfare, Sun, on the other hand, insisted on the need for peaceful class reconciliation as the source of social progress. To prevent capitalist monopoly, Sun proposed a mechanism of progressive taxation on the one hand and public ownership of public utility services on the other. His policy on land control and 'land to the tillers' represents a peaceful alternative to Marxist violent confiscation of private property. Sun's approach was more successful and practical, therefore, than that of Marx, Lenin and Mao Zedong: Mao's rural commune failed while Taiwan succeeded in its land reform. His doctrine has been implemented with flexibility by the Nationalist government to bring about an economic morale of prosperity and high per capita income as compared to the deplorable suffering of the Chinese people under Mao's rule. In his lectures in 1924, Sun specifically warned that Marxism was inapplicable to China. At that time, there was little or no industrial development or capitalist threat in China. He was sure that China could easily prevent all the evils of the free enterprise economy. In conclusion, it is fair to say that much of what he advocated has proved to be accurate and useful. He was a moderate revolutionary, a reconciliationist of cultural differences and a progressive thinker who, unfortunately, did not live to see the revival in the study of this revolution of 1911 in the PRC sixty years after his death.

Furthermore, Sun was a man of peace. He negotiated for peace with Yuan Shih-Kai in 1912 to avoid more blood. To satisfy Yuan's amibition in exchange for peace and for Yuan's acceptance of the new republic, Sun resigned his post as provisional president of the young republic in March 1912. Thirteen years later, he journeyed from Canton to Beijing via Japan while ill, in order to unify the country by peaceful agreement with the warlords to avoid a military expedition which was being prepared by Chiang Kai-shek in 1925. Unfortunately, he died at the warlord's capital on 12 March 1925. Since then, Sun has been venerated by the entire nation. No other modern Chinese leader of any political persuasion has been able to match his knowledge, personality, tolerance, vision, sincerity, and gracefulness. Had China had his helmsmanship for two more decades, many tribulations, civil wars and national sacrifices might have been avoided. In the early 1920s, people of all classes in China, youth and intellectuals, especially the communists, believed in him, supported his leadership for the realisation of his Three Principles of the People. Had it been implemented while he was still alive, it could have brought to China the long-expected democracy, rapid industrial development, and the general modernisation of the country much earlier than what is now happening under Deng Xiaoping. Sun believed in popular democracy and basic fundamental human rights. He was not as doctrinaire as Mao Zedong was, who wanted to 'brainwash' and punish his opponents. Nor was he a leader who allowed a violent temper to get in his way. What he stood for, such as a pluralistic open society with constitutional rights and freedoms guaranteed for all, seems to be exactly what the Chinese students and intellectuals are demonstrating for in 1980s in the streets of Shanghai and Beijing. They do not want science and technology without democracy and freedom. Likewise, Chinese people in Taiwan today are demanding political reform – the removal of martial law, grant of freedom of association, press freedom and a genuine two-party system of democracy. Whether under bourgeois democracy or proletarian dictatorship in China or anywhere else, people of all races are crying out for the opportunity to speak their minds. Minds cannot be 'brainwashed' forever. This, in short, is the message of Sun Yat-sen and his revolution of 1911. Taiwan's experiment under the late Chiang Ching-Kuo may provide the required result. A few events in Taiwan deserve discussion.

8.3.1 The Emergence of the DPP in 1986

The emergence of the Democratic Progressive Party can be counted as one of the most eventful surprises in the ROC since 1949. Given the existence of martial law and the potential for war in the Taiwan Strait, development of political opposition against the Nationalist Party can be divided into five stages: 1) 1945–51, the period of confusion, instability and ambiguity in ROC's external relations when the government adopted a severe attitude against the emergence of any political opposition: 2) 1951–61, still no opposition forces emerged after an aborted effort by Chen Lei to organise a second party, and the government eagerly reached out to influence every existing group on the island; 3) 1961–71, when Wen-Shing magazine alone was able to voice some intellectual liberalism on the one hand, while the government was scoring in economic and social progress simultaneously; 4) 1971–81, a critical stage when new anti-government magazines and greater participation in election politics opened up new channels to reach the masses whose favourable curiosity brought warning and alertness to the government. Both street demonstrations and arrests were occurring; and 5) 1981-present, there is now a greater number of political participants. a large number of anti-government publications, factional developments among the opposition forces and press freedom, etc. And the government party has become more used to criticism and willing to share elective offices with opposition groups. Opposition forces seem to represent exclusively the interests and sentiment of the 13 million local population *vis-à-vis* the 5 million people who followed the KMT to Taiwan in 1949. Potential for physical street violence has been apparent. The line of political division is unfortunate. With the DPP leadership at their disposal, many Taiwanese young voters can compete openly for popular support. The following factors may help to promote non-violence: 1) President Chiang was determined to share power and leadership peacefully within the constitutional framework; 2) the new party appears determined to follow peaceful elections to acquire political power, and 3) Taiwan's friends and foes abroad do not want the island to become embroiled in violent chaos. Friendly countries and the tourist industry hope to continue their profitable economic and trade relations with Taiwan. Besides, Taiwan is not another Philippines. There is rapid economic growth and the standard of living is high. Almost everyone has a strong stake in 'progress through stability', and an emerging middle-class majority is likely to protect its vested interest through peaceful transition in politics. It would, however, be suicidal if the new DPP failed to integrate in the coming years to become a rational and effective party. It will also suffer from incalculable difficulties if it fails to meet late President Chiang's wishes and, especially, his three conditions: 1) be supportive of the Constitution; 2) be anti-communist in policy, and 3) reject the independence movement. Despite an internal factional struggle, all the leaders of the DPP must not follow the separatist movement. The future of a likely healthy two-party democracy depends on the

DPP's capacity to grow to provide alternative government peacefully and without inviting external interference. For example, its party policy platform and constitution, as it now stands, can lead to many future difficulties. The DPP insists on 'Taiwan's future to be determined by the residents only' and on its 'opposition to any agreement between the CCP and the KMT on Taiwan's future'. It has so far failed to cut clean from those advocating Taiwan's independence from China. Nor has the DPP platform declared, beyond doubt, its support for the ROC constitution. These are fundamental issues that concern all Chinese everywhere, especially those high officials in the PRC and the ROC. The future of a healthy party system now depends on how the DPP guides itself. It may alienate itself from the support of the middle-class majority who are also native-born Taiwanese in origin – 1987 may prove to be more critical to the expectation of a two-party democracy than any previous year.[7] The development within the DPP leadership will be less critical if its moderate faction can rise to the majority in intra-party decision making. N. S. Kang, the well-known leader of the moderate faction, is far more dedicated to building a democratic infrastructure in the electoral and legislative process than on other issues. But its radical wing is eager to confront the KMT and more willing to rely on street demonstrations to achieve its goals.[8]

The other danger to democracy in Taiwan may emerge from the conservative wing within the Nationalist Party. Since September 1986, when the DPP was first organised in violation of martial law, it has tried to convince the government to take severe measures against the 'illegal party'. These conservative elements can make it very difficult for the ruling party to tolerate and cooperate with the DPP. As die-hard anti-communists, the leaders are incapable of tolerating those who advocate Taiwan's independence. Now President Chiang Ching-Kuo is no longer at the helm, they may not be able to interrupt the KMT decision making. In future years, however, they must be dealt with by President Li. If the DPP deviates from its present policy course in favour of separatism. President Li will have a new crisis on hand against his fellow Taiwanese of the DPP.

8.3.2 The KMT Stand on Reunification

Despite the peace overtures from the PRC, and some US$700 million of indirect trade through Hong Kong, President Chiang Ching-Kuo's policy toward the PRC was still the 'three nos approach: 'No compromise. No contact and No negotiation'. He was prepared to wait 'until the Communist Party is overthrown'.[9] On the other hand, the PRC intensifies rapidly its campaign for early unification. The Beijing authority has designated unification as one of its major agenda issues for the 1980s. Even lowering the ROC flag and hoisting the PRC flag would seem to satisfy the PRC government. Many people in Taiwan, under the existence of martial law and the restriction on freedom of press, were deeply concerned about the deadlock but unable to speak out. Such anxiety for the citizens of Taiwan today resembles that of Hong Kong a few years ago. In many ways, the people of Taiwan have both doubt and fear concerning the PRC's eventual decision to attack Taiwan with military forces. They simply have many questions. The ROC today maintains a force of 500,000 men who are well equipped and trained in battlefield experience. It could be suicidal for the PRC to launch a military attack without interrupting its own four modernisations. Thus, there is no solution is sight. Professor C. T. Chang of National Taiwan University estimated that at least 90 per cent of the people in Taiwan are anti-communist. However, a large majority among them are in favour of trade, mail and shipping services directly between Taiwan and mainland China. They are also in favour of mutual exchange visits of among newsmen, academicians and families. According to the current policy, however, anyone who trades directly with the PRC can be tried for treason and subjected to the death sentence. But how long can the ROC restrain the pressure for contact from within and without? What will happen now when Chiang is no longer in office? How to respond to the DPP stand against any negotiation by the KMT government? Who can say when the PRC decides to use military means to achieve unification? Can the PRC succeed through diplomatic channels to deny Taiwan's arms purchases from abroad?[10] If the democratisation process in Taiwan creates uncertainties and anxiety for the PRC, it may very well adopt the military option to prevent a future crisis in Taiwan. For example, many Taiwan citizens are eager to replace the current members in the Legislative Yuan, Control Yuan, and the National Assembly who were elected in 1947 on the mainland and have long lost any claim to represent any one. If the KMT should allow them to be replaced suddenly and totally through local elections in Taiwan, the KMT will most likely lose its control of these organs. A political crisis for its legitimacy to govern would become imminent. But there is, indeed, no valid justification for this 'longest parliament' to last any longer. They are very old people now and physically too weak to attend to their duties vigorously. Even their gradual death is rapidly contributing to an emerging crisis. Secondly, now the press controls are lifted, public discussions of many sensitive issues will be aired. This new freedom of inquiry may also create problems and crises that cannot be resolved. In short, many issues in Taiwan tend to generate crises, tensions, and frustrations as a result of democratisation and party politics in a pluralistic society that may hasten the PRC's choice of a military option to prevent deterioration on the island.

Political opposition forces, including the DPP, may not be quite as expected as interested in democracy itself. They are undoubtedly more interested in the transfer of political power through the election process. The KMT leadership, they believe, can be replaced or ousted in a future election defeat. Its only way to retain power may lie in military control through declaration of an emergency which is legally possible under the new National Security Law, which was passed in 1987 to replace the martial law. However, all the enlisted men and their officers below the rank of generals are native-born Taiwanese who will be forced to choose in their loyalty between the KMT and their own indigenous brethren. Such a future state of affairs for the KMT is very unpalatable. In short, it will lose political power and leadership because of its own success in democratisation which the KMT cannot afford not to promote. In either case, the KMT, being on the minority side, may in time lose power unless it is able to integrate itself into the local majority to compete on equal footing with the DPP. Some overseas Chinese writers assert that the KMT itself, in fact, is promoting Taiwan's independence.[11] They concluded that the only way out for the KMT is to negotiate with the PRC for a long-term peaceful co-existence. On the other hand, the PRC's Chairman of the National People's Congress (NPC), Peng Zhen, has declared that 'Beijing rests its hope on the KMT and also on the 19 million Chinese people in Taiwan for contacts and discussions for reunification'.[12] Peng emphasised in his speech the PRC's readiness to receive representatives of any party, organisation and individuals who are in favour of reunification. This represents a major shift from the PRC's previous position to negotiate only with representatives of the KMT.

8.3.3 Succession issue in Taiwan

This issue legally found its constitutional answer in the 1984 presidential election. President Chiang chose Li Teng-hui as vice-president of the ROC. Li had a strong academic background before becoming the mayor of Taipei and the governor of Taiwan. He is a native-born Taiwanese. Beyond this limited experience, he has no other credentials to compete with other notables who are far better prepared in their experience, ability and leadership in the Nationalist Party. On the other hand, the power and leadership of the future presidential office depends on who occupies the seat. When the late President Chiang Kai-shek held the title, the office was the most powerful seat in the leadership. His successor, C. K. Yan, did not have the same command of power. When Premier Chiang Ching-kuo moved up to the presidency eight years ago, the office again became more powerful. In Chinese politics on both sides of the Taiwan Straits, the informal arrangement is often more important in the exercise of leadership role than the constitutional designation. In fact, whoever, exercises the supreme power in the ruling party commands the highest authority to act despite what office in the government he may hold. We must consider Vice-president Li's authority to rule in the future through his relations with the KMT Party. Because of his lack of close relations with the party, his authority as president of the republic under the constitution may not carry him too far. Since 1988, he has become the president. Therefore, there is no succession problem. The KMT elected him the Party Chairman also.

Many question can be asked about President Li. For example, how has he been groomed to tap various sources of power in preparation for his future leadership? How is he ranked inside the KMT internal leadership role against him? Is he by nature or training a great fighter for power? How would the new DPP opposition think of his as president? There are no answers yet to these questions. The general informal discussion in Taiwan gives a sense of crisis of transition in leadership beyond late President Chiang Ching-Kuo. In fact, many other individuals may be competing for the position and a better opportunity to become the real future decision-maker in the party and the government. This very uncertainty produces anxiety and crisis in future leadership. President Li appears in charge as both the ROC government leader and the KMT party Chairman.

8.3.4 Conclusion

The legacy of the revolution of 1911 may be summarised as follows. It was a short period of experiment in democratic government. Yet through Sun's doctrine and his influence, modern China learned about the Western democratic system of government, individual dignity and human rights in an open and pluralistic society. The Republic of China, under President Chiang Kai-shek, fought to unify the country after 1925, and to resist and defeat Japan in the end to regain Chinese sovereignty over Taiwan. During the 1930s, China regained sovereign control over her lost rights through renegotiation to abolish the 'un-equal treaties'. These included customs rights and foreign concessions in many coastal cities. He expanded education, built transportation, and made preparation against foreign aggression.

Due to its own corruption and other factors, the ROC government was defeated in 1949 on mainland China. But Sun's legacy has continued in Taiwan. The ROC government succeeded in peaceful land reform and in economic development. Now the experience of success should be taken as positive reference in China's modernisation under the communist leadership. Taiwan's success has already become a model example for many developing countries in the world. It must not be sacrificed after reunification in some future time. Taiwan is part of China; so is the legacy a part of Chinese experience in modernisation. Sun's doctrine of revolution has brought prosperity to the people in Taiwan. It should be of aid and reference to Deng's 'Socialism with Chinese Characteristics'.

8.4   SOCIALISM WITH CHINESE CHARACTERISTICS

Before some concluding remarks on the communist legacy or tradition in China, it is important to remind oneself that the world knows China by her Confucian civilisation and traditional institutional stability in social structure and in political transfer of dynastic changes through the 'Mandate of Heaven'. The glory of China was partly from its cultural achievement and partly from its well-structured system of human relations which centred on the extended family with rigid discipline. This traditional way of life was not feudalistic or antiquated in the usual sense. The values and style of the Chinese traditional way of life are on the contrary, rich and humane. The cultural system of China for 2000 years remained unaffected, pure, original and continuous until the 1840s when the country was forced to open up to the outside world. Sun Yat-sen's doctrine of revolution aimed at preserving China's own cultural identity, while learning from the democratic West those things China lacked – popular sovereignty, liberties and equality, science and industry. Chinese culture, to Sun, is the foundation of her 'national spirit'. His theory of Chinese nationalism is based on it. The leaders of the revolution of 1911, from all factions and including the late President Chiang Kai-shek and his son, campaigned to preserve Chinese culture through Chiang's New Life Movement in the 1930s and in the 1960s again in Taiwan through a Cultural Renaissance Movement. Contrary to this, Mao Zedong launched a cultural revolution in 1960s to condemn Confucius and Chinese culture.

Secondly, despite the different policies toward the indigenous cultural legacy, the leaders themselves of the revolutions both of 1911 and 1949 acted in their behavioural mode very much like those in traditional China. They think in the same pattern as the ancients did in their concerns and motivations. Many leaders of both revolutions could not even modernise and modify their own habits against personal misuse of authority. Revolutionaries at all levels before and after 1949 have tended to demonstrate, for example, the following indigenous traits: (1) Nepotism toward relatives and friends; (2) imperial and authoritarian attitudes toward the rule of law; (3) personalisation in major policy decision-making in disregard of institutional settings and administrative procedure; (4) balancing of factional conflicts among subordinates relative to maximisation of their own personal exercise of power and leadership and (5) lack of control of their own violent temper – to name just a few. These traditional traits are demonstrations of personal trust, selfishness, skills, and strategies and tactics in leadership and in politics. And revolutions cannot change much in cultural depth and substance. Revolutions in an ancient but well-developed cultural environment can only change the superficial and the obvious things to satisfy the grievances of the revolutionaries. Whatever their success or failure, Sun Yat-sen and Chiang Kai-shek are, in many ways, highly respected statesmen for their respect of Chinese culture. But Mao Zedong and the Gang of Four of the cultural revolution are generally condemned by many Chinese for their 'excessively untraditional or anti-historical behaviour'. China under Deng Xiaoping has clearly reversed Mao's mistakes in many areas – in education, in rural and urban reform, in intellectual policy and governmental reform. It is likely that future historians will judge Deng as one of the most outstanding revolutionary statesmen in modern China. He has saved the Communist Party. He is correcting the mistakes committed by the party before 1978. Consciously or not, he is following the message of the traditional legacy – the virtues of moderation and a sense of historical relevance.

Thirdly, Deng owes it to the one billion Chinese people to develop and describe his own ideology of reform. 'China under Deng' cannot be sufficiently understood or even correctly observed without the guidance of an ideology explaining his reform. This he has not yet provided. Since 1978, China scholars throughout the world have heard from Beijing that Marxism is not applicable to some of the contemporary problems of China. They have heard also that 'practice is the sole test of truth' and Deng's promises to build 'socialist legality or rule of law and socialist democracy, different from Western democracy'. There are great difficulties in ascertaining what these terms mean. On the other hand, the four cardinal principles seem to be 'unpredictably applied' from time to time either in severity or in leniency. Without clarification, the people cannot follow his leadership with assurance. For example, the nationwide student demonstration in January 1987 for 'democratic reform' was either good or bad, tolerable as appeared at first or intolerable as later proved true.[13] Official confusion leads to actual frustration. Perhaps, the time is not right yet in intra-party factional politics for Deng to announce an 'ideology of reform'. If the four cardinal principles are followed literally (Democratic Centralism, Party leadership, socialist path, and Marxism-Leninism-Maoism), there would be little hope for any genuine degree of democracy in the foreseeable future. If so future student street marches are likely to be unavoidable while the political system remains closed. Finally, without mutual adjustment in their political ideologies, the ROC and the PRC can not easily achieve talks on their unification which both are pledged to carry out eventually.

Having made these three aspects of observation, the next concluding remark is on the success and the problem of Deng's economic reform. Generally speaking, the success of the last nine years of reform in both rural and urban areas have greatly improved the living conditions of the people. There is strong incentive to work and manage for still greater achievement in the economic fields. Economists and policy officials have acquired greater experience in the past eight years. They are, with much confidence, able to accurately forecast the performance of the economy. However, much more remains to be dealt with in continuing the reform between macro-economic planning and micro-economic execution throughout the economy. New problems have been discovered in the relation between economic decision-making on the other hand and political interference on the other. Separation of the communist party from the operation of the government remains critical to reform success. Planning on 'socialist command economy' may still inadvertently or intentionally affect the individual and the collective sectors of the economy. Balance in the economy between the consumption needs of the one billion people and capital accumulation requires constant adjustment and correction. Great debate goes on concerning the ownership of means of production. Continuing improvement over enterprise autonomy and its relation to macro-economic planning requires more experience, better understanding and clear division of authority and responsibility.

Economic performance can be divided as follows: (1) the recent economic success; (2) continuing economic problems; and (3) a short macro-analysis of the economic reform.

8.4.1   Recent Economic Success

Today in China, the people have more purchasing power. Stores are full of consumer goods. Demands for consumption remain higher than the market can supply. Prices of rare articles rise faster because there are more consumers who want them. The trend is toward marketisation and privatisation on daily goods and services. There is much less regulation in this daily service economy. Food grain growth and cotton production both are so greatly increased that a rationing system is no longer used. Statistics show great success in many production fields.

1986, for example, registered an overall steady growth. There was good harvest in the rural economy. Total grain output was reported at 390 million tons, an increase of 10 million tons over the previous year. Livestock breeding, aquaculture and fishery and many other consumer goods all registered satisfactory growth.[14] The total agricultural output was expected to reach 303.8 billion yuan, a 4.4 per cent growth over 1985. Rural industry grew in 1986 by 21 per cent more than in 1985, reaching a total of 330 billion yuan. In industry, 'overheating', as in the previous two years, was arrested. The total industrial output was expected to reach 980 billion yuan with an 8.7 per cent gain over 1985. Production of major raw materials, steel, copper, cement and iron, for example, all recorded a 10 per cent increase. There was a clear satisfaction over the balance between heavy and light industry. Gradually, but not satisfactorily, the PRC has achieved better control over capital investment. Some 194 billion yuan went into investment of 'fixed assets in state-owned' areas in 1986. It represented 15 per cent more than in 1985 which had reached a 41.8 per cent of 1984 growth. Some 200 export-oriented light industrial and textile projects were completed in 1985. They could earn an annual income of $US400 million in foreign currencies. In 1986, some ninety production centres were organised to produce electrical machines for export. Exports rose 14.7 per cent over previous year, while imports were kept at the level as planned. Trade deficit, thus, was $US4 billion less in 1986 than in the previous year. A drop in oil prices on the international market adversely affected the trade deficit. Sources of credit in bank deposits in the year rose to 56 billion yuan more for a total of 218 billion yuan which were available for industrial and agricultural production and construction. In short, some years are better than others because of luck; other years may suffer from greater international trade or other financial difficulties, in addition to natural disasters or droughts and floods in the agricultural sector. The economy is now much better managed since Deng's reforms of 1978. Improved methods in statistical collection and interpretation has represented a giant step forward in the management field.

8.4.2 Continuing Economic Problems

In my interview on 13 July 1986, Mr Luo, a senior economist of the Economic Planning Commission for thirty-five years, summarised several major problems:[15]

1. In recent years, industrial expansion has remained steady; but the rate of efficiency has not kept pace. It even declined in some sectors;
2. Rapid enterprise expansion may cause and has caused abnormal behaviour in efficiency performance and market instability. There must be better control over the rate of investment, consumption credit, volume of lending, foreign exchange regulation, and increase in exports and elimination of unnecessary imports;
3. In order to succeed in enterprise autonomy, its profit or loss must be made as the central link of economic reform. Each enterprise must learn budget responsibility;
4. There is the need of the market supply being in excess of consumer demand to create conditions for competition among enterprises aginst each other and to avoid the present excessive demand that minimises the sluggish lack of competition among suppliers;
5. Adjustment of control systems to help build a scientific macrostructure in the economy;
6. Need for further research and knowledge in enterprise behaviour, quality products, and standardisation; and finally
7. Improvement in the inspection system on false reports, commercial misinformation, revenue deception, warehouse management, product quality test, etc.

Elswhere, reports indicate that there is still a tendency toward excessive investment in fixed assets. In some areas, excessive taxes unduly sap the vitality of state-owned enterprises. People's consumption patterns change too fast. It creates problems for production structure and product mix. In 1987, the second year of the Seventh Five-year Plan, some 5800 new products entered the market. On the other hand, additional problems of 1986 have been released by the State Statistical Bureau in January 1987. They are listed as follows:[16]

1. 'Revenue from industrial and commercial enterprises declined'. Production costs rose 6 per cent in 1986 while profit and taxes delivered to the states declined by 0.3 per cent. There was no marked improvement in product quality. Circulation costs of state-owned commercial enterprises rose by 4.6 per cent. Enterprises were not making full use of their capacity;
2. Budget deficit. 'More and more enterprises fell behind in delivering their tax payment and profit to the state while increasing their expenditures';
3. Balance between import and export. 'China's import payments exceeded export revenues in both 1984 and 1985 ... This unfavourable situation grew worse in 1986'. In all, trade deficit was $U8.6 billion for 1986;
4. 'Over-building and shortage of capital'. 300 billion yuan went into fixed assets investments in 1986. The next two years in capital construction will cost, as estimated, 840 billion to complete projects already under way at the end of 1986 without starting any new ones: and
5. 'Imbalance of supply and demand.' China's failure to change production processes and the mix of items has meant that many products in domestic demand turned out to be in short supply.

The Statistical Bureau's report concludes that 'industrial production growth in 1987 is likely to stay at 1986 levels. Multi-level reforms will help strengthen management of industrial enterprises, adapt their production to market demand and mobilise their workers' enthusiasm for production.'

Many Chinese economists recognise the positive results of urban economic structural reform. But they see a series of difficulties has forced the government to slow down the pace of reform and to return to both adjustment and stabilisation measures. These economists have come to agree, as a theoretical breakthrough on the urgent need to deal with the issue of 'socialist public ownership of the means of production'. They have urged a new policy to allow all kinds of 'non-socialist' ownerships to compete. One professor at Beijing University concluded: 'The success or failure of economic structural reform rests on reform of socialist ownership, not price reform'.[17] They agreed generally that structural reform must begin with the fundamental issue, not the minor aspects. These PRC economists formulated their own conclusion as follows: (1) breakthroughs on economic structural reform lie in the system of ownership; (2) other forms of ownership can co-exist with the 'ownership of the whole people and collective ownership of groups'; (3) forms of ownership are part of the process of development in socialist ownership concept – socialist ownership concept should not be 'an inflexible dead one'; (4) other structures of specific ownerships must be considered besides the official simple categorisation of ownership of means of production; and finally (5) they reject the theory that collective ownership is suitable only for manual workers and reject further the concept that collective ownership is a transition stage between individual owner-ship and ownership by the whole people. This is a dangerous threat to the long-term existence of both collective and individual ownerships. Collective ownership has by nature an enormous capacity for economic adaptation. It should not be considered as a transition stage to be absorbed eventually into ownership by the whole people.[18] In short, these economists seem to argue in reverse of the present half-way reform policy, as declared in October 1984, which thought that ownership and management could be separated to allow management autonomy without ownership. Real structural reform includes ownership reform as well. Ownership contributes to greater freedom for planning by the enterprise itself. Thus unity of ownership and management will contribute to more management efficiency and greater profit making. This is, of course, a very serious debate. For example, if the state or the whole people should give up ownership in the socialist economy, how could the government impose its macro-economic planning on the whole economy? The debate must turn to the main thrust of the 1984 policy on urban economic structural reform.

8.4.3 A Short Macro-analysis of the Economic Reform

The PRC's economy before 1979 was influenced by two basic factors: the Soviet pattern of structure and Mao Zedong's radical mistakes. The setbacks resulted from Mao's mistakes in the great leap, rural communes, the cultural revolution and the Soviet cut-off of economic aid. There was also undue emphasis on rate of growth, concentration on heavy industry, imbalance in rapid development against consumption and tertiary services. Deng's emphasis since the early 1980s has been in the improvement of living conditions of the people. This shift was aimed at the following : (1) better economic results; (2) balanced development with emphasis on new technology, energy production, rural improvement, and expansion in transport and communication; and (3) enterprise renovation and management improvement of existing enterprises for better quality products and efficiency rating. The Soviet model of economic structure unduly concentrated on bureaucratic and administrative control and planning. In addition, the Chinese economy before 1980 was also adversely affected by the defence need in military supplies.[19] Thus, the economic structure was overly centralised and also unduly committed to Mao's extreme notion of egalitarianism.

As a result, during the first thirty years after 1949, economic decision-making was totally dominated by the central government. The operating units throughout the country took orders from high officials. The day-to-day production targets and distribution orders were issued through administrative channels in the state bureaucracy. The government was interested in high statistics only, with little regard for quality of products, incentives to work, need for wage or salary differentials, and the new science for management efficiency. Party ideology gave orders to technical experts who had no right to disagree on orders given. The ultimate result was an economic paralysis and the philosophy of 'big rice bowl' mentality. No one wanted to work without rewards. The government itself became enterprises and distributors. There was little need for marketing. No one had anything to sell. There was no money to buy. Starvation in desolate and remote frontiers was not uncommon. Economic power was totally in the control of the government. This was Mao's China.

Deng's China must change to make progress, to redeem the government from popular disaffection, to undo the damage of the cultural revolution, and most important of all, to catch up with the rest of the world in living standards and in science and technology. Urban economic reform was one of the central thrusts for change and progress. After the satisfactory result in doing away with Mao's communes in rural China and some examples of reform experiment in urban economy, the 1984 broad reform plan was finally announced to convert the economy into a 'socialist commodity economy'. It was a small step in retreat from over-centralisation. By definition the new 'socialist commodity economy' was to be biased toward 'public ownership of the means of production'.[20] This would allow some free market under a central macro-economic plan. However, the market mechanism has been a dynamic force to slowly, but steadily, affect the central planning and the demands of the consumers who, with increased work incentives and higher income, have generated new activities in the economy. Socialist relations of production under public ownership is now itself subject to continuous debate for the purpose of common prosperity and efficient performance. Thus, the process of reform is dynamic. Private economists contribute also to the continuing dialogue of the reform. The success of the reform has persuaded government planners to adapt to new reform measures. For example, the emergence of individual, collective and other forms of ownership and management have been so succssful that the socialist command sector of the economy is forced to learn from the private market. In short, the main features of the 1984 urban reform are as follows: (1) previously unified state control has given way to a 'multi-layered decision structure' which expects the government to limit itself to macro-economic planning only; (2) the old egalitarianism has given way to a new system of distribution which merges 'incentives with social justice'; (3) there is today a separation of function between government and the enterprises, less vertical command between higher and lower government agencies and closer relations horizontally between enterprises; and finally (4) direct regulation through administrative orders has given way to indirect regulation by economic methods of market forces under centrally planned guidance. The new economic system focuses on vitalisation of enterprises through greater opportunity for competition.[21]

'Socialism with Chinese Characteristics' is still in a process of evaluation. Each new five-year plan has incorporated a number of new goals and fresh changes annually. Marxist ideology is competing or giving way to economic rationalism. Lenin once groped to implement Marxism without being able to 'describe what socialism is'.[22] The Chinese Communist Party blindly adopted the Soviet model without questioning its applicability. Unlike Yugoslavia and other socialist states in East Europe, the PRC allowed Mao Zedong to try and to fail. During Deng's first return to government in 1973, still under Mao's leadership, he had helped Zhou Enlai to propose the programme for the four modernisations.[23] Two years before the 1984 urban reform was launched, Secretary-General Hu Yaobang in his speech to the party's Twelfth National Congress categorised the Chinese character-istics of socialism on seven major points: (1) abolishing the system of exploitation; (2) public ownership of the means of production; (3) remuneration according to work; (4) planned commodity economy; (5) political power in the hands of the working class and other labouring people; (6) highly developed productive forces and labour productivity which will eventually be higher than in capitalist countries; and (7) socialist ethics cultivated under the guidance of Marxism.[24]

Many Western economists have observed the Chinese economy. Some are quite optimistic about the outcome of reform, while others are much less so. Some are even pessimistic. A few already see the *de facto* breakdown of public ownership in favour of 'privatisation of property rights'. The users of public property are private persons, peasant families, collective firms, and provinces. There must be a continuous search for a balance between plan and market, public and private property or commodity. In other words, the PRC is experi-menting with innovation in rational choice. The final product many be rightly called 'Socialism with Chinese Characteristics'. The reformers can speed up or slow down according to the new 'unleashing' of market forces or depending on the control of opposition faction within the ruling party itself. For example, 1986 was designated as a year of relaxation. Premier Zhao Ziyang wanted a year to 'consolidate, digest, supplement and improve what had been achieved earlier in the way of economic changes'.[25] The government for a while, however, seemed to have lost control of investment, consumption funds, currency and credit, import and export, and even cadre discipline in the nineteen months following the announcement of the 1985 reform plan. Thus, there was the 'overheating' of the economy in 1985. Meanwhile, reform changes were introduced, such as new wage and price policy, labour contract system, experimentation in the financial capital market, extension of macro-economic control measures and levers, industrial-commercial tax system, and the improvement of domestic conditions for foreign investment. Given this large volume of change, there was a need for a period of 'digestion and adjustment'. In conclusion it can be said that, especially among Western economists, economic reform will continue to face challenges from a variety of sources. The reform itself, however, has been a success. But the intractable difficulties are summarised by one US economist as follows:[26]

Most of the more intractable difficulties experienced by the Chinese system are due to the half way nature of the changes so far. Not unlike Hungary, China has almost arrived at the state of neither plan nor market, with the market striving to dominate agriculture and the plan still dominant in industry. This represents an unstable condition in which the many remaining old and new systemic elements work at odds. In other words, China's policy makers are facing a fundamental choice that can not be avoided by systemic half measures ('adjustments'). The choice is to either move all the way to the market, or revert to administrative command.

Unfortunately, there are other political and ideological considerations, in addition to the need for prudence in the reform movement. The success in the rural economy has already paved the way for successful industrial changes. But greater preparation is needed to move more successfully and more rapidly toward marketisation and privatisation in the urban sector. One of the critical preconditions in determining the pace in economic reform is political support among factions of the Communist Party. There cannot be any economic reform if that political support is lacking for Deng Xiaoping or his successors in future decades. Deng does not want to split the party into factions. He also refuses to purge the opponents of the reform. Both political and economic reforms must be 'peaceful'. His reform is a long-term movement which he has equated with 'peaceful revolution'. For example, he called off the recent student demonstrations in thirteen major cities for 'faster political reform and more democracy' after the demonstrations had provoked a serious resistance from the conservative element within the party.[27] The resistance within the party was plotted to challenge Deng and his faction, not to make any concessions to the students. Instead of protecting his reformist colleagues, Deng removed his potential successor, Party Secretary-General Hu Yaobang in January 1987. The reform programme will, no doubt, slow down. Premier Zhao Ziyang has already announced a limit on importation of unnecessary merchandise, and a reduction in project spending. This reduction can only be interpreted as retreat by Deng in the face of strong intra-party resistance. A nationwide ban against demonstrations has been imposed. The press has suddenly turned against student demonstrations. In short, there cannot be an economic reform without a political reform. The two must march forward hand in hand. Fear of Western 'bourgeois liberalism' can lead to political instability which can instantly disrupt economic reform. Jaime A. Florcruz has reported the following on the government's change of attitude from approval of the demonstration to its ban two weeks later:[28]

> Astonishingly, some local officials at first spoke approvingly of the anti-government actions ... By the time the Peking protests ended, a government controlled media blitz was underway. Television, radio and newspapers hammered away at variations on a theme: while the students might have a well-meaning desire for more democracy, they should desist from actions that threatened the country's stability and unity. More than once the spectre of the Cultural Revolution was raised.

In other words China is following 'its own way of modernisation' – that is 'Socialism with Chinese Characteristics'.

There are, indeed, many Chinese characteristics: such as size of population, landscape and resources, lack of arable land, way of life and a low living standard, pockets of poverty and backwardness, a long indigenous Confucian legacy, the challenge of the revolution of 1911, the failure of the Soviet economic model in China, and so on. For China to accept any foreign model of modernisation, there are major difficulties, whether a Western, East European, or even Japanese model. China is China, and she will experiment with things in her own way. Foreign experts, friends or foes, should be able to appreciate this uniqueness of the Chinese tradition, which was never historically influenced by the outside world except by Buddhism from India. One Chinese economist from the ROC has commented on the PRC's economic reform to emerge as a 'mixed model' by following a number of principles:[29]

1. 'Insist on socialist principles';
2. 'Throw out the Soviet economic structure';
3. 'Imitate from the Hungarian economic model';
4. 'Absorb the American enterprise management model';
5. 'Learn from the Japanese developmental experience';
6. 'Learn from Taiwanese economic success';
7. 'Integrate indigenous practical characteristics'.

Economic reform on such a scale will take decades to accomplish. It cannot reach its predicted goals unless there is first a success in political-institutional reform, or at least, both political and economic reforms should advance together to achieve 'progress through stability', which has been the strategy of Taiwan in its economic miracle.

8.5 IS POLITICAL REFORM POSSIBLE AFTER HU YAOBANG?

As Sun Yat-sen's revolution of 1911 and the May 4th Movement of 1919 had insisted, Chinese modernisation and reform must include political democracy. Sun promised a Western model of 'Bourgeois democracy'. Mao Zedong in his writing promised a new doctrine of 'People's Democratic Dictatorship', but in Mao's definition it means 'democracy for the people, and dictatorship for the enemies of the people' simultaneously. He developed a classification of who are the people and who are the enemies of the people. For example, the people consist of the workers, the peasants, the progressive intellectuals and others who are in favour of Mao's revolution. The enemies of the people are those who are opposed to his revolution, such 'National bourgeois', landlords, warlords, the opportunists and others who are, by definition, counter-revolutionaries. What did Mao do in carrying out his promise of 'democracy for the people'? And how do those people, as workers and peasants and progressive intellectuals, feel about democracy after thirty years under Mao since 1949? At least, many do remember today that violence was employed and millions were executed both during rural land reform and as spies, saboteurs, Kuomintang agents and counter-revolutionaries. Mao ignored the provisions of his 1954 constitution on civil and political rights of the citizens. He purged hundreds of thousands of the 'rightists' in 1957, and again during the ten years of cultural revolution. There was no grass-root election or any genuine effort to justify his government by popular sovereign consent.

Since 1978, government under Deng Xiaoping has promised the Chinese people 'socialist democracy' and 'socialist legality'. Does this mean government by popular consent and a rule of law with judicial independence? In practice this has meant several different things. For example, popular elections under Deng have been held at village, township and up to county level. Deng has welcomed back the other small democratic parties which had existed before and after 1949 but were ousted during the cultural revolution.[30] Today, they co-exist with the Communist Party in the Chinese People's Political Consultative Conference (CPPCC). The CPPCC now meets regularly each year as a deliberative body in the same building, the people's hall, where the National People's Congress (NPC) meets. However, the CPPCC does not have constitutional power. It has, on the contrary, only an advisory capacity. Deng's socialist democracy has meant tolerance toward direct and constructive popular criticism. Anyone who visits China and mingles among intellectuals, students, and in rural areas will detect a relaxed atmosphere and open exchange of policy evaluation. There has been repeated assurance of the new liberal policy toward writers, artists, religious leaders, church organisations, teachers, and there is now a greater degree of academic freedom for discussion. In many respects, Deng's 'socialist legality' implies also a new reform policy toward judicial exercise of power, support for a new legal profession, restoration of law schools and legislation of new criminal and civil procedural codes, and so on. The trend appears to be in the direction of institutionalisation of political and legal stability. In time, the rule of law may replace the rule of man. However, there is a long way toward a system of democracy and a system of legal, and objective justice guaranteed by the state. For example, a democratic constitution must be approved by a majority of the people directly. Political decision should not replace legal judgement. No individual or party should be above the laws of the state. The court system and judicial decisions must not serve as instruments of any political party. These are some obvious aspects of 'the rule of law' in any democractic country. Furthermore, the rule of law, or socialist legality, is inseparable from a genuine political democracy which itself must recognise and protect basic civil liberties and universal human rights as enshrined in the Declaration of Human Rights Charter of 1948. There are, of course, special obstacles in China to the realisation of both political democracy and judicial independence. For example, the ancient Confucian state disregarded positive law in favour of morality. Today Marxist ideology places the morality represented by the Communist Party above positive law as the 'guardian of the revolution'. In the ancient Chinese tradition, collectivism of family, clan, and village identity was far more important for protection than the recognition of the individual person and his 'inalienable rights'. But the revolution of 1911 and the contemporary universal demands for liberties and equality seem to have forged in China an irreconcilable and irreversible requirement for such constitutional rights. As people's living standards rise, demands for rights and equality will be likely to grow stronger, although the realisation of such rights may take a very long time to achieve. When that day comes, China will have acquired a new tradition. It is in this long perspective that the future generations will eventually see an emergence of such a true democracy that all believers in Sun's doctrine and his revolution will live happily in a unified and peaceful China.

However, China under Deng Xiaoping does have a short-term problem with the concept of 'socialist democracy' and 'socialist legality'. There have been many moments of tension and oppression since 1978 when Deng achieved leadership in his party. For example, the movement for 'democracy by wall posters' in 1978, suppression of novelist writer Bai Hua, the arrest of Wei Jinsheng and his friends for their dialogue on democracy, to cite just a few, have stirred up enormous frustration and debate in recent years. There has been, since Deng's ascension, a general assumption and hope for gradual and steady progress toward opening up of the political system without major set-backs. This hope rested on Party Secretary General Hu Yaobang who has been viewed as an open-minded interpreter of 'Marxism, Leninism and Mao Zedong Thought' to which the party insists on adhering. Nearly all observers expect the Secretary-General to succeed Deng when he someday chooses to retire. But recent political unrest, from December 1986 to January 1987, has resulted in Hu Yaobang's partial downfall. The development of his downfall is an excellent illustration of the reality of politics and factions inside the Chinese Communist Party (CCP). A summary discussion of its highlights will help understanding the internal pressures and counter-pressures which have affected Deng's decision to remove Hu from his post. There can be many aspects about Hu's removal that the outside world can not accurately interpret or speculate. This newest leadership crisis surrounding Hu over the student demonstrations has been analytically reviewed in many newspapers around the world. The following summary will follow the chronological development from early December, 1986 to 27 January 1987. In fifty days, the entire crisis came to an end but with implications that may last.

8.5.1 The Crisis of Hu Yaobang's Downfall

In China, university students are always concerned about national affairs and the destiny of their country in a hostile world of competing nations. Campus organisations often support street demonstrations which register their protests against various matters. During the summers in recent years, the government has helped college students and post-graduates to visit factories and farms, etc., to acquire accurate information so as to avoid misunderstandings. There are times when rumours spread about students being arrested and detained. For example, it was reported that more than 100 students were arrested on 18 September 1986, the day Japanese aggression commenced in Manchuria fifty-six years ago.[31] But in fact no such arrests ever happened in 1986. In December 1986, university students in Hefei, Anhui Province, demonstrated for the right to nominate and vote for their own candidates against a single-candidate ballot as approved by the government. As a result, one of their most respected advocates for greater democracy and free press, the Vice-president of the University and Professor of Physics, Fang Lizhi, was elected. Immediately, tens of thousands of college students in Shanghai took up the cause and demonstrated. They even debated with the mayor of the city on his right to hold public office without popular election and their general rights to openly voice their opinions on public issues. The mayor was most accommodating and supported the right to demonstrate.

Fang Lizhi is known nationwide as one of several spokesmen for intellectual freedom. As reported in *Beijing Review*,[32] he insisted on the right of scientists to discuss 'unreasonable aspects of the West or the East'. Fang believes in free inquiry as a tradition among physicists and the practice can be traced back to Galileo and Copernicus. Fang's insistence on free inquiry influenced student demonstrations to spread unexpectedly and suddenly to many other major cities in ten provinces. The final result of this unrest was Hu Yaobang's downfall as the designated successor of Deng Xiaoping. Hu was accused by the leftists in the Communist Party for his failure to suppress student demonstrations. The chronology of the crisis emergence and a few comments are recorded as follows:

The first stage

The government was first found to be very accommodating rather than repressive as in the past decades, and the students restrained their own demands on improvement of campus conditions. After more than 30,000 demonstrators in Shanghai had demanded more democracy and after some violence had occurred in the middle of December 1986, the student movement for more democracy began to spread rapidly to other cities. Some of their minor demands were being quickly met. But the demonstration was expanding to include greater demands. Some police arrests and beatings were reported. Student placards read 'Long Live Democracy' or 'Give Us Freedom'. However, the students' motives seemed peaceful; and they did not make any formal demands beyond the communist system. The reform group under Deng Xiaoping could choose to use such student demands to advance political reform against the opposition faction within the party.[33] The students indicated clearly that 'they support government reforms, and that their only demands were for meaningful participation in campus life and local election'. The *People's Daily* in Beijing even encouraged the students 'to promote popular election and some of the Western ideas of democracy.' By late December, the government's attitude toward the demonstration still remained 'lenient and unclarified'. Unofficial reports considered the demonstrations the best response to the anti-reform leftist faction. Nearly all newspapers throughout the country supported the broad democratic causes of the student marches before the end of December. As late as 26–27 December, students in Beijing University began to march on the streets. They chanted the Communist Internationale, the National Anthem, and complained that the Communist Youth League 'cannot represent their needs'. Large-letter wall posters appeared on many campuses in Beijing. The mayor of Beijing had earlier publicly declared 'there would be no arrests if students should demonstrate, and that the Constitution provides the freedom to march.'[34] But as participation in demonstrations spread, the city suddenly issued new regulations to demonstrators to register their marches five days beforehand and not to march in certain areas of the city. The Press in Hong Kong began to comment that such demonstrations 'would be limited against challenges to communist party authority'. The foreign press also at first considered that the demonstration was government-induced and supported to 'help Mr. Deng carry out reform in the political structure.' But the *New York Times* report commented: 'The pro-democracy demonstrations over the last several weeks have revealed a depth of discontent among the elite of China's youth unsuspected until now... But many intellectuals have insisted that responsibility in the work place must be accompanied by political rights. Yet the absence of liberalization in daily life has become increasingly apparent to students. They have no decision in who their representatives to student councils are, no role in picking student candidates for local people's congresses. No freedom to choose where they will work after graduation.'[35] As students raised the level of demands for greater democracy, newspapers in Beijing began to advise students not to 'deviate from the leadership of the Communist Party'. Demonstrations in Nanking were even more open. The students and a few city workers openly 'attacked the party dictatorship and held debates and seminars in the streets'. Chinese newspapers abroad echoed the student demands and voiced the 'incompatibility of economic freedom with political dictatorship'. 'Freedom of press' was emphasised by Nanking student demonstrators.

The Second Stage

By 30 December 1986, the government became gravely concerned about the scope of student demands. Newspapers suddenly changed their stands. The *Workers Daily* accused students of thinking of 'the capitalist world as paradise, and downgrading socialist society as hopeless and without a future'. The Xinhua News Agency quoted five conservative faction leaders who had accused 'Western thoughts in China have become a flood of disaster'. General Wang Zhen accused his opponents for advocating 'total Westernisation'. The *People's Daily* stated that 'capitalist democracy is a form of bourgeois control in service of private capital'. On the other hand, a *Time* magazine weekly correspondent in Shanghai warned that student demonstrations could 'add difficulties to Deng's economic reform... unless Deng can manage student demands skilfully, severe suppression is quite likely'. United Press reported that Chinese newspapers began to accuse the 'Voice of America' broadcast for 'Skilful encouragement of students to demonstrate and the Nationalist Government underground agents to conspire in the student movement.'[36] The *People's Daily* on New Year's day made a special declaration in support of the party's 'Four Cardinal Principles' and warned the students not to make impractical demands. Still, thousands of students marched in Beijing's Tienanmen Square in a demand for human rights. Clearly, the government had adopted a suppression policy. Deng Xiaoping was reported to have blamed Hu Yaobang for mishandling the demonstrations and for not giving orders to prevent any further unrest.

Deng was being confronted by the conservative faction in a power struggle. A purge seemed necessary. Deng had to choose between 'his success in economic reform with acquiescence from the leftists' or immediate political concessions to the students' cause. Hu Yaobang became Deng's 'scapegoat to protect his own leadership'. By 6 January most campuses had become quiet. Students returned to their classes with disappointment. It had been a demonstration movement in support of Deng's reform, but it ended in defeat at the hands of Deng himself.[37] The *Far East Economist* properly commented that three weeks of student demonstration had led to a head-on conflict between party factions. The conservative group seized the opportunity to move to the offensive against Deng's reform group. Students, on the other hand, burned and condemned newspapers for misjudging the purpose of their demonstration. Advisers from Premier Zhao Ziyang's office warned students that any further demonstration would affect the progress of economic reform.[38] By 9 January all major newspapers escalated attacks against 'Bourgeois liberalisation'. The *Beijing People's Daily* advocated future emphasis in the school curriculum on the 'Four Cardinal Principles'. The next day news revealed the military leaders had taken a strong position to prevent 'Bourgeois liberalisation' and pledged loyalty in support of the 'Four Cardinal Principles.'[39] Newspaper editorials in Hong Kong quoted unidentified sources from Beijing that Deng had issued a directive to deal with student demonstrations. They were: (1) firm attitude toward students; (2) fair and just handling of any issue; and (3) an interest in understanding problems of the students. There was general agreement that the conservative group had won, but the reformers suddenly realised that additional major political reform was essential to greater future success in economic achievement. This was only a temporary strategic retreat. Rumours were spreading that Hu Yaobang might be the victim to end the crisis since Deng spoke publicly on the mishandling of the demonstrations.

The Fall of Hu Yaobang and Other Purges

Since 29 December Hu chose not to appear in public or to receive guests. Physical fatigue was cited for his official absence for more than two weeks. The news media emphasised Deng's own decision not to retire. Many other well-known names associated with support for democratisation were cited as potential victims for a purge of limited scope.[40] On 15 January action was taken to replace the President and Vice-president of the University of Science and Technology at Hefei, Guan Weiyuan and Fang Lizhi, for their failure in administrative duty and their own participation in the student demonstration in early December. Other victims included the Party Minister of the Propaganda Department and the Director of Information Division. Wang Ruowang, the well-known novelist of Shanghai, and Liu Binyan, a long-time critic and correspondent of the *People's Daily*, were removed to be soon expelled from Party membership. The next day news quoted Deng saying 'at least during the next twenty years, we must oppose bourgeois liberalism'. Control over literature and arts will be, no doubt, intensified. Economic and political reform will slow down. Party members will be severely disciplined in the future for violation of party constitution.[41] Finally on 16 January 1987, Hu Yaobang personally admitted his mistakes in managing the student unrest and tendered his resignation as Secretary-General of the Party at the full meeting of the Party's Political Bureau. His resignation was reportedly accepted unanimously. However, he retains his membership in the Political Bureau and on its Standing Committee, as well as his membership in the Party's Secretariat. Premier Zhao Ziyang took over as Acting Secretary-General.[42] Meanwhile, Deng himself publicly reaffirmed the government's policy to keep China open to the outside world and to continue on economic reform. In addition, the final action was taken in late December to strip the three so-called anti-party intellectuals, Fang Lizhi, Wang Ruowang, and Liu Binyan, of their party membership. The fall of these three served as a warning to others. Deng's devotion to reform remains unabated. Hu Yaobang has been re-elected in October 1987 a member of the new Political Bureau. Hu is reported to be assigned a new high post in early 1988. Political reform seems accelerating its pace since the Thirteenth Party Congress in October 1987. Deng wins again.

The Short-Run Consequences of Hu's Fall
Students and intellectuals in China are dismayed and disappointed. Moreover, Deng's own economic reform did slow down in 1987. Deng's image was temporarily damaged in the minds of the intellectuals who will probably choose to remain silent for a long while. The Chinese media has proved itself once again to be a totally obedient instrument on behalf of the party. The burning of the *People's Daily* on Beijing University campus spoke well for the 'demerit of news media' in China. Hong Kong indirectly has been much affected by Hu's downfall. Prices on the stock market reacted sharply, moving downward upon the news on Hu's fall. He had been the most important right-hand man to guard the party on Deng's behalf. Hu's own natural disposition toward liberal ideals and democratic political reform has convinced many intellectuals and students of his sincere promotion of 'meaningful Socialist democracy' and his implementation of the constitutional rights of the people as enshrined in the 1982 constitution. Hu has shown himself to be Deng's architect in developing ideological debates, such as that surrounding 'practice as the sole test of truth', and to be the one to adjust Marxism-Leninism to meet 'Chinese characteristics'. Besides, Deng is already 83 years old. His own leadership, without Hu, is now far more critically needed than before. Deng has to fight more battles in the frontline against the leftist faction inside the party. In this Deng has succeeded up to the 13th

Party Congress in October 1987. Chao Ziyang seems a new articulate ideologist for Hu's place unless the latter is restored to share Chao's power. New Secretary-General Zhao Ziyang is more experienced in the administrative side of the government than in party ideology.

It was widely believed in early 1987 that Deng would map out a new strategy in personnel reshuffle before the next major confrontation with the leftist faction at the 13th Party Congress. For example, Hu has been treated with high honour and visibility at the 13th Party Congress, and he may yet return to other powerful role to work closely with Zhao Ziyang as the new Secretary-General if they both can agree privately to join forces beyond Deng's departure. It is simply inconceivable that Hu's close relation with Deng has suffered beyond repair and that Hu's talent and influence should be lost to the reform group and to Deng personally. Since 1977, Hu has placed many friends in party high posts.

In the long-term, the reform group has found, through the recent student demonstration, how eager and impatient China's future leaders and present intellectuals are in favour of gradual democratisation. They did not ask for Western institutional restructure, nor multi-party politics. They even did not directly challenge the 'Four Cardinal Principles'. They quite modestly asked for meaningful local election with multiple candidates to choose from. They want some freedom to speak out and to receive fair and honest press coverage. Deng and his group should realise the country is far more ready for his promised political reform than he is prepared to accept. If he does take a giant step in the area of political-structural reform, he will have more support than he needs, provided he can successfully handle the Marxian leftists within the party. The post-Hu halt in political relaxation can only be considered a temporary one. Deng's economic reform cannot succeed without political reform regarding decentralisation. On the contrary, and with disappointment, Deng and Zhao both have recently reasserted that 'China needs more opening to the outside world ... and the country's mistakes were due to demanding too much and moving too fast'.[43]

It has been obvious after the 13th Party Congress that the reform group has taken the major leadership posts within the party. If Hu Qili, a protégé of Hu Yaobang, can protect in the next ten years his position in the party, he may in time emerge to succeed Zhao Ziyang, who was 68 years old in 1987, to become Secretary-General (Zhao is ten years older than Hu Qili). In strategy, Deng took a tough stand against the students in January 1987 in order to take an equally tough stand against his opponents within the party to defend his economic reform and his own leadership position in the party.[44] In any case, even after Deng, demands for democratic reforms will not end but may suffer from many small sacrifices. In my judgment, theoretically, economic and political reform must proceed together. Ideally, political reform should lead the way.

On 31 July 1986, four months before the recent student demonstration, Vice-premier Wan Li and Deng's friend and also a member of the powerful Political Bureau of the Party, made a speech entitled 'Making Policies Democratically and Scientifically – An Important Problem of Political Restructuring'. He made many major points in that much-quoted speech, including the following:[45]

making policy by democratic and scientific means has not received enough attention in this country. One of the obstacles to this comes from traditional ideas about authority. It also reflects the main defect of the existing political structure, namely, the over-centralisation of power in the leadership and the resulting imperfect policy-making procedures. It is therefore most important in the political restructuring to bring socialist democracy into full play and to adhere faithfully to democratic and scientific approaches in policy making ... to develop a scientific approach, it is necessary first to create a political environment in which democracy, equality and the free exchange of views and information are the norms of life. Leaders must respect other people's democratic rights to air their opinions without fear, including, of course, those that contradict their own ... Only in an atmosphere of complete academic and political freedom can one hope to form true judgements and feel free to speak out and argue with others ... Political research must be conducted on the basis of facts and truth, not subject to the blind worship of any authority or to the will of any individual leader.

Socialist legality, or rule of law essentially, can not be possible, if the party exists in sovereign command dominating all other organisations and people. Robert E. Bedeski wrote also that, 'A basic contradiction between socialist legality and party sovereignty remains. The former should mean equality before the law.'[46] Eventually the party must modify the 'Four Cardinal Principles' to avoid this contradiction when politics within it becomes ready to accommodate such long-awaited modification. Progress in economic pluralism will create country-wide demand, rural and urban, for genuine political participation. On the other hand, even without the 'Four Cardinal Principles', the Communist Party will remain, for a long time, the single dominant party in the

PRC. In East Asia, there can be modified democracy under a single party domination. Japan under the Liberal Democratic Party (LDP) since 1955, Taiwan under the Kuomintang Party since 1949, and Singapore under the People's Action Party since 1959, have all practised Western democracy with various degrees of modification. Why can this not be possible in the PRC, given the increasing demand for it from the people?

It seems also necessary to redefine and rejuvenate Chinese traditional values with a modern sense of virtue and utility. 'Socialism with Chinese Characteristics' must be an open concept to accommodate worthy traditional values. It should be able to integrate change and continuity with a global perspective. Deng's political and economic reforms must be properly synthesised to permit internal institutional harmony. Secondly, the three basic political and cultural traditions, one indigenous and two revolutionary, must, in time, be synthesised into a new eclectic and pluralistic system with emphasis on the preservation of its indigenous foundation. Thirdly, the PRC's modernisation must not yield to current political convenience and political in-fighting among ruling factions. Humanistic values must not be sacrificed to the ideological inflexibilities of Marxism. Modernisation, furthermore, cannot avoid the need to conform to global trends toward a world culture which, in time, will affect the parochial values of all national cultures and ideologies. 'Socialism with Chinese Characteristics' is an excellent and practical approach. It must, first of all, succeed in a synthetic effort to integrate modern revolutionary values with Chinese cultural tradition. And finally, whatever the ideological labels, western democracy or Marxist socialism, modern foreign revolutionary philosophies must reconcile on the basis of Chinese cultural tradition. This implies a long way for the Communist regime to adjust to the genuine aspirations of the people in both spiritual and material terms. However, the grand reform since 1978 has been, indeed a 'Peaceful revolution' in itself, although the road ahead remains rough and zig-zagged. In comparison, what is currently transforming in Taiwan as an advanced industrial-political community is itself a model-setting. And what is happening in the PRC is quite another model-setting. The two models, originally inspired to succeed in making China into a modern industrial and democratic state through either the Western democratic revolution or the Communist proletarian dictatorship, have both come a long way and there is still far to go yet. The leadership of both regimes must reflect in terms of what the Chinese people have sacrificed, and what they want in their future. Both regimes have had their share of failures. Both are capable of self reform. They both must, in the interest of the nation, put aside their mutual antagonism. It seems hopeful lately that both appear moving toward each other. For example, exchange of visits and indirect trade are welcome beginnings in 1987, and can generate new opportunities for mutual accommodations in the interests of eventual reunification. The ROC under President T. H. Li must not move toward separatism to avoid the PRC's decision to unite both by military means. The PRC must consolidate its leadership under Chao Ziyang to reduce dependency on Mr Deng as crisis arbiter and to subdue the conservative-leftists in the interest of accelerating political reform, which is a necessary precondition in ultimate economic reform success. On the other hand, short-run economic success does breed new needs in political reform. Preference is for politics to lead economics to maximise efficiency in reform progress.

Notes and References

1 Introduction

1. *Beijing Review*, 8 April 1985, p. 6 (also ibid., 15 July 1985, pp. 6–11).
2. Ibid., p. 7.
3. These trips brought me and my visiting party to Guangzhou, Guilin, Kunning, Zhengdu, Chongqing, Xian, Taiyuan, Beijing, Tiangin, DaQing Oilfield, Harbin, Changchun, Zhenyang, Anshan, Dalian Shanghai, Hangzhou, Suzhou Wuxi, Changsha, Wuhan and Yanan. At each place I had both escorted and unescorted interviews of my own choosing.
4. See *Toward the Year 1997: (Hong Kong's Future*, Hong Kong: Qiong Pao Cultural Enterprise, 1983).
5. Hungda Chiu and others (eds.) *China's Unification and the Question of Negotiation*, (Rushing, NY.; World Journal Books, 1982).
6. *Beijing Review*, 24 September 1984, p. 6, and pp. 20–21.
7. Ibid., 17 June 1985, p. 8.
8. See the government document announced on 20 October 1984 on 'Enterprise Management Decision-making'. *People's Daily*, Beijing, 25 October 1984.
9. Robert A. Scalapino, paper read at the Symposium on the East Asia-Pacific Base Area Economic Development, 9 and 10 September (Berkeley: University of California, 1985).
10. For greater understanding, see Dorothy J. Salinger *Three Visions of Chinese Socialism* (Boulder, Col.: Westview) and also Frederick C. Teiwes (1984) *Leadership, Legitimacy and Conflict in China: From a Characteristic Mao to the Politics of Succession* (London: Macmillan, 1984).
11. See James L. Watson (ed.) *Class and Social Stratification in Post-Mao China* (London: Cambridge University Press, 1984).
12. 18 September 1985, *People's Daily*, Beijing.

2 Deng's Return and Reform

1. David W. Chang, *Zhou Enlai and Deng Xiaoping in Chinese Leadership Succession Crisis* (Lanham, Md.: University Press of America, 1984), p. 126.
2. Ibid., pp. 153–4.
3. The 'Gang of Four' was used for the most radical group under Mao's wife, Jiang Qing. They sought to succeed Mao and Zhou at the expense of the moderate group within the party. The radical leaders included also Zhang Chun Qiao, Yao Wenyuan, Wang Hungwen. All of them are still in gaol after their trial in 1980–1.
4. Deng Xiaoping, *Collected Works of Deng Xiaoping: 1975–82* (Deng Xiaoping Wen Xuan, People's Press, Hsinhua Co. 1983), pp. 1–3, also pp. 15–24.
5. Ibid., pp. 13–14.
6. Deng Maomao, 'My Father's Days in Jiangxi' *Beijing Review*, 3

September 1984, pp. 17–18. See also *People's Daily*, 22 August 1984. The English version is a shorter summary of the Chinese language version in *The People's Daily*.

7. David W. Chang, *Chinese Leadership Succession Crisis* ch. 4, pp. 197–206.
8. Ibid., pp. 209–27.
9. *The Resolution of the Central Committee of the Chinese Communist Party on some Historical Problems Since 1949* (Beijing: Hsinhau Bookstore, The People's Press, 1981, in Chinese).
10. Ibid., pp. 21–2.
11. Ibid., p. 25.
12. David W. Chang, *Chinese Leadership Succession Crisis*, pp. 218–20.
13. Fang Shei-chun, *Hu Yaobang and Chinese Communist Politics* (Taipei: Liu Hsueh Press, 1983, pp. 11–49).
14. *San Francisco Examiner*, 18 September 1985.
15. Ibid., 29 September 1985. See also *China Daily*, 29 September 1985. (English edition published in the USA).
16. *The People's Daily*, 30 September 1985.
17. *The People's Daily*, 14 December 1984.
18. *Workers Daily*, 4, March 1984.
19. Ibid., 11 March 1981.
20. Editorial office, Worker's Press, *Persistence on the Four Cardinal Principles*, (Beijing: Workers Press) 1 May 1981 (Chinese).
21. Hsinhua Book Store, *Deng Xiaoping Wenxuam, 1975–1982* (Beijing; The People's Press, 1983) pp. 35–6.
22. Ibid., pp. 131–43.
23. Ibid., p. 151.
24. *Beijing Review*, 23 September 1985, p. 4
25. Editorial office, *Beijing Review, China After Mao: A Collection of 80 Essays*, 1984, p. 54. See also: *Learning From the Constitution of the 12th Party Congress*, by the Research Centre of the CCP Secretariat, December 1981 (Beijing: Hsinhua Press, 1981).
26. Chen Yun, *Guang Ming Ribao*, 18 September 1982 (an influential daily newspaper in Shanghai)
27. *Beijing Review*, 30 September 1985.
28. Deng Xiaoping, *Selected Works of Deng Xiaoping, 1975–1982* (Beijing: Foreign Language Press, 1984), pp. 394–7.

3   New Political Orientation and Economic Development

1. David W. Chang, *Zhou Enlai and Deng Xiaoping in Chinese Leadership Succession Crisis*, ch. 3, pp. 111–52.
2. *The People's Daily*, Beijing 17 December 1984. See also *Christian Science Monitor*, 'Moscow Weeps as Peking Pulls Down Marxist Bridge', 14 December 1984. At first, the The People's Daily said 'We cannot use Marxist and Leninist works to solve our present day problems'. This sentence was modified as 'to solve all of today's problems' on the next day.

3. See the resolution of 27 June 1981, Sixth Plenum of the Eleventh Party Congress.

4. Deng Xiaoping, *Selected Works of Deng Xiaoping, 1975–1982* Beijing: Foreign Language Press, (1983), especially speeches since December, 1978.

5. Ibid., pp. 297–9.

6. Deng Xiaoping, 'Implement the Policy of Readjustment, Ensure Stability and Unity', 25 December 1980. Also see ibid., pp. 335–53.

7. Deng's preferred definition of democratic centralism is: use 'collective decision making against any single person who alone has the final say in all decisions' and that 'the party members are subordinate to the organisation, the minority to the majority, the lower party organisations to the higher and all constituent organisations and all members to the central committee'.

8. Those main rules and points for good military discipline also stressed the relations of the guerrilla army and the peasants in addition to internal unity. In October 1947, the army issued them again as follows. Three main rules: obey orders in your action, take no needle or piece from the peasant property, and turn in all things captured; and eight points: speak politely, pay fairly for what you buy, return everything you borrow from the people, pay for anything you damage, do not hit or swear at people, do not damage crops, do not take liberties with women, and do not mistreat captives.

9. His many other speeches and central documents on party reforms can be found in Deng Xiaoping *Selected Works on Deng Xiaoping*, 27 September 1975, pp. 47–50, 4 October 1975, pp. 51–2, 15 September 1978, pp. 141–4, 29 February 1980, pp. 259–68, and in many other speaking occasions he often stressed the need of party reform and unity.

10. Deng Xiaoping, *Selected Works of Deng*, pp. 192–5.

11. Ibid., pp. 53–4.

12. For further documentation on Deng's new political orientation and economic development, other government and party documents reflect his emphasis in policies. For example, *Major Documents Since the 3rd Plenum of the 11th Party Congress* (Shi, Uijie, Sanzhong Quanhui Yilai Zhongyao Wenxian Jainbian)(Beijing: People's Press, 1983), is a good source book.

13. Xue Muqiao, *China's Socialist Economy* (Beijing: Foreign Language Press, 1981), p. iii.

14. Ibid., p. 9.

15. Ibid., p. 9.

16. Ma Hung, *The New Strategy for China's Economy* (Beijing: New World Press, 1983), p. 20.

17. Ibid., pp. 9–30.

18. For details see Xue Muqiao, *China's Socialist Economy* ch. VII, pp. 163–95.

19. Ma Hung, *The New Strategy for China's Economy* p. 26.

20. Hu Yaobang, *Report to the 12th Party Congress*, The Twelfth National Congress of the CPC (Beijing: Foreign Language Press, 1982), p. 15.

21. Ibid., p. 24.

22. *The People's Daily*, Beijing, 21 October 1984. Also see the first half of
    Chapter 6 of this book.

4 Broad Implementation of the New Economic Strategy

1. *China's Economic Structure Reform–Decision of the CPC Central Committee* (Beijing: 1984 Foreign Language Press). This long and detailed document is relied on in this analysis.
2. Ibid., p. 10.
3. Ibid., p. 14.
4. Ibid., p. 29.
5. Ibid., p. 30.
6. Zhao Ziyang '*Report on Government Work*', *The Third Session of the Sixth National People's Congress*, (Beijing: Foreign Language Press, 1985), 1st edn p. 10.
7. Ibid., p. 15.
8. Ibid., p. 19.
9. Ibid., p. 22.
10. Ibid., p. 28–34.
11. *The Third Session of the Sixth National People's Congress: Main Documents*, (Beijing: Foreign Language Press, 1985), p. 48.
12. Ibid., p. 57.
13. Ibid., p. 62.
14. Ibid., pp. 63–6.
15. Wang Bingqian, *Report on the Execution of the State Budget for 1984 and on the Draft State Budget for 1985*, (Beijing: Foreign Language Press, 1985), p. 69.
16. Ibid., pp. 76–7.
17. Ibid., pp. 81–8.
18. Zhang Xingxiang, State Industrial and Commercial Administration, made the announcement in Beijing, 16 November 1985. See *People's Daily*, 16 November 1985, and also San Francisco Chronicle, 17 November 1985, A-14; China is to build 30,000 free markets in five years. Every community of 20,000 people should have at least one such free market.
19. Zhao Ziyang, 'The Draft Plan for the Seventh Five-year plan, 1986–90', *Guang Ming Ribao*, 19 September 1985.
20. The entire document was published in Chinese in the daily publication, *Guang Ming Tibao*, 26 September 1985. The English translation is my own to summarise the major points not discussed so far on economic reform and development. Quotations from the document may not be footnoted each time in the next several pages.
21. Xue Muqiao, welcome speech. Conference on Chinese Economic Development, 6 September 1985, Chongqing, China. The speech in Chinese language was obtained by the author through Librarian C.P. Liu at the Centre for Chinese Studies at University of California Berkeley, in November 1985. Translation into English is my own. Thanks to Liu and Annie Chang of the Centre Library.
22. Ibid., p. 2.

23. Ma Hung, 'Speech at the Conclusion of Chongqing Conference on Chinese Economy', September 1985. This was made available to this author through the Institute of East Asian Studies at the University of California, Berkeley. My special thanks are due to the IEAS as a visiting scholar in the autumn of 1985.
24. Ibid., p. 5–6.
25. See *Renmin Ribao*, overseas edn, 21 September 1985.

5   Rural Economic Development

1. The ancient management of Well-field system was innovated in the Zhou Dynasty. The government divided a large piece of land into nine equal shares. #letter resembles the shape of the nine-unit together. Eight families each farmed their private pieces. The central, ninth piece of land was royal land, jointly farmed by them all for royal income free of charge. It was a form of taxation on their private piece.
2. Fei Xiaotong (Fei Shiao Tung), *Chinese Village Close-up*, (Beijing: New World Press, 1983), pp. 198–9.
3. Professor W. R. Geddes wrote a monograph published in 1963, *The Peasant Life in Communist China*. It also dealt with the same village Professor Fei had studied since 1936.
4. Ibid., pp. 13–14.
5. Ibid., p. 87.
6. The General Office of the Central Committee of the Communist Party of China (ed.), *Socialist Upsurge in China's Countryside*, 1st edn (Beijing: Foreign Language Press, 1978), p. 5.
7. Li Kai and Ching Shen in *The People's Daily*, 28 November 1955.
8. Fei Xiaotong, *Chinese Village Close-up*, p. 122.
9. Ibid., 'An Interpretation of Chinese Social Structure and Its Changes.' 1946. pp. 124–57.
10. Yu Guanguan (ed.), *China's Socialist Modernisation* (Beijing: Foreign Language Press, 1st edn 1984), pp. 207–70; 'Agriculture' by Zhan Wu and Liu Wenpu, pp. 209–11.
11. Ibid., p. 217.
12. Xu Dixin, *China's Search for Economic Growth: the Chinese Economy Since 1949* (Beijing: New World Press, 1982), (in Chinese)
13. Ibid., pp. 36–7.
14. Liang Wensen, 'Balanced Development of Industry and Agriculture', *China's Search for Economic Growth*, see Ibid., pp. 45–6.
15. Ibid., p. 55.
16. Statement by Vice-premier Yao Yilin, Chinese Agricultural Bao, 11 July 1982.
17. Lu Xieyi, *Golden Age of Rural Economic Development: A Study of Family Responsibility System*. Nanzhou: Kan Xu Province People's Press, Nanzhou, 1983), p. 1.
18. Ibid., p. 2.
19. Ibid., p. 14.
20. Ibid., pp. 38–40.
21. Christopher S. Wren, 'China Announces Sweeping Changes to Create a Freer Economic System', *The New York Times*, 21 October 1984. See

also *Beijing Review*, No 25, 24 June 1985, p. 26, 'An Economist on Socialist Commodity Economy', an interview with Liu Kuoguang, Vice-president of the Chinese Academy of Social Sciences.

22. My interview with Hu Qili took place in the Xinzhiang reception room of the People's Hall in Beijing on 7 July 1985. He had just returned from an inspection tour into southwest rural China. See also *Cheng Ming Monthly*, June 1984, p. 59.

23. See 'Marxist Theory gets a Shave, a Limo and a Three-piece Suit', *San Francisco Examiner*, 22 September 1985. Section A, page 7.

24. Peng Xianchu, 'The Collective is Alive and Well at Wanyu,' *China Reconstructs*, September 1982. Also see Wang Xinmin 'Cultural Center Livens Up Commune', *China Reconstructs*, May 1981.

25. Andrew Watson. 'New Structures in the Organization of Chinese Agriculture: a Variable Model', *Pacific Affairs*, vol, 6, no. 4, Winter, 1984–5, pp. 621–45.

26. See 'Nongye Jingji Wenti,' (in Chinese) no. 2, Feb, 1982, Beijing, pp. 3–7.

27. See 'New Trends in the Development of China's Rural Cooperative Economy', *Jingji Yanjiu*, no. 11, 1983.

28. Liang Liang, 'County Government Seat: its Construction and Development', *Chinese Economic Problem Bi-Monthly*, March 1985, pp. 2–6.

29. See *Jingji Wenti Tansuo*, April 1985, no. 4. See also 'Circular of the Central Committee of the Communist Party of China on Rural Work During 1984', *China Quarterly*, March, 1985, p. 133.

30. Y. Y. Kueh, 'Second Land Reform in China', *China Quarterly*, March 1985, p. 131.

6 Chinese Urban Economic Reform and the Case of Shenzhen

1. See Ma Hung, *New Strategy for China's Economy*, esp. ch. 2, pp. 31–82 (Beijing: New World Press, 1983).

2. Xue Muqiao, *China's Socialist Economy*, ch. 9, pp. 234–65. (Beijing: Foreign Language Press, 1981). See also *Beijing Review*, no. 14, p. 8, April 1985.

3. The China Handbook Editorial Committee, *Economy*, (Beijing: Foreign Language Press, 1984). (translated into English by Hu GengKang, Liu Bingwen and others). p. 3.

4. Peasant households in mutual aid teams of early private cooperatives by growth percentages between 1950 and 1956 as follows: 1950 (10.7), 1951 (19.2), 1952 (40.0), 1953 (39.5). 1954 (60.3), 1955 (64.9), and 1956 (97.2). See the handbook series title *Economy*, p. 19, 1984. Point system was adapted to local circumstances.

5. The China Handbook Editorial Committee, *Economy*, p. 40.

6. Ibid., p. 42.

7. Ibid., p. 52; see also *Beijing Review*, no. 5, p. 4, February 1985.

8. Ibid., p. 54.

9. Decision of the Central Committee of the Communist Party of China on Reform of the Economic Structure, adopted by the Twelfth Central

committee of the CPC at its Third Plenum on 20 October, (Beijing: Foreign Language Press, 1984).

10. The Eighth National Congress of the Communist Party of China, (Beijing: Foreign Language Press, 1956), vol. II, pp. 175–6.
11. Yu Kuangyuan (ed.), *China's Socialist Modernisation* (Beijing: Foreign Language Press, 1956), Vol. II.
12. Ibid., p. 48.
13. China Handbook Editorial Committee, *Economy*, pp. 68–9.
14. Yu Kuangyuan, *China's Socialist Modernisation*, p. 8.
15. The Thirty-Three subsidiary branches represent the long-term development of greater Shenzhen special zone. These thirty three branch companies are: Nan Shan Development Co., Zhan Hua Construction Material Co. Ltd, Honey Lake Country Club; Shenzhen Golf Club Co. Ltd, Su Fa Union Co., Tutian New Town Development Co. Ltd, Hong Kong Restaurant; Shenzhen Railway Station Development Co. Ltd, Head Co. of Shenzhen special economic zone Development Co., Shenzhen Classic Project Design & Decoration Co., Real Estate & Properties Co., Shenzhen International Arcade; Regal Freight Service Co., Shenzhen Lian Cheng (Wen Jin Du) Joint Development Ltd, Sang Hing Hong Filling Station Ltd, Shen Xi Building Decoration Co., Machinery Installation Division of Shenzhen Properties & Estate Co., Shenzhen Lian Hua Industry & Trade Co., Duacheng Develoment Co., Zhen-tung Air-Conditioning and Engineering Co., Xiao Meisha Beach Vacation Camp Development, Shenzhen Properties Management Co., Hua Hui Aluminium Fabricating & Engineering Co., Shui Bei Industrial District, China–Japan Automobile Engineering Co., Sanho Limited; Xin Fa Enterprise Co. Ltd, Wan Lai Renovation and Furniture Co., Oriental Pearl Cooperation Development Co. Ltd, Shenzhen Chia Tai Conti Ltd., Texaco Petroleum Products Distributor Ltd, and Shenzhen Cement Enterprise Co. Ltd.
16. My interview with deputy director of Shekou Industrial Zone took place on 13 July 1985 at his office. Chen himself was instrumental in Shekou's development. I am grateful to him. Some of the statistical figures and quotations in the next several pages have been taken directly from my taped interview.
17. *Shekou Investment Guide*, 1984, p. 18.
18. *Beijing Review*, no. 13, p. 23, March 1985, which reviews the Chuhai development at the Western end of the Pearl River Delta. Chuhai and Shantou are the other two special economic zones in Guangdong Province, while Xiamen, the fourth special economic zone, is located in Fujian province.
19. *Shenzhen University*, a university publication which explains the uniqueness of the University, published in April, 1985, p. 8. (It was created in 1984 to meet the special needs of the special economic zones in techonology and management science).
20. Fang Sheng, 'My View on Some Economic Problems in Special Zones', *Journal of Shenzhen University*, vol. 1, no. 1, 1984, pp. 3–7.
21. Ibid., p. 7.

22. Fang Sheng, 'Is Chinese Special Economic Zone a Capitalist Development? – Answer to the Question of a Foreign Friend'. This was given to me to read during the interview. I am not aware of its publication outside China anywhere yet. See p. 7. (Fang is a well-known economist.) The essay advocates a mixed or pluralistic economy for China.
23. *China's Foreign Economic Legislation* (CFEL), vol. 1, no. 1, published by Foreign Language Press, Beijing, 1982 and 1984 (second printing). It includes some twenty-two different laws, regulations, and procedures governing foreigners, their investment, income, profit, whether in joint venture or individually.
24. CFEL, vol. 1, no. 1, p. 2, articles 3 and 4.
25. Ibid., p. 7.
26. CFEL, p. 36–7.

7 'One Country, Two Systems'

1. *Mirrow Monthly, Toward the year 1997: the Future problems of Hong Kong, A special Issue*, (Hong Kong: The Mirrow Cultural Enterprise Co., July, 1983), p. 173.
2. Ibid., 174.
3. Hungdah Chiu (ed.), 'The 1984 Sino-British Settlement on Hong Kong: Problems and Analysis', in *Symposium on Hong Kong: 1997, Occasional Papers/Reprints Series in Contemporary Asian Studies*, no. 3, 1985, pp. 1–13; and the Joint Declaration itself of 26 September 1984.
4. See the Joint Declaration and Article 31 of the PRC constitution.
5. Ibid., p. 13.
6. Hong Kong Government Information Services Publication, No. 6/1985, February 4–10, p. 1.
7. Ibid., no. 10/85, 11–17 March 1985, p. 2.
8. Ibid., no. 39/85, 30 September–6 October 1985, p. 1.
9. Ibid., no 44/85, 4–10 November 1985, p. 1.
10. Hsing Kuo-chiang, 'The Drafting of a Basic Law for Hong Kong', *Issues and Studies*, vol. 22, no. 6, June 1986, pp. 1–4.
11. *International Daily News*, San Francisco (Chinese language), 25 December 1985.
12. Editorial essay, Ibid., 27 December 1985, p. 2.
13. Ibid., 17 December 1986.
14. See also Ambrose Y. C. King, 'The Hong Kong Talks and Hong Kong Politics', *Issues and Studies*, vol. 22, no. 6, 1986, pp. 52–75.
15. Ibid., p. 74; and also Kuan Hsin-Chi and Lau Siu-Kai, 'Hong Kong in Search of a Consensus', *Occasional Paper, The Centre for Hong Kong Studies*, (Hong Kong: The Chinese University of Hong Kong, November 1985), p. 23.
16. Harry Harding, 'The Future of Hong Kong', *China Business Review*, vol. 12, no. 5, September–October 1985, pp. 30–7.
17. *Beijing Review*, vol. 29, no. 49, 8 December 1986, p. 5.
18. See I-Ching Tsou, 'The CCP's 'One Country, Two Systems', *Studies in*

Communism, vol. 12, no. 7, 15 July, 1986, pp. 1–9. This is a negative view representing Taiwan's position.

19. *Beijing Review*, 5 October, 1981, p. 10, 'Chairman Yi Jianying's Elaboration on Policy Concerning Return of Taiwan to Motherland and Peaceful Reunification'.

20. *Beijing Review*, vol. 21, no.1, 5 January, 1979.

21. Hungdah Chiu, 'Prospect for the Unification of China: an Analysis of the Views of the Republic of China', *Occasional Papers/Reprint Series in Contemporary Asia, Law School of the University of Maryland*, no. 3, 1985, pp. 81–92.

22. Ibid., p. 88.

23. Sun Yun-suan, *United Daily News* (international edn), 12 June 1982, p. 3.

24. Li Shenzhi and Zi Zhongjun, 'Taiwan in the Next Ten Years'. Speech given at the Seminar of the Council of Atlantic Organization, New York, 1985. The chief author is the Vice-president of the Chinese Academy of Social Sciences, Beijing, China. He was an expert and participant in foreign policy of the PRC since Zhou Enlai's time. This long paper represents the PRC spectrum on the Taiwan tangle.

25. Ibid., p. 7 (of the original Chinese version)

26. Ibid., p. 8.

27. Huan Xiang, foreign diplomat and former Vice-president of the Chinese Academy of Social Science. Presently he is the advisor of the Foreign Policy Research Group of the State Council. Our interview took place on 12 July 1985.

28. The author of this policy paper, Li Shenzhi granted me an interview on 10 July, 1985, in Beijing. He gave me a copy of his paper to the Seminar of the 1985 Atlantic Organization in the United States. My interview lasted for three hours and focused on this paper. I did not see the second author, Zi Zhongun, of the same article. (See Ibid., p. 17.)

29. Zhang Hongzeng, 'U.S. Taiwan Relations Act Viewed Against International Law', in *Selected Articles from Chinese Yearbook of International Law*, (Beijing: China Translation & Publishing Corporation, 1983), p. 189. See also two statements made by a U.S. State Department spokesman on 6 and 10 February 1981.

30. Ibid., p. 191.

31. Taiwan: Hearings, Spring, 1978, 2979, *Congressional Record* pp. 48–9.

32. Hungdah Chiu, James C. Hsiung and Ying-Mao Kau (eds.), *Anthology on Reunification and Negotiation between the PRC and the ROC*, 135–16, 39th Ave. (Flushing, New York: *World Daily Journal*, Book Division, 1982), pp. 1–4.

33. This five-point conclusion is the summary of a conference held in Washington, DC on 17 April 1982. Some nine main speakers were heard. The views of the participants have long been known to intellectual Chinese in the United States through their own personal publications.

34. John F. Copper and George P. Chen, 'Taiwan's Elections: Political Development and Democratisation in the Republic of China, *Occasional papers/Reprints Series in Contemporary Asian Studies*. no. 5,

1984, School of Law, University of Maryland, chs 1 and 4, esp. pp. 57–8 on election statistics.
35. Ramon H. Myers, 'Political Change and Democracy in the Republic of China, 1986', unpublished paper. Hoover Institution of War, Revolution and Peace, Stanford University, p. 4. This paper provides a good evaluation of changes in 1986 and other details on the formation of the Democratic Progressive Party.
36. Ibid., p. 12.
37. A. James Gregor and Maria Hsia Chang, 'The Taiwan Independence Movement', in *Political Communication and Persuasion*, vol. 2, no, 4, 1985, pp. 363–91.
38. Douglas Mendel, *The Politics of Formosan Nationalism* (Berkeley and Los Angeles: University of California Press, 1970), p. 249.
39. Ibid., p. 147.
40. Ibid., p. 149.
41. A. James Gregor and Maria Hsia Chang, 'The Taiwan Independence Movement', pp. 371–75.
42. Peter Kien-hong Yu. 'The Taipei-Washington-Peking Triangle: the Taiwan Experience as a Catalyst for China's Reunification', *Asian Outlook*, vol. 21, no. 8, August 1986, pp. 17–19.

8 Conclusion: Revolution, Continuity and Synthesis

1. John K. Fairbank and Edwin O. Reischauer, *China: Tradition and Transformation*, ch. 4. (Boston: Houghton Mifflin 1978), pp. 59–65.
2. Ibid., pp. 346–96.
3. C. P. Fitzgerald, 'The Chinese View of Their Place in the World', *Chatham House Essays*, London: Oxford University Press, 1964), pp. 1–14.
4. Joseph P. Jiang, 'Traditional Chinese Political Culture: Its Characteristics and Influence in the Future' (in Chinese, published in Taipei, Taiwan), *Oriental Magazine*, Spring, 1981, vol. 15, no. 12. pp. 10–14, and no. 13, pp. 20–7.
5. David W. Chang, 'Sun Yatsen's Doctrine and the Future of China', a paper presented at the 27th Convention of American Association of Chinese Studies, 2 November 1986, Pittsburgh. p. 18.
6. Ibid., pp. 25–40.
7. *International Daily News* (Chinese). San Francisco, 10 December 1986. Also *Sino Express Weekly*, New York, 8 December 1986.
8. Ibid., 3 January, 1987, pp. 2–3. See also New York Times; 6 December 1986 on the election in Taiwan on 6 December 1986.
9. Chiang Ching-Kuo, National Day Message, 10 October 1985. See also the editorial of *International Daily News*, 27 December 1985, p. 2.
10. Professor Hung-Mao Tien, 'Three Crises Before the People of Taiwan', *The Chinese Tribune*, no. 199, 27 November 1985. p. 1.
11. *The Chinese Tribune Weekly*, Los Angeles, 30 April 1986, p. 4.
12. *International Daily News*, 6 November 1986.
13. *Beijing Review*, 'Intellectual and Intellectual Ideology' A Dialogue

between Fang Lizhi and Dai Qing of *Guangming Ribao*, vol. 29, no. 50, 15 December 1986, pp. 16–18, See also *Milwaukee Journal*, 28 December p. 7A. 'Chinese Student Discontent A Surprise', by Edward A. Gargan of the New York Times.

14. Ibid., vol. 30, no. 2, 12 January 1987, pp. 17–19.
15. Luo spent five hours with me at my hotel in Beijing. I am grateful to him for his insight through working experience in thirty-five years with the Economic Planning Commission as a senior economist. The interview took place on 13 July 1986 in Beijing at the Nationality Hotel.
16. *Beijing Review*, vol. 30, no. 1, 5 January, 1987, pp. 20–21.
17. *International Daily News*, 30 May, 1986, p. 2.
18. Ibid., and also *Beijing Review*, vol. 29, no. 49, 8 December 1986, p. 14–15. 'Socialist Features Reexamined' by Zhao Yao who argues on behalf of the current reform policy which allows only the separation of ownership from management and the state must retain the ownership of the enterprises.
19. Liu Guoguang, 'Major Changes in China's Economy', *Beijing Review*, 8 December 1986, pp. 15–17.
20. The central idea of the definition of socialist commodity economy came from a resolution of the third plenary session of the Twelfth Central Committee in 1984.
21. See *Journal of the Postgraduate School of the Chinese Academy of Social Sciences*, no. 3, 1986 by Liu Guoguang, Vice-president of the Chinese Academy of Social Sciences. He is an economist.
22. Lenin's speech in 1918, Seventh Congress of the RCPCB, *Collected works of Lenin*, vol. 27. p. 151.
23. David W. Chang, *Zhou Enlai and Deng Xiaoping In the Chinese Leadership Succession Crisis*, chapter IV, esp. pp. 218–46. University Press of America, Nanham, MD., 1984.
24. See also *Beijing Review*, vol. 29, no. 49, 8 December 1986, p. 14.
25. Jan S. Prybyla, 'Economic Development in the People's Republic of China, 1985–86', A conference paper presented at the 1986 meeting of the American Association of Chinese Studies, Pittsburgh, 1–3 November 1986, p. 2.
26. Ibid., p. 26.
27. Michael S. Serrill 'Proud Legacy of Youthful Protest', New York Times Magazine 5 January 1987, pp. 51–2.
28. Ibid., p. 51.
29. Yu-chen Chen, 'An Assessment of Economic Reform In Mainland China Since 1979', Chung-Hua Institute for Economic Research, *Modern Economic Study Series*, no. 8, Taipei, Taiwan, January 1985, esp. ch 5, pp. 133–63, p. 138.
30. There had been no less than ten small democratic parties in China before 1949. Two of them went to Taiwan to support Chiang Kai-Shek (the China Youth Party, and Democratic Socialist Party). The eight parties invited by the Communist Party to underwrite the Common Program as the Constitution for the period of 1949–54.
31. *International Daily News*, 7 December 1986.
32. *Beijing Review*, vol. 30, 15 December 1986. p. 15.

33. *International Daily News*, 22 December 1986, editorial, p. 2.
34. Ibid., 27 December p. 10
35. Edward A. Gargan, 'Chinese Student Discontent A Surprise', *The Milwaukee Journal*, 28 December 1986, p. 7A. (Gargan is New York Times Correspondent in Beijing).
36. *International Daily News*, 3 January 1987, p. 1.
37. Ibid., 6 January 1987, p. 4.
38. Ibid., 6 January 1987, p. 12.
39. Editorial of *Army Daily News*, 8 January 1987.
40. *International Daily News*, 12/14 January and *Asian Weekly Outlook*, 12 January 1987.
41. Ibid., 16 January, 1987, p. 12 and also *Beijing Review*, 'Minister Wang Meng on Campus Situation', vol. 30, no. 1, 5 January 1987, p. 6 and 22.
42. *International Daily News*, 17 January 1987, p. 1.
43. Thomas A. Sanction, 'As crackdown Campaign goes On Peking Purges Liberals and Slows Economic Reforms', *Time Magazine Weekly*, 2 February 1987, pp. 45–6.
44. Ibid., 26 January 1987, pp. 25–6.
45. Wan Li, 'Democracy and Science Vital to Good Policy Making', *Beijing Review*, vol. 29, no. 29, pp. 28–31.
46. Robert E. Bedeski, 'Socialist Legality and Citizenship in China: the 1979 Election Law and Its Implementation'. A paper presented at the Regional Seminar on Chinese Studies, University of California, Berkeley, October 1985, p. 5.

Index